THE NAVAL
OFFICER'S
GUIDE

THE NAVAL OFFICER'S GUIDE

TWELFTH EDITION

CDR Lesa A. McComas, USN (Ret)

NAVAL INSTITUTE PRESS
Annapolis, Maryland

Naval Institute Press
291 Wood Road
Annapolis, MD 21402

Library of Congress Cataloging-in-Publication Data
McComas, Lesa A.,
  The naval officer's guide / Lesa A. McComas. — 12th ed.
    p. cm.
  Includes bibliographical references and index.
  Rev. ed. of: The naval officer's guide / William P. Mack, Harry A.
Seymour, Jr., and Lesa A. McComas. 11th ed. c1998.
  ISBN 978-1-59114-501-1 (hardcover : alk. paper) 1. United States.
Navy—Officers' handbooks. I. Mack, William P., 1915- Naval officer's
guide. II. Title.
  V133.M28 2011
  359.00973--dc22
                        2010047021

Printed in the United States of America

19 18 17 16 15 14 13 12 11   9 8 7 6 5 4 3 2 1
First printing

Unless otherwise noted, all photos are from official U.S. Navy sources.

Sep. 1st

12, 13, 16

CONTENTS

PREFACE

The *Naval Officer's Guide* is a collection of information and advice for officers in the U.S. Navy, intended to serve primarily as a resource from their preparation for commissioning through their years as junior officers.

In the decade since the eleventh edition was published, considerable changes have taken place in the organization and policies of the Department of Defense and the Navy. The rise of irregular challenges, increased emphasis on joint and interagency operations, introduction of numerous technological innovations, and the natural evolution of traditions and social norms further contributed to the need to completely revise and update the twelfth edition. Mindful of the legacy of this reference, I made every attempt to retain the original inspiration of the first author, Rear Admiral Arthur Ageton, as well as the accumulated wisdom of the other authors who have shared in the development of the various editions over the years.

Although I am solely responsible for any remaining errors or oversights, I am particularly grateful to my colleagues and shipmates at the Johns Hopkins University Applied Physics Laboratory who reviewed and "sanity checked" this edition. The Reserve, retired, and active-duty officers who contributed significantly to the review process include Commander Chris Cook, Lieutenant Lew Cooper, Commander Dru Daubon, Commander Fred Goldhammer, and Commander Steve Phillips.

THE NAVAL
OFFICER'S
GUIDE

CHAPTER ONE

THE UNITED STATES NAVY

Seapower is our heritage. . . . Seapower is not merely a fleet of ships and planes. Seapower reaches into every phase of our national life. It means domination of the sea and the air above it. In order to maintain such power the fruits of our farms, the minerals of our land and the products of our factories must flow into the sinews of maritime strength.

—Fleet Admiral Chester W. Nimitz

The widest use of the sea, integrated fully into our national strength, is as important to America in the age of nuclear power and space travel as in those stirring days of the birth of the Republic.

—President John F. Kennedy

The United States Navy has served the American people with distinction and pride for more than two hundred years, in times of peace and war. The United States is fundamentally a maritime nation and has always maintained an active role in keeping open the sea lines of communication that connect us to our allies and trading partners.

Twenty years ago, the strategic landscape was fundamentally changed by the fall of the Berlin Wall and the end of the Cold War. No longer solely focused on the open ocean, "blue water" role in which the Navy had so successfully served as a counter to the former Soviet Union since the end of World War II, today's Navy is actively engaged in deterring and controlling conflicts among smaller regional powers, and protecting vital U.S. interests and the interests of our allies. In more recent years, wars in Afghanistan and Iraq, counterpiracy operations off the coast of Somalia, and the rise of other irregular threats around the world have demanded new capabilities to counter threats in the littorals. This focus requires increased flexibility, mobility, and rapid response.

One of the most significant changes taking place in recent years has been the increasing emphasis on joint and interagency operations, an emphasis that enables the United States to bring to bear all of the elements of national power in a coordinated manner. The "Naval Service," encompassing the Navy, Marine Corps, and Coast Guard, is working closely together, guided by the 2007 Maritime Strategy and 2010 Naval Operations Concept, both documents jointly signed by the Chief of Naval Operations, the Commandant of the Marine Corps, and the Commandant of the Coast Guard.

These documents articulated six enduring core capabilities for the Naval Service: forward presence, maritime security, humanitarian assistance/disaster response, sea control, power projection, and deterrence. The Navy plays a key role in each.

Forward Presence. The Navy maintains forward-deployed or stationed forces overseas to demonstrate national resolve, strengthen alliances, dissuade potential adversaries, and enhance the ability to respond quickly to contingency operations.

Forward presence is accomplished through the periodic formation and deployment of expeditionary strike groups and the establishment of Global Fleet Stations in key regions. Naval forces are deployed for specific exercises and operations of limited duration, with the ability to re-aggregate into adaptive force packages to eliminate geographical and service seams based on mission requirements.

Forward-deployed forces conduct cooperative engagement and maritime security operations and deterrence and also combat terrorism. Presence enables the Navy to provide immediate crisis response for maritime security, noncombatant evacuation operations, humanitarian assistance and disaster response, and maritime ballistic missile defense.

Maritime Security. These operations are conducted to protect sovereignty and resources, ensure free and open commerce, and to counter maritime-related terrorism, transnational crime, piracy, environmental destruction, and illegal seaborne immigration.

The Navy counters piracy, terrorism, weapons proliferation, drug trafficking, and other illicit activities short of war. The United States is committed to preventing such irregular and transnational threats and to upholding domestic and international law in the global commons through activities including engagement in global maritime partnerships and participation in the U.N.'s International Maritime Organization.

Humanitarian Assistance and Disaster Response (HA/DR). Humanitarian assistance to the local populace provided by predominantly U.S. forces in conjunction with military operations and exercises is specifically authorized by Title 10, U.S. Code (USC), sec. 401, and funded under separate authorities. Assistance provided under these provisions is limited to medical, dental, veterinary, and preventive medical care provided in rural areas of a country; construction of rudimentary surface transportation systems; well drilling and construction of basic sanitation facilities; and rudimentary construction and repair of public facilities. Assistance must fulfill unit-training requirements that incidentally create humanitarian benefit to the local populace.

The Navy is uniquely capable of providing rapid and sustained assistance to other nations, including deliberate actions as well as those in response to a crisis.

Sea Control. Sea control comprises employment of naval forces, supported by land and air forces as appropriate, in order to achieve military objectives in vital sea areas. Such operations include destruction of enemy naval forces, suppression of enemy sea commerce, protection of vital sea lanes, and establishment of military superiority in areas of naval operations. The establishment of sea control permits the use of the sea as maneuver space and is an essential precondition for decisive power projection ashore.

The ability to operate freely in blue water is critical. Threats, including mines, nuclear and diesel submarines, small-boat attacks, and cyber threats that target command, control, computer, intelligence, and satellite systems can be posed by blue-water near-peer competitors as well as smaller states and non-state actors.

Power Projection. Power projection is the ability of a nation to apply all or some of its elements of national power—political, economic, informational, or military—to rapidly and effectively deploy and sustain forces in and from multiple dispersed locations to respond to crises, to contribute to deterrence, and to enhance regional stability.

Strike operations, executed primarily by the nuclear-powered aircraft carriers' (CVNs) embarked air wings, and surface- and sub-surface–launched land attack missiles, are the principal means of gaining and maintaining operational access.

The projection of power ashore includes strikes using missiles, aircraft, or unmanned vehicles; amphibious operations using assault aircraft and landing craft; and irregular operations including raids, non-combatant evacuations, personnel recovery, reconnaissance, and advance force operations to conduct certain amphibious missions. Sealift capability to rapidly concentrate and sustain forces is a key enabler of joint and combined power projection campaigns.

Deterrence. Effective deterrence is a means to prevent and deter conflict with state and non-state adversaries through both nuclear and conventional means. Both credible and scalable, deterrence requires a comprehensive effort that includes all elements of national power. Collectively, forward presence, maritime security, humanitarian assistance and disaster response (HA/DR), sea control, and power projection support deterrence.

An arresting-gear officer aboard the aircraft carrier USS *Dwight D. Eisenhower* (CVN 69) observes flight deck operations as an F/A-18F Super Hornet lands.

As the 2007 Maritime Strategy notes, preventing war is preferable to fighting wars. While ballistic missile submarines remain a key component of deterrence, other deterrence activities include theater security cooperation and ballistic missile defense. Forward-based and forward-deployed forces, space-based assets, sea-based strategic deterrence, and other initiatives all serve to deter potential adversaries.

The Officer's Role

Some junior officers join the Navy out of a sense of patriotism and duty; some join with the goal of obtaining education and skills to prepare them for civilian careers after their initial obligations are over; some enter the Navy out of the necessity of finding jobs or as a means of financing their college educations; some simply want to "see the world" before settling down into more mundane careers. If you count yourself among these latter categories, you are far from alone—few senior officers can look back on their first days in the Navy and say that they always knew they would stay for twenty or thirty years.

The Navy offers a unique opportunity to the young men and women who become commissioned officers. Regardless of your designator and specialty, within your first few years you will receive training and hands-on experience to become qualified in some technical specialty, and you will learn to lead the men and women in your charge to accomplish a mission that is of vital importance to your country. You may find yourself surprised at the magnitude of the sense of accomplishment you feel when you achieve a new milestone or are entrusted with a new responsibility, be it qualifying as engineering officer of the watch, landing on the deck of an aircraft carrier for the first time, or conning your submarine out of a crowded harbor. Many of the experiences you will have over the next few years have no counterpart in the civilian world.

The opportunity for you to succeed is there, but you will have to earn your success every step of the way. When you report to your first duty station after completing your initial schooling you may feel that your education as an officer is complete, but in fact it will have only just begun. From then on, it will be largely up to you to find out what you need to know and to set about learning it. You will be guided to some extent by the Navy's formal watch qualification programs, and there will be many people willing to help you learn, including senior petty officers and more experienced officers, but no one will push you. You must push yourself—set goals for yourself and work at achieving them, and then set higher goals.

After earning your initial warfare qualification, you may feel the temptation to slack off and relax for the remainder of your tour. If you choose to do this, you will not only be letting down your superiors and shipmates who are depending on you to take the next step in your development, but you will be robbing yourself of the opportunity to learn something you may never have another opportunity to learn. If you find yourself in a rut, look for new opportunities: ask to be rotated to a new department, volunteer to take on a demanding collateral duty, work on a new watch qualification. This kind of initiative is the way in which outstanding senior officers begin to establish their service reputations early in their careers.

As you become more senior, you should constantly have an eye on your next career milestone: selection for department head, executive officer, commanding officer, major command. For each step, find out what you need to do to be competitive for selection, and make sure you do it and do it well. Chapter 17 offers additional information on career planning. The ultimate goal of any unrestricted line officer is command at sea; as you become more senior, the book *Command at Sea* will provide valuable guidance to help you work toward this goal.

From the time you receive your commission, your education and professional development are largely up to you, and they represent the keys to success in a very complicated and technical profession. Contrary to what you might expect, extra effort on your part will not have a negative effect on your ability to perform your regular duties; you will find, over and over, that the more you do, the more you can do. That is what this profession is all about.

Naval Operations Concept 2010 (excerpt)

Who We Are. The Naval Service is comprised of the active and reserve components and the civilian personnel of the United States Navy, the United States Marine Corps, and the United States Coast Guard.

We are, first and foremost, men and women dedicated to the service of our Nation in peace and war. We are an all-volunteer force instilled with a warrior and guardian ethos. Our people are the foundation of our mission success. They possess willpower, creativity, inspiration, reason, knowledge, and experience to overcome adversity and accomplish any task. They exemplify the values of honor, courage, and commitment.

We are an instrument of national power, employed to prevent conflict and, if necessary, prevail in war. We are organized, trained, and equipped primarily to operate and fight at and from the sea. The qualities that allow us to prevail in war also contribute to conflict prevention. These qualities include speed, flexibility, agility, scalability, readiness, mobility, self-sustainability, and lethality.

What We Believe. We believe that the future is uncertain and that the United States will be threatened by a variety of state and non-state adversaries, current and emerging. We believe that both state and non-state adversaries are likely to employ a hybrid of conventional and irregular methods to counter the United States' advantage in conventional military operations. Thus, we must be prepared to overcome a range of adversaries, employing a variety of capabilities and tactics.

We believe that naval forces uniquely contribute to overcoming diplomatic, military, and geographic impediments to access, while respecting the sovereignty of nations. Even as security, stability, and the global economy become more interdependent, resistance to a large U.S. military "footprint" abroad will continue to increase. Naval forces provide the ideal means in such a security environment to accomplish a wide variety of missions conducted independently or in concert with joint, interagency, international, and non-governmental partners that share the United States' interest in promoting a safe and prosperous world.

We believe that preventing war is as important as winning, and that prevention activities will constitute the most likely application of naval power.

Where We Operate. The Naval Service operates in the maritime domain, which consists of the "oceans, seas, bays, estuaries, islands, coastal areas, and the airspace above these, including the littorals." The littoral is comprised of two segments. The seaward portion is that area from the open ocean to the shore that must be controlled to support operations ashore. The landward portion is the area inland from the shore that can be supported and defended directly from the sea.

A number of common, non-doctrinal terms also describe aspects of the maritime domain. Blue water refers to the open ocean; green water refers to coastal waters, ports, and harbors; and brown water refers to navigable rivers and their estuaries. The complexity of the maritime domain, which encompasses the confluence of water, air, land, as well as space and cyberspace, is infinite in its variations. As a result, operations in the maritime domain are inherently challenging. The magnitude of this challenge increases as the proximity to land increases, with the most complex cases being operations that transition between water and land.

This is the environment in which naval forces thrive.

Naval forces will continue to be in high demand across the range of military operations (ROMO), largely because they effectively bridge the seams between water, land, and air. Leveraging our strong historic interdependencies, we task organize Navy, Marine Corps, and Coast Guard resources to achieve the requisite blend of capability, capacity, and legal authorities to suit the given situation and mission. Similarly, command relationships are tailored to each operation, based on the mission specifics.

As we train for and conduct missions, we are mindful that the maritime domain is a precious resource shared by the global community. We will conduct effective combat training, using live and simulated methods, while ensuring that we sustain our naval preeminence and our record of good environmental stewardship.

What We Provide the Nation. The Naval Service provides the Nation a multi-purpose team whose capabilities are applicable across the ROMO. While most frequently employed to prevent conflict, we are manned, trained, and equipped to prevail in combat. We provide:

- Persistent presence, operating forward while respecting the sovereignty of others. Naval forces conduct military engagement and security cooperation to build partnerships; prevent and deter conflict; communicate our Nation's intent; conduct crisis response and limited contingency operations; and when necessary, facilitate the introduction of additional naval, joint, or multinational forces, as well as interagency, multinational, or non-governmental organizations.

- Self-sustaining, sea-based expeditionary forces, the Nation's preeminent, combined-arms teams. Uniquely tailored to fight and win from the sea, we are manned, trained, equipped, and ready to operate without reliance on ports or airfields in an objective area. For the Naval Service, "expeditionary" is not limited to being "an armed force organized to accomplish a specific objective in a foreign country." Rather, being expeditionary is one of our defining characteristics—we are ready to fight when we "leave the pier," persistently forward postured, and self-sustaining throughout our deployments.

- Maritime domain expertise, fully cognizant of the complexities of the water, air, and land environments and their interfaces. We are the only force skilled at operating in this maneuver space. We fight by achieving access, establishing local sea control, and projecting power ashore as part of a joint or multinational team. We effectively employ a range of lethal and non-lethal capabilities to counter both conventional and irregular challenges in the maritime domain as well as space and cyberspace.

- Flexible force options, scalable with respect to capability, capacity, and legal authorities. Our forward posture is a cost-effective means of proactively influencing events and responding to crises. When required, these naval forces can be rapidly reinforced by other naval forces surged from globally dispersed locations. Our inherent mobility, organizational agility, and self-sustainability provide combatant commanders with a variety of options, including the ability to command and control joint task forces from afloat and ashore, across the ROMO.

- Expanded deterrence, through credible, maneuverable, forward deployed and scalable power projection capabilities—including ballistic missile defense and nuclear strike—and prevention activities that build capable partners and address the causes of instability and conflict.

- Joint, multinational, and interagency enabling forces that facilitate the integration and application of all elements of national power.

CHAPTER TWO

CORE VALUES, ETHICS, AND CONDUCT

*Nearly all men can stand adversity, but if you want to test a man's
character, give him power.*

—President Abraham Lincoln

I am a United States Sailor.
I will support and defend the Constitution of the United States of
*   America and I will obey the orders of those appointed over me.*
I represent the fighting spirit of the Navy and those who have gone
*   before me to defend freedom and democracy around the world.*
I proudly serve my country's Navy combat team with Honor, Courage,
*   and Commitment.*
I am committed to excellence and the fair treatment of all.

—The "Sailor's Creed"

The above creed applies equally to all Sailors, from seaman recruit to admiral. Although drafted in the 1990s, these words embody the traditions and values that have guided our Navy and the men and women who have served in it since its inception. As an officer, you will not only be expected to uphold the standards that apply to all members of the Navy, but in view of the "special trust and confidence" placed in you, to exceed them.

Honor Concept

Whatever your commissioning source, you have probably already been exposed to some form of honor concept or code. The "Honor Concept" used by the Brigade of Midshipmen at the U.S. Naval Academy reads as follows: "Midshipmen are persons of integrity: They stand for that which is right. They tell the truth and ensure that the full truth is known. They do not lie. They embrace fairness in all actions. They ensure that work submitted as their own is their own, and that assistance received from any source is authorized and properly documented. They do not cheat. They respect the property of others and ensure that others are able to benefit from the use of their own property. They do not steal."

A typical Naval Reserve Officer Training Corps (ROTC) "Concept of Honor" for midshipmen reads as follows:

> Never before has the individual character of the American Sailor and Marine weighed so heavily on the calculus of potential conflict. For all the intrinsic excellence of our technology, experience demonstrates that its successful employment in battle continues to depend upon the integrity, courage, commitment, and professional excellence of those called to bring it to bear in defense of freedom. With ruthless efficiency and finality, the awesome violence of modern warfare distinguishes forces filled with these attributes from those rendered hollow by their absence. Unlike previous conflicts in our history, technology no longer permits us the luxury of awaiting the first battle to determine whether our forces are ready. The pace of conflict will afford us little, if any, chance to profit from our mistakes.
>
> Military systems, which often operate under extreme duress, are built on a foundation of absolute trust and fidelity. You don't learn that when you get to the fleet; you take it to the fleet. This may seem to be a harsh standard, but it's not that difficult to understand what your obligations are.
>
> For the Naval Reserve Officers Training Corps midshipman, those obligations are succinctly stated in the following honor code: A midshipman does not lie, cheat or steal.

These ideals were intended to serve as a foundation upon which to begin your training as a Navy officer. Once you become a commissioned officer you do not become exempt from these standards but will continue to build on them throughout your career.

Core Values of the United States Navy

Throughout its history, the Navy has successfully met all its challenges. America's Navy began during the American Revolution, when on 13 October 1775, the Continental Congress authorized a few small ships, creating the Continental Navy. Esek Hopkins was appointed commander in chief and twenty-two officers were commissioned, including John Paul Jones.

From those early days of the Navy, certain bedrock principles or core values have carried on to today. They consist of three basic principles.

Watchstanders track contacts from the combat information center aboard the amphibious dock landing ship USS *Pearl Harbor* (LSD 52).

Honor: "I will bear true faith and allegiance . . ." Accordingly, we will: Conduct ourselves in the highest ethical manner in all relationships with peers, superiors and subordinates; Be honest and truthful in our dealings with each other, and with those outside the Navy; Be willing to make honest recommendations and accept those of junior personnel; Encourage new ideas and deliver the bad news, even when it is unpopular; Abide by an uncompromising code of integrity, taking responsibility for our actions and keeping our word; Fulfill or exceed our legal and ethical responsibilities in our public and personal lives twenty-four hours a day. Illegal or improper behavior or even the appearance of such behavior will not be tolerated. We are accountable for our professional and personal behavior. We will be mindful of the privilege to serve our fellow Americans.

Courage: "I will support and defend . . ." Accordingly, we will have: courage to meet the demands of our profession and the mission when it is hazardous, demanding, or otherwise difficult; Make decisions in the best interest of the Navy and the nation, without regard to personal consequences; Meet these challenges while adhering to a higher standard of personal conduct and decency; Be loyal to our nation, ensuring the resources entrusted to us are used in an honest, careful, and efficient way. Courage is the value that gives us the moral and mental strength to do what is right, even in the face of personal or professional adversity.

Commitment: "I will obey the orders . . ." Accordingly, we will: Demand respect up and down the chain of command; Care for the safety, professional, personal and spiritual well-being of our people; Show respect toward all people without regard to race, religion, or gender; Treat each individual with human dignity; Be committed to positive change and constant improvement; Exhibit the highest degree of moral character, technical excellence, quality and competence in what we have been trained to do. The day-to-day duty of every Navy man and woman is to work together as a team to improve the quality of our work, our people, and ourselves.

These are the CORE VALUES of the United States Navy.

The Code of Conduct for Members of the United States Armed Forces

This code was created by Executive Order in 1955 and amended by several subsequent Executive Orders. It governs the conduct of military members in combat and captivity.

I. I am an American, fighting in the forces which guard my country and our way of life. I am prepared to give my life in their defense.

II. I will never surrender of my own free will. If in command, I will never surrender the members of my command while they still have the means to resist.

III. If I am captured I will continue to resist by all means available. I will make every effort to escape and aid others to escape. I will accept neither parole nor special favors from the enemy.

IV. If I become a prisoner of war, I will keep faith with my fellow prisoners. I will give no information or take part in any action which might be harmful to my comrades. If I am senior, I will take command. If not, I will obey the lawful orders of those appointed over me and will back them up in every way.

V. When questioned, should I become a prisoner of war, I am required to give name, rank, service number and date of birth. I will evade answering further questions to the utmost of my ability. I will make no oral or written statements disloyal to my country and its allies or harmful to their cause.

VI. I will never forget that I am an American, fighting for freedom, responsible for my actions, and dedicated to the principles which made my country free. I will trust in my God and in the United States of America.

Conflicts of Interest

The Federal Acquisition Regulations (FAR) prescribe special responsibilities for those exercising fiduciary responsibilities on behalf of the federal government.

> Government business shall be conducted in a manner above reproach and, except as authorized by statute or regulation, with complete impartiality and with preferential treatment for none. Transactions relating to the expenditure of public funds require the highest degree of public trust and an impeccable standard of conduct. The general rule is to avoid strictly any conflict of interest or even the appearance of a conflict of interest in Government-contractor relationships. While many Federal laws and regulations place restrictions on the actions of Government personnel, their official conduct must, in addition, be such that they would have no reluctance to make a full public disclosure of their actions.

The FAR specifically prohibits the solicitation or acceptance of any gift or favor from anyone seeking government business with the employee's agency, anyone conducting activities regulated by the employee's agency, or anyone with interests that may be substantially affected by the performance or nonperformance of the employee's official duties.

In addition, Navy members are prohibited from participating personally and substantially in an official capacity in any particular matter in which they have a financial interest, if the particular matter will have a direct and predictable effect on that interest. This prohibition also includes interests of a spouse, child, general partner, organization in which a member serves (e.g., as a director or trustee), or anyone with whom the member is seeking or negotiating future employment.

If you find yourself in a situation in which a conflict either exists, or could be perceived to exist, you are required to seek the opinion of an ethics counselor (normally a Judge Advocate General [JAG] officer), disqualify yourself from taking action on the matter, and provide written notice of the conflict to your superior requesting to be excused from any responsibility for decisions affecting the situation.

General Conduct Issues

Outside Employment. Commanding officers (COs) generally require subordinates to obtain permission prior to seeking outside employment, and Navy members' outside employment may not interfere or conflict with their military duties. Employment by a defense contractor, or other employer doing business with the military, could result in a conflict-of-interest situation (see above).

Drug- and Alcohol-Abuse Prevention. Alcohol and drug abuse undermines combat readiness and is incompatible with the maintenance of high standards of performance. The Navy's approach to eliminating alcohol and drug abuse includes detection, deterrence, prevention, education, intervention, and treatment. The Navy's "Right Spirit" campaign is designed to deglamorize alcohol use and requires all leaders to set the right personal example and command climate. The drinking age for Navy and Marine Corps members is twenty-one, although this may be relaxed to conform with the laws in a host country.

All Navy members are responsible not only for monitoring their own alcohol use, but also for looking out for signs of abuse in their shipmates. This includes being aware of the warning signs of alcohol abuse and intervening before a shipmate consumes an excessive amount or drives while under the influence of alcohol.

Any alcohol-related misconduct, such as a conviction for driving while intoxicated, is likely to have career-ending consequences, particularly for an officer. However, because alcohol abuse is considered to be a treatable condition, in the absence of any misconduct, self-referral or command-referral for alcohol dependence or abuse should not be viewed as detrimental when recommending a member for promotion, command screen, or special assignment.

Nonalcoholic beverages must always be provided as an alternative whenever alcoholic beverages are served at a command-sponsored function, and for those who drink, moderation is expected.

The Navy's "zero tolerance" policy toward illicit drug use prohibits Navy members from wrongfully possessing, distributing, or abusing drugs; being in possession of drug abuse paraphernalia; or being under the unauthorized influence of prescribed drugs. The Navy's drug abuse policy applies to all members regardless of whether foreign, state, or local ordinances exist that may permit the use, possession, distribution, or prescription of certain controlled substances. Navy members are also prohibited from using products or deceptive practices to provide a false-negative result on a urinalysis test.

The cornerstone of the Navy's drug abuse prevention program is random urinalysis testing required of everyone, regardless of pay grade. You may be tasked with acting as a witness during such a test at your command, and you will certainly be tapped on a regular basis to provide samples for testing. It is your responsibility as a leader to set the example by demonstrating your wholehearted support, regardless of whatever short-term personal inconvenience such testing may cause.

Fraternization. The Office of the Chief of Naval Operations has issued the OPNAV Instruction 5370.2 series, "Navy Fraternization Policy," which lays out the Navy's regulations concerning personal relationships between Navy members of different pay grades or within the same chain of command. The following is an excerpt from that instruction: "Personal relationships between officers and enlisted members that are unduly familiar and that do not respect differences in rank and grade are prohibited and violate longstanding custom and tradition of the Naval Service. Similar relationships that are unduly familiar between officers or between enlisted members of different rank or grade may also be prejudicial to good order and discipline or of a nature to bring discredit on the Naval Service and are prohibited."

The instruction clarifies that fraternization does not refer strictly to dating relationships between personnel of disparate pay grades, but in fact is a gender-neutral concept. Any relationship between a senior and a junior that results in, or gives the appearance of, favoritism, loss of objectivity, preferential treatment, personal gain, or which otherwise undermines the morale and discipline of a command is prohibited. This prohibition can include business relationships as well as social relationships. Improper fraternization between instructors and students is also prohibited, regardless of rank. The responsibility for preventing inappropriate relationships rests primarily with the senior, although both members involved in such a relationship can be held accountable for their conduct.

Although marriage does not forgive any previous fraternization that may have preceded the marriage, there are legitimate circumstances under which an officer may be married to an enlisted member, as when the officer was promoted from the enlisted ranks following the marriage. Navy members who are married or have other familial relationships with personnel of different ranks or grades must maintain the requisite respect and decorum while on duty or in uniform in public.

Fraternization policy is not meant to preclude all social interaction between seniors and juniors. Command-sponsored functions, such as division or command picnics, can foster morale and esprit de corps, and it is not considered inappropriate for a senior to join a group of subordinates for an occasional celebration of an achievement or other notable event. Seniors must take care, however, to maintain the proper level of professional propriety in all such interactions, and to ensure their participation does not cross the line into routine socializing.

Gambling. Small wagers (e.g., card games, pools on sporting events) based on personal relationships, transacted entirely within assigned government quarters and not in violation of local law, are permissible. However, gambling is prohibited onboard ship and whenever it would violate *Navy Regulations* or the Navy's policies prohibiting fraternization between seniors and subordinates.

Sexual Harassment. Sexual harassment is defined as a form of sex discrimination that involves unwelcomed sexual advances, requests for sexual favors, and other verbal or physical conduct of a sexual nature when

    a. submission to or rejection of such conduct is made either explicitly or implicitly a term or condition of a person's job, pay, or career; or

    b. submission to or rejection of such conduct by a person is used as a basis for career or employment decisions affecting that person; or

    c. such conduct has the purpose or effect of unreasonably interfering with an individual's work performance or creates an intimidating, hostile, or offensive working environment. For military members, the workplace may include conduct on or off duty, twenty-four hours a day.

Any person in a supervisory or command position who uses or condones implicit or explicit sexual behavior to control, influence, or affect the career, pay, or job of a military member or civilian employee is engaging in sexual harassment. Similarly, any military member or civilian employee who makes deliberate or repeated unwelcomed verbal comments, gestures, or physical contact of a sexual nature is also engaging in sexual harassment.

To combat sexual harassment as well as other forms of inappropriate behavior, the Navy has developed a three-tiered zone approach to classify behavior:

- Red-zone behavior is always unacceptable. This behavior includes asking for sexual favors in return for favorable supervisory decisions (termed "quid pro quo," Latin for "this for that"), making supervisory decisions based on a person's race or gender, sending "hate" mail or explicit unwanted messages of a sexual nature, and, as the most extreme example, assault.

- Yellow-zone behavior is that which would be regarded as inappropriate by most people and includes making racial, ethnic, or sexual comments or "jokes," violating personal space, or touching someone in a sexually suggestive way.

- Green-zone behavior is that which is always acceptable and includes performance counseling, normal social interaction, polite compliments, and touching that could not reasonably be perceived in a sexual way.

Minor infractions of a "yellow-zone" nature, particularly between peers, should normally be dealt with under the Navy's informal resolution system. Under this system, individuals have three options and may use any or all as necessary to resolve the conflict:

(1) Under the direct approach, the individual would approach the person whose conduct is of concern and, politely and respectfully, explain the situation and request the individual refrain from further such conduct.

(2) Alternatively, a member may choose to send a letter to the offender, placing the same information in writing.

(3) The individual may ask a third party, usually a friend or co-worker, for assistance.

When a subordinate feels threatened or intimidated by a senior's conduct, the subordinate may request redress through the chain of command. When the senior is the subordinate's immediate superior, a request to see the next senior member in the chain of command is appropriate.

The informal resolution system is not meant to replace disciplinary action against serious offenders. Red-zone behavior, which often represents a violation of the Uniform Code of Military Justice (UCMJ), should always be immediately reported to the chain of command.

Hazing. Hazing is the mistreatment of trainees or juniors by those entrusted to oversee their training and development, regardless of rank, and is defined as any conduct whereby a military member or members cause another military member or members to suffer or be exposed to any activity which is cruel, abusive, humiliating, oppressive, demeaning, or harmful. Whether an individual consents or volunteers is immaterial and does not render an incident of hazing any more acceptable.

Specific actions that are clearly prohibited include playing abusive tricks; threatening or offering violence or bodily harm to another; striking; branding; taping; tattooing; shaving; greasing; painting; requiring excessive physical exercise beyond what is required to meet standards; "pinning"; "tacking on"; "blood wings"; or forcing or requiring the consumption of food, alcohol, drugs, or any other substance. In short, any behavior that causes or has potential to cause an individual or group to be embarrassed, humiliated, or injured represents a serious breach of the trust the Navy has placed in the trainer or supervisor. Those in the Navy who are engaged in the indoctrination, training, or supervision of more junior members are expected to use the power of their positions wisely and compassionately, for the good of the Navy and the individuals entrusted to them.

There is a common misperception that a certain degree of hazing is an essential element of effective military training; such a perception represents a serious misunderstanding of the concept of hazing. Rigorous training and stern discipline, when used to improve the performance of trainees or junior members, remain legitimate and beneficial training tools; harassment or humiliation of trainees or juniors for the amusement and personal gratification of their instructors or seniors does not now have, and indeed has never had, a legitimate place in any training or indoctrination program.

Initiation Ceremonies. Any form of initiation ceremony must be approved by the chain of command. Two commonly authorized initiation ceremonies are crossing-the-line, for crossing the equator, and chiefs' initiations for new chief petty officer selectees. To ensure such ceremonies enhance rather than damage the command climate, the CO should personally be involved in their planning and execution.

CHAPTER THREE

PERSONAL ADMINISTRATION

*Your personal records are you, as far as the Navy is concerned, until
you have had time to create a service reputation. Therefore, make
sure your records are complete, accurate and include all of your
qualifications and achievements.*

—Admiral Chester Nimitz

*A few moments spent taking care of your dependents' affairs will give
you peace of mind and your loved ones a settled future.*

—Vice Admiral Charles Melson

Officer Records

Of all of the responsibilities you will hold in your career, none will be more uniquely important to you than the proper maintenance of your personal records and those of your family members. These records will play a key role in your personal and professional success.

Electronic Service Record (ESR). You are responsible for establishing an ESR account on the Navy Standard Integrated Personnel System (NSIPS), located on the Navy Marine Corps Intranet (NMCI), and ensuring the accuracy of the information in your record. This record contains emergency contact information on your assignment and training history, personal awards, family data and insurance beneficiary information, and other key data. Individuals in your administrative office or chain of command can access your record if they have a need to do so as part of their official duties.

Medical and Dental Records. The medical department on board your ship, or the nearest Navy medical and dental clinics, will normally maintain these records. Although electronic record keeping is increasingly being used to supplement paper records and ensure continuity of care when records are not available, paper records still remain in use. Before checking out of your command, you will need to make sure to pick up these records so that you can hand-carry them to your next duty station. Your medical record will also include a separate shot record to enable your medical department or clinic to quickly determine when you are due for new immunizations.

Because your health record is government property, you must surrender it to the appropriate office rather than maintain it yourself. For this reason, whenever you are treated for anything significant, it is a good idea to make copies of the appropriate pages of your medical record and retain them in a safe place for future reference in the event your record is ever misplaced. In addition, it is a good idea to make a complete copy of your records prior to separation or retirement.

Official Military Personnel File (OMPF). This record is maintained on the Electronic Military Personnel Records System (EMPRS). Because the information in your OMPF is used by selection boards, it is important to ensure it is accurate and complete. The process for reviewing your record prior to a selection board is discussed in chapter 17.

Detailing. The process by which you are issued orders requires balancing three factors: personal desires, career development, and the needs of the Navy. Because these factors can sometimes conflict, it's beneficial for you to temper your personal desires with a clearheaded understanding of both the normal career progression for your designator, and current operational realities. Two officers at Navy Personnel Command (NPC) are directly involved in every set of orders you receive: your detailer and the placement officer who represents your next command. Your detailer is your representative in the negotiating process with the placement officer. Conversely, the placement officer is the Navy's representative, whose primary purpose is to ensure that the needs of the Navy are met during this process. Well in advance of the date you expect to transfer, you should establish communications with your detailer to make sure that he or she is aware of your particular desires for your next set of orders, and that you are aware of the billets that are likely to be available, taking into consideration your qualifications, experience, and career progression needs. Chapter 17 discusses this process in greater detail.

Prior to discussing your preferences with your detailer, you should file a preference card, listing your preferred billets, geographic areas, and commands, to allow your detailer to research the options available to you. The duty-preference card can be an actual card that you fill in and mail, or you may submit the same information electronically.

Officer Data Card (ODC). NPC produces the ODC from the active-duty Navy officer automated record. The ODC provides up-to-date information in an easy-to-use format that detailers and placement officers use in the distribution process and for consideration by various selection boards.

The ODC is prepared for all active-duty officers and may be reviewed online at http://www.bol.navy.mil. Review your ODC carefully for accuracy, and determine whether any updates or changes are necessary. If changes are required, print the document, circle items requiring correction in red, and indicate the correct information on the change form. To make corrections, you must return the ODC to the appropriate NPC code along with substantiating documentation (certified copies of appropriate documents). If no corrections are required, your administration office will place the ODC in your service record with a signed annotation that it has been verified as correct.

Full-Length Photograph. Within three months of your acceptance of each promotion, you must submit a full-length color photograph to NPC attached to NAVPERS form 1070/884. This photograph must be taken in service dress khaki (uncovered), three-quarter face (left shoulder forward), with your name, designator, social security number, and the date of the photograph displayed on a board in the foreground. Photographs may be mailed or submitted electronically.

Because your photograph will be used by selection boards to evaluate your general level of physical fitness and military bearing, it is important that it project a sharp military appearance. More information on the full-length photograph is in chapter 17.

Fitness Reports (FITREPs). The Navy requires that all officers and enlisted personnel be regularly and formally counseled on their performance. For officers and senior enlisted personnel, these evaluations are called fitness reports, or FITREPs.

The FITREP system evaluates every officer in each of the following areas:

- Professional expertise
- Command or organizational climate/equal opportunity
- Military bearing/character
- Teamwork
- Mission accomplishment/initiative
- Leadership
- Tactical performance

Performance traits are measured on a five-point scale, from 1.0 ("below standards") to 5.0 ("greatly exceeds standards"). A grade of 3.0 ("meets standards") represents performance to full Navy standards, with higher grades reserved for performance that significantly exceeds those standards. Reporting seniors must substantiate all grades of 1.0, two or more grades of 2.0, or any mark below 3.0 in Command or Organizational Climate/Equal Opportunity with explicit comments.

The FITREP form also provides a five-step promotion recommendation scale: "significant problems," "progressing," "promotable," "must promote," and "early promote." A recommendation of "early promote" does not require the officer receiving it to actually be eligible for early promotion, nor does it guarantee early promotion. Officers of the same pay grade and designator in a single command are ranked against each other in the same competitive group. There are strict limits on the number of officers within a competitive group who can be ranked in the top two promotion categories: a maximum of 20 percent of any group may be categorized as "early promote," and for pay grades above O-3, a maximum of 40 to 50 percent (depending on pay grade) may be in the combined categories of "early promote" and "must promote." Additional restrictions on assignment to promotion categories apply for officers in pay grades O-1 and O-2.

The purpose of a FITREP is to serve as a vehicle for your CO to clearly and succinctly communicate to the Navy your suitability for promotion and increased responsibility. Because of space constraints, comments on a fitness report must be brief and to the point. A well-written fitness report contains comments, written in bullet form, that are fact-based and specific, and that reflect quantifiable or documented achievements.

To enable a promotion board to fairly evaluate an officer's fitness report grades, the reporting senior's average FITREP grade is provided to the board. This practice also helps to prevent grade inflation; a 4.0, "above standards" grade from a CO whose average grade is 3.3 will carry much more weight with a selection board than one from a CO whose average grade is 4.5.

Pay and Allowances

Types of Compensation. The two broad categories of regular compensation are pay and allowances. In general, pay is taxable and is intended to compensate members for the performance of duty. Allowances are generally not taxable and are intended to reimburse members for certain costs, such as for meals, lodging, or travel.

Pay. The primary component of the pay for most military members is basic pay. The amount of basic pay, which is set in law, is based on pay grade or rank and years of service, and the same pay table is used for all of the uniformed services. Basic pay is augmented by special pays for certain types of duty, including career sea pay, submarine duty incentive pay, aviation career incentive pay, hazardous duty incentive pay, and imminent danger/hostile fire pay. Additional types of pay, such as medical and dental pay, aviation and nuclear retention bonuses, and reenlistment bonuses act as an incentive to help retain officers and enlisted personnel with specialized skills.

Allowances. Basic allowance for subsistence (BAS) compensates members for the costs of food when a government mess is not provided.

In lieu of government quarters, you will be authorized basic allowance for housing (BAH), based on your pay grade and the most recent survey of actual local housing costs. It is a good idea to find out what the local BAH rate is before beginning your housing search so that you know what kind of quarters you can afford. Bear in mind that in addition to your rent or mortgage payment you will also need to keep room in your budget for utilities, insurance, and commuting expenses. In principle, BAH should reimburse a typical officer or enlisted member for 75–85 percent of out-of-pocket housing rental costs (including utilities) in a given geographic area.

Another common type of allowance is the family separation allowance (FSA), payable to servicemembers with dependents, who are assigned away from their permanent duty stations.

When Paid. Payday for all members falls on the first and fifteenth of each month. When the first or fifteenth falls on a Saturday, Sunday, or holiday, payday is held the weekday before.

Pay Increases. The basic pay tables are designed to provide periodic pay raises (often called "fogeys"), normally every two years. Your pay raise dates are based on the anniversary date of your entry into active duty, called the pay entry base date (PEBD), or simply pay date. You will also receive significant increases in pay each time you are promoted to a higher rank. In addition, Congress normally authorizes an annual cost-of-living increase, which normally takes effect on January 1. Housing allowances are also adjusted annually, based on the housing costs in each geographic area.

Direct Deposit. You will be required to have your pay deposited directly into your bank account, rather than receiving an actual check on payday. This saves the government the effort and expense of drafting and distributing paychecks, and it can allow you to provide your spouse with rapid access to your funds even when you are on deployment.

Allotments. You may withhold set amounts from your pay for charitable contributions to the Navy and Marine Corps Relief Society (NMCRS) or Combined Federal Campaign (CFC), to make loan or insurance payments, or for deposits to bank accounts or other investments. Amounts withheld for these purposes are automatically transferred to the designated recipients.

Pay Record. The Defense Finance and Accounting Service (DFAS) maintains all pay records electronically. Each month you will receive an electronic leave and earnings statement (LES) that reflects your compensation and leave activity over the previous month. You should review your LES for accuracy. LESs are only retained online for twelve months, so you may want to also print a copy or save it to your own computer as a permanent record.

You will normally receive your LES on the same day as the mid-month payday. Figure 3-1 shows a sample LES. Some of the information included in the LES is as follows:

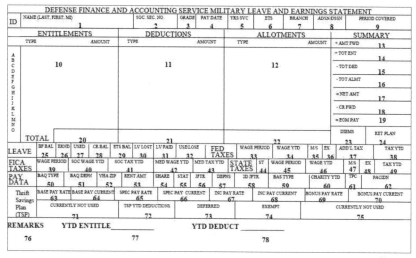

Figure 3-1 Leave and Earnings Statement

- The top section (sections numbered 1–9 in figure 3-1) includes your name, social security number (SSN), pay grade, pay date (or PEBD), years of active service, expiration of term of service, branch, disbursing station symbol number, and the period covered (normally, one month).

- The entitlements section (10) includes the types of entitlements and allowances you are receiving (e.g., base pay, BAS, etc.), their amounts, and the total amount of entitlements. If more than fifteen different types of entitlements are included, the overflow is printed in the remarks section.

- The deductions section (11) includes the types of deductions taken from your pay (state and federal taxes, etc.), their amounts, and the total amount of deductions.

- The allotments section (12) includes the types, amounts, and total amounts of your allotments.

- The summary section (13–19) adds the amount carried over from previous unpaid pay and allowances to the current month's entitlements and subtracts the total deductions and allotments to arrive at the net pay amount. This amount, less any amount to be carried forward to the next month, represents your net end-of-month pay.

- The day initially entered military service (DIEMS [23]) is used solely for the purpose of identifying a member's retirement plan eligibility. RET PLAN (24) indicates which retirement plan the member is under.

- The leave section (25–32) includes the leave balance brought forward from the beginning of the fiscal year or your first day of active duty, whichever was later; the amount of leave earned during the reporting period (2.5 days per month); the amount used during the reporting period; any leave lost during the period (under most circumstances, any unused leave in excess of 60 days is lost at the end of the fiscal year); leave paid to date; and leave projected to be lost if not taken in the current fiscal year.

- The federal tax section (33–38) includes wages earned during the current reporting period that are subject to federal income tax withholding (FITW); FITW wages earned to date; marital status; number of exemptions; additional taxes withheld in excess of the calculated amount from the appropriate tax tables; and cumulative total of FITW withheld throughout the calendar year.

- The Federal Insurance Contributions Act (FICA) tax (39–43) and state tax (44–49) sections contain similar information for these taxes.

- The pay data section (50–62) includes the type of BAH entitlement (with dependents/without dependents/partial, etc.); a letter code that indicates the type of dependents for which BAH is paid; the zip code used to compute BAH; the amount of your monthly rent or mortgage payment; the number of individuals (exclusive of dependents) sharing the housing cost; the number of your dependents, and codes to indicate the location(s) for which cost of living allowance (COLA) is paid; the type of BAS (this is blank for officers); cumulative charitable contributions for the calendar year; and the unit identification code used to represent your command.

- The Thrift Savings Plan (TSP) section (63–75) contains the percentages of base, special, bonus, and incentive pays elected for TSP contributions; the dollar amount of TSP contributions deducted for the year; the total dollar amount of TSP contributions that are deferred for tax purposes; and the dollar amount of TSP contributions that are reported as tax exempt to the Internal Revenue Service (IRS). TSP is discussed in more detail later in this chapter.

- The remarks section (76) contains additional information, including general notices, explanations of starts and stops, and other pertinent announcements.

- The final section includes the cumulative total of all entitlements for the calendar year (77) and the cumulative total of all deductions for the calendar year (78).

It is your responsibility to carefully review your LES and to promptly report any errors or questionable entries to your disbursing officer or Personnel Support Detachment (PSD). You can review your LES at any time via the Internet, at https://mypay.dfas.mil/mypay.aspx. Whenever an error in an officer's pay account occurs and the officer had received an LES for that period, the Navy assumes that the officer had sufficient understanding of the pay system to have been aware that the error occurred. (The same assumption is not always made for enlisted personnel.)

Travel Expenses. Whenever you are ordered to travel, either in conjunction with a permanent change of station (PCS) move, or for a brief period as temporary additional duty (TAD), you will be authorized certain travel entitlements, including mileage (if you are authorized to use your own vehicle), standard lodging and meal costs (i.e., per diem), and certain incidental expenses. If you are required to fly on a commercial airline, the government will normally provide you with a plane ticket directly.

Frequent travelers are provided with credit cards to use for their travel expenses. All travelers must file detailed travel claims, including certain receipts, upon completion of travel in order to receive compensation.

Medical Benefits

Although all active-duty members are eligible to receive treatment at military clinics and hospitals, dependents and retirees may have limited access to these facilities depending on the demand in the local area. The TRICARE system was designed to ensure adequate health care would be available to all dependents and retirees. The Defense Enrollment Eligibility Reporting System (DEERS) provides a means to rapidly verify a dependent's eligibility for health care. Although dependents are automatically enrolled in DEERS when they receive their military dependent identification cards, it is imperative that you update your dependents' information any time there is a change in your family status—for example, new address, marriage, child birth/adoption. Failure to do so could result in your dependents being denied their entitlements.

Active-duty servicemembers must enroll in TRICARE Prime (described below), but other beneficiaries such as family members and retirees have several options for seeking care under the TRICARE program, each with a different cost-sharing feature and level of flexibility.

TRICARE Prime. This option is similar to most civilian health maintenance organizations. There is no annual fee for dependents of active-duty members (although there is a small fee for retirees) and no annual deductible, which, along with minimal copayments, make it the least expensive option. However, it is also the least flexible option. All TRICARE Prime users must utilize a single primary care manager (PCM), which may be either a network civilian provider or, if available, a military treatment facility (MTF). This provider treats routine ailments and authorizes any additional tests, treatments, and referrals that may be necessary. Enrollment in TRICARE Prime is not automatic and must be initiated by the member or dependents.

TRICARE Standard and Extra. Under TRICARE Standard and Extra beneficiaries have almost complete freedom to choose their own health care providers. However, this option has a significant annual deductible as well as an annual benefits cap, and the beneficiary bears 15–25 percent of all outpatient costs. TRICARE Standard refers to non-network physicians; use of TRICARE network physicians under TRICARE Extra can result in smaller out-of-pocket costs. All dependents and retirees are automatically eligible to participate in TRICARE Standard and TRICARE Extra.

TRICARE for Life. TRICARE for Life (TFL) is TRICARE's Medicare-wraparound coverage available to all Medicare-eligible TRICARE beneficiaries, regardless of age, provided they have Medicare Parts A and B. When Medicare is your primary insurance, TRICARE acts as your secondary payer, minimizing your out-of-pocket expenses. TRICARE benefits include covering Medicare's coinsurance and deductible.

Emergency Treatment. Although under normal circumstances active-duty members receive all of their health care from MTFs, you may always seek emergency treatment from the closest emergency room. After seeking such care, contact your local health benefits adviser (who is normally attached to a military hospital or medical center) as soon as possible to arrange for payment of the bills.

Dental Care. Active-duty members receive free dental care from military dentists, although such care is rarely available to dependents and retirees. Active-duty members may enroll their dependents in the TRICARE dental plan, which provides some benefits for a minimal annual cost. Currently, TRICARE dental benefits are offered via United Concordia. Enrollment for dependents is not automatic, and there is a monthly premium for participation.

Death and Burial

Servicemembers' Group Life Insurance (SGLI). Every member on active duty is entitled to purchase term life insurance coverage in amounts up to $400,000 under the SGLI program. The cost for this insurance is $0.065 per month per $1,000 coverage. In addition, all servicemembers are charged $1.00 per month for mandatory traumatic injury protection coverage. The cost of SGLI compares very favorably with that of most commercial life insurance policies, and unlike many such policies, includes coverage for deaths resulting from aviation accidents or combat action.

Family Servicemembers' Group Life Insurance (FSGLI). This program provides life insurance coverage to spouses and dependent children up to a maximum of $100,000 for spouses and $10,000 for dependent children. Enrollment is automatic unless FSGLI coverage is specifically declined or reduced by the servicemember.

Notification and Arrangements. Whenever an active-duty member dies, the Navy assigns a casualty assistance calls officer (CACO), who is frequently accompanied by a Navy chaplain, to notify in person the member's primary next of kin (usually the spouse, or the parent of a single member). Officers and senior enlisted members serving in a particular geographic area may be assigned as collateral duty CACOs for that area. These individuals receive training to enable them to assist the families with paperwork, funeral arrangements, and payment of benefits. Once assigned to a member's family, the CACO remains available to assist them full-time for as long as is required. When a secondary next of kin, such as a parent or adult child, is located in a different geographic area, another CACO may be assigned to notify and assist him or her.

Dependency and Indemnity Compensation. Dependency and Indemnity Compensation (DIC) provides continuing financial support to a deceased member's surviving spouse and dependent children. Spouses who later remarry may lose their entitlement to DIC, although such remarriage does not affect the children's entitlements.

Burial. For service-related deaths, the Department of Veterans Affairs (VA) will pay up to $2,000 toward burial expenses, and if the servicemember is buried in a VA national cemetery, some or all of the cost of transporting the deceased may be reimbursed. For non–service-related deaths, the VA will pay up to $300 toward burial and funeral expenses and $300 to help defray interment costs. The VA will also provide a flag to each deceased servicemember's family, and, if the member is buried in a private cemetery, a marker.

Miscellaneous Benefits

Legal Assistance. Legal services offices on most installations provide free legal advice and counseling for active-duty members, but they cannot represent members in court.

Because no Navy member should be without a will, Navy Legal Services Offices will prepare wills free of charge, and frequently arrange visits aboard soon-to-deploy ships to ensure that all crew members onboard have the opportunity to have their wills drawn. These offices can also draft powers of attorney for service-members, free of charge.

DoD Military Spouse Preference Program. This program provides priority in the employment selection process for military spouses who are relocating as a result of their military spouse's permanent change of station. Spouse preference may be used for most vacant civil service positions in the Department of Defense (DoD) and applies only within the commuting area of the spouse's permanent duty station. It is not limited to the branch of the military in which the spouse is serving or to only those who have previously worked for the federal government. Preference does not obligate the government to create jobs or make jobs available especially for military spouses; nor does it guarantee employment.

Educational Benefits. The Navy offers servicemembers a wide variety of opportunities to further their academic studies. These programs are discussed in detail in chapter 17.

Personal Financial Management

Budgeting. The simplest way to establish a budget is to list all of your income, including pay, allowances, and investment income. Then list your expenses, including your rent or mortgage, commuting costs, mess bill and other food expenses, utilities, insurance, taxes, and loan payments. The difference is your discretionary income, some of which you will probably need to pay for uniforms and other work-related expenses. If you find you are spending more than this difference on a regular basis and are beginning to accumulate credit card and other debt, you may be headed for trouble.

Savings and Investment. As soon as you receive your commission, you should plan to implement a savings and investment strategy. You should establish a short-term savings account, equal to several months' pay, to take care of unexpected bills and emergency expenditures. This account should be very accessible and safe, such as a bank or credit union savings account. In addition, you should establish a long-term investment program to enable you to buy a home, continue your education, or pursue other long-term goals. This type of account does not need to be as liquid as your short-term savings, and if you are willing to accept a higher risk, over the long run you can obtain a higher rate of return with mutual funds or individual stocks and bonds than you can with savings accounts or other insured vehicles. In addition to these investments, it pays to begin planning for your retirement needs early in your career; establishment of a traditional or Roth individual retirement account (IRA) is a smart move for any officer. You may want to consider consulting with a professional investment counselor to assist you in developing your investment strategy.

The Thrift Savings Plan (TSP) is similar to the 401(k) retirement plans offered by many private employers, and can provide a valuable supplemental source of retirement income. As a defined contribution plan, the retirement income that you will someday receive from your TSP account will depend on how much you contribute to your account and on the earnings on those contributions. You may elect to contribute any percentage of your basic pay, up to the IRS maximum limit ($16,500 as of 2010), and invest it in a variety of funds including government securities, fixed income, common stock, and other options.

Insurance. SGLI and FSGLI were discussed earlier in this chapter. Taking into account the size of your family and the amount of your outstanding debts and expenses (e.g., house payments), you may determine that you need to obtain additional insurance. A number of associations specialize in insurance policies for military members. Before purchasing any life insurance, make certain it does not exclude from coverage deaths that occur due to combat action or aviation mishaps.

Loans and Credit. It is advisable to have a general-purpose credit card, which is safe and convenient and can provide a ready source of cash in an emergency. It is good practice to pay off your credit card bills in full every month to avoid accumulating debt and paying the generally high-interest rates associated with these cards. You may eventually desire to obtain additional credit, such as for a car loan or mortgage payment. Be sure to pay your bills promptly to help build a good credit rating.

CHAPTER FOUR

MILITARY COURTESY, HONORS, AND CEREMONIES

*A naval ceremony should follow the long-established rules for its
execution carefully and exactly. Such attention to detail honors those
who, long before us, established the ritual, and all those who, past,
present, and future, take part in that same ceremony.*

—Fleet Admiral Chester Nimitz

Any profession has its standards of appropriate courtesy and decorum, but
this is particularly true in the Navy. As an officer, you will be expected to
be familiar with the fundamentals of military honors, ceremonies, customs, and traditions. Not only must you be comfortable with these procedures
yourself, but you must be prepared to properly instruct and supervise your subordinates. Military "smartness" is a much valued trait in the Navy. You will find your
mastery of the subject tested daily, starting when you step aboard the quarterdeck
of your first command.

Fortunately, the information you will need on a day-to-day basis is relatively
easy to master, and you will normally have time to research and rehearse for major
ceremonial events, such as changes of command and official visits from dignitaries. *Navy Regulations* (available in every command), *Naval Ceremonies, Customs
and Traditions*, and *Watch Officer's Guide* are several publications that might prove
useful when preparing for such events.

Courtesy

Honors and ceremonies are based on the societal principle of courtesy, which
implies politeness and considerate behavior toward others.

Military Courtesy. Military courtesy is a more codified extension of the system of civilian courtesy, and its strict obedience is important to the maintenance of discipline. Military courtesy and mutual respect and consideration operate from senior to junior as well as from junior to senior. Seniors must treat juniors with fairness and compassion just as juniors must treat seniors with respect and obedience.

The Salute. The hand salute, performed at the meeting of a junior and a senior who is an officer, is the most basic act of military courtesy. The salute has been handed down through the ages and is an integral part of military life. The senior is as much obliged to return it as is the junior to render it. You should learn to execute a sharp salute, as a sloppy salute is nearly as discourteous as a failure to salute. Figure 4-1 displays the proper procedure. You must also understand the circumstances under which salutes are required, as well as those in which salutes are not appropriate. Figure 4-2 illustrates some of the more common situations.

Enlisted members do not exchange salutes except under special circumstances, as when one of the members is standing watch as officer of the deck (OOD). You will normally salute with your right hand, unless an injury or other reason makes this impracticable, in which case you should salute with your left hand. The custom of offering left-handed salutes under such circumstances is unique to the Navy and Marine Corps; Army and Air Force personnel never salute with their left hands. When under arms, Navy members render the appropriate salute for the type of arm.

Figure 4-1 The Hand Salute

IN GENERAL

ENLISTED MEN SALUTE OFFICERS AND JUNIOR OFFICERS
SALUTE SENIOR WHEN MEETING, PASSING NEAR, WHEN ADDRESSING
OR BEING ADDRESSED

WHEN SEVERAL OFFICERS ARE
SALUTED, ALL SHALL RETURN IT

WHEN OVERTAKING A SENIOR,
THE SALUTE SHALL BE GIVEN WHEN
ABREAST, WITH "BY YOUR LEAVE, SIR."

OFFICERS AND ALL ENLISTED MEN NOT IN FORMATION SALUTE
DURING HONORS TO THE FLAG OR PLAYING OF NATIONAL ANTHEM

WHEN REPORTING (COVERED)

GUARDS SALUTE ALL OFFICERS
PASSING CLOSE ABOARD

Figure 4-2 When to Salute/When Not to Salute

Juniors salute first. Seniors in uniform and covered (wearing a hat) must return all salutes; at other times seniors must appropriately acknowledge salutes, such as with a nod or verbal greeting. Uncovered members do not salute, except when failure to do so would cause embarrassment or misunderstanding. This is another circumstance in which the custom followed by members of the Navy and Marine Corps differs from the custom followed by Army and Air Force members, who do render salutes when uncovered.

Navy Regulations sets forth the occasions on which salutes must be rendered. Members of the Naval Service render salutes to senior officers of the armed forces of the United States, the National Oceanic and Atmospheric Administration (NOAA), the Public Health Service (PHS), and foreign armed services.

All persons in the Naval Service must salute all officers senior to themselves on each occasion of meeting or passing near or when addressed by or addressing such officers, with the following exceptions:

- On board ship, salutes may be dispensed with after the first daily meeting, except for those rendered to the CO and those senior to him or her, to visiting officers, to officers making inspections, and to those officers when addressed or being addressed by them.

- At crowded gatherings, or in congested areas when normal procedures for saluting are impracticable, salutes must be rendered only when addressing, or being addressed by, a more senior officer.

- Members at work or engaged in games must salute only when addressed by a more senior officer, and then only if circumstances warrant.

- Members in formation must salute only on specific command to the formation. Normally, only the person in charge of a formation will salute.

- When boats pass each other with embarked officers or officials in view, the senior officer or boat officer and coxswain in each boat exchange salutes. More information on boat etiquette is included later in this chapter.

Wearing of Covers. Navy personnel in uniform normally wear headgear at all times when outdoors, except at sea (at the discretion of the CO), when doing so could create a safety hazard (as during flight operations), or at religious or funeral services. You should always uncover when entering any mess or berthing area or sick bay, unless you are conducting an inspection. As a general rule, you should normally uncover when indoors unless you are attending an official military function at which headgear is prescribed or are under arms or on watch.

General Notes on Salutes and Other Military Courtesies. Salutes are normally exchanged at a distance of no less than six paces, although twenty-five paces is not considered excessive. The junior remains at the salute until the senior returns the

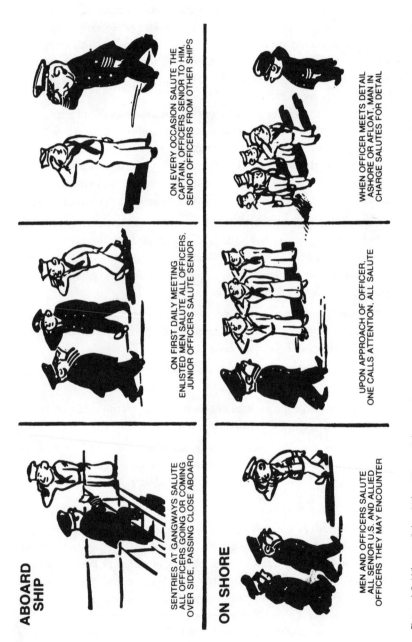

ABOARD SHIP

SENTRIES AT GANGWAYS SALUTE ALL OFFICERS GOING OR COMING OVER SIDE, PASSING CLOSE ABOARD

ON FIRST DAILY MEETING ENLISTED MEN SALUTE ALL OFFICERS. JUNIOR OFFICERS SALUTE SENIOR

ON EVERY OCCASION SALUTE THE CAPTAIN, OFFICERS SENIOR TO HIM. SENIOR OFFICERS FROM OTHER SHIPS

ON SHORE

MEN AND OFFICERS SALUTE ALL SENIOR U.S. AND ALLIED OFFICERS THEY MAY ENCOUNTER

UPON APPROACH OF OFFICER, ONE CALLS ATTENTION, ALL SALUTE

WHEN OFFICER MEETS DETAIL ASHORE OR AFLOAT, MAN IN CHARGE SALUTES FOR DETAIL

Figure 4-2 When to Salute/When Not to Salute (continued)

IN BOATS

ENLISTED MEN RISE AND SALUTE WHEN AN OFFICER ENTERS OR LEAVES

OFFICERS RISE AND SALUTE WHEN A SENIOR ENTERS OR LEAVES

WHEN OFFICER PASSES NEAR, OFFICER OR PETTY OFFICER IN CHARGE SALUTES. IF NONE PRESENT, MEN DO

VEHICLES

RENDER SALUTES DUE THEM TO ALL OFFICERS IN VEHICLES (IF SAFETY PERMITS)

WHEN COLORS ARE SOUNDED MAN IN CHARGE OF DETAIL SALUTES; OTHERS AT ATTENTION

PASSENGERS IN CARS RENDER AND RETURN SALUTE (DRIVER: NO, IF SAFETY IS INVOLVED)

Figure 4-2 When to Salute/When Not to Salute *(continued)*

DO NOT SALUTE

WHEN UNCOVERED
(WITHOUT HEAD DRESS)

WHEN IN RANKS
(IF ADDRESSED, COME TO ATTENTION)

AT OARS IN A
PULLING BOAT

WHEN ENGAGED IN
GAMES OR ATHLETICS

WHEN CARRYING ARTICLES
IN BOTH HANDS

IN PUBLIC CONVEYANCES
WHEN OBVIOUSLY INAPPROPRIATE

AT MESS (IF ADDRESSED BY
OFFICER, SIT AT ATTENTION)

IN PUBLIC PLACES WHERE INAPPROPRIATE
(THEATRE, HOTEL, RESTAURANT, ETC.)

WHEN PART OF A
DETAIL AT WORK

Figure 4-2 When to Salute/When Not to Salute *(continued)*

salute or the senior is well past. Conversely, seniors must always be alert to salutes rendered from farther away than the minimum distance. Juniors should always accompany their salutes with greetings such as "Good morning, Lieutenant," or "Good evening, ma'am," which should be returned by the senior.

When you are overtaking a senior, approach to the senior's left, salute when abreast, and say, "By your leave sir (ma'am)." You may pass the senior after he or she returns your salute and responds with "Very well," or "Permission granted."

If you are seated when approached by a more senior officer, you should rise and salute. When your hands are full so as to prevent a salute, or when you are uncovered, you should greet the senior with a verbal salutation such as "Good morning, sir (ma'am)." When you are covered, you should salute whenever you recognize a senior officer, regardless of whether the senior is covered or in uniform. Under such circumstances, the senior should nod or speak to you to acknowledge the salute.

When formally addressing, or being addressed by, a senior, stand at attention. If covered, salute when first addressed and again upon the conclusion of the instruction or conversation, and stand at attention throughout the conversation unless otherwise directed by the senior. You should rise, uncover, and stand at attention whenever a senior visits your stateroom or office.

If anyone observes an officer or high-ranking civilian approaching an area where his or her passage would otherwise be blocked, he or she should give the command "Gangway." Enlisted personnel should not use this word to clear a passage for themselves or for other enlisted persons but should say "Coming through," or something to that effect. When the command "Gangway" is given, the senior petty officer in the vicinity is responsible for seeing that it is carried out.

Always use "sir" or "ma'am" after "yes" or "no" when conversing with senior officers. Many senior officers use these terms as a matter of courtesy when conversing with junior officers. Also add "sir" or "ma'am" to any routine statement, request, or report to a more senior officer, such as "The watch is relieved, ma'am," or "I request permission to leave the ship, sir."

A junior never initiates a handshake, but waits for the senior to do so. Juniors walk, ride, or sit on the left of seniors they are accompanying; juniors open doors for seniors, passing through last when practicable.

The place of honor is to the right. Accordingly, when you walk, ride, or sit with a senior, take position alongside and to the left of the senior.

Officers enter boats and automobiles in inverse order of seniority, unless the senior indicates he or she desires other arrangements. Juniors always allow seniors the most desirable seats. Although the traditional seat of honor is in the rear of a vehicle, in practice many seniors prefer to ride in the front passenger seat.

Small-Boat Etiquette

Figure 4-3 illustrates some of the more common rules of boat etiquette. You should master them thoroughly prior to riding in a boat or being assigned to serve as a boat officer. The following general rules apply:

- Juniors normally board first and leave last, unless given an order to the contrary. Juniors must ensure that there is sufficient room left in the boat for seniors; if there is not, juniors should leave the boat without being asked and wait for the next one.

- The most desirable seats in any boat are in the stern. Juniors must move forward as necessary to give seniors more room astern.

- Juniors rise when seniors embark, unless it is unsafe to do so.

- For safety reasons, all personnel must keep their hands and arms inside the boat. All officers and petty officers are responsible for ensuring that junior personnel on the boat do not become loud or unruly or otherwise cause a hazard or distract the coxswain and boat crew from the safe operation of the boat.

- All personnel on a boat should step carefully and avoid walking on varnished areas.

- The senior unrestricted line officer in a boat should identify himself or herself to the boat officer and coxswain. This officer is responsible for the safe and proper operation of the boat but should leave the normal operation to the boat officer and coxswain unless it is necessary to intervene in an emergency.

Responsibilities of Boat Officers. Boat officers are normally assigned to each boat operating in an unfamiliar port, in periods of poor visibility or bad weather, at night, when senior officers or other dignitaries are embarked, or at other times as prescribed by the CO or higher authority. When you are assigned as a boat officer, you are responsible for the safe operation and navigation of the boat and must ensure that the coxswain is aware of and ready to execute the appropriate rules of etiquette. Just as military courtesy must be observed between individual juniors and seniors, similar courtesies must be observed between "junior" boats and boats carrying more senior officers or dignitaries. These rules include the following:

- No junior should overtake and pass a senior without permission.

- The senior officer or boat officer and coxswain in the junior boat salute passing seniors; the senior officer or boat officer and the coxswain in the senior boat return the salute. Other passengers do not salute but, if practicable, sit in a position of attention facing the direction of the boat being saluted. The coxswain and saluting officer rise to salute unless doing so would be hazardous.

Figure 4-3 Boat Etiquette

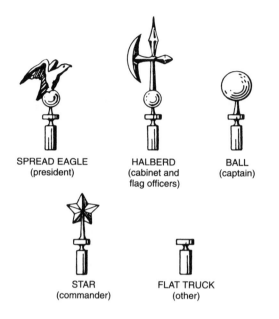

SPREAD EAGLE
(president)

HALBERD
(cabinet and
flag officers)

BALL
(captain)

STAR
(commander)

FLAT TRUCK
(other)

Figure 4-4 Boat Staff Insignia

- When approaching a ship or landing, a junior boat gives way to a senior boat.
- The coxswain must haul clear of the ship or boat landing while waiting for passengers and must not allow the crew to leave the boat.
- The crew must not lounge in the boat while it is running.
- A boat crew should be outfitted in the same uniform, which must be clean and properly worn.
- During colors, the boat stops and disengages the clutch, and the senior officer or boat officer and the coxswain stand at attention and salute. Other passengers remain seated at attention. During gun salutes, the procedures are similar, although only the person being honored rises.

Boat Appearance. The reputation of a ship is based, in part, on the smartness and appearance of its boats and boat crews. An alert, well-uniformed crew is the first step in this direction, as a sharp crew will take pride in their boat. Chrome and fancywork may further enhance an already sharp boat but are not substitutes for cleanliness, preservation, and neatness. Boats should have a full complement of safety devices and life jackets, as well as flags and flagstaff devices, and coxswains should understand their use.

Boat Hails. In the days prior to World War II, large ships normally anchored or moored to buoys, even when in home port. Under such circumstances, boat operations were far more common than they are today, and the system of boat hails developed to allow the OOD to determine the seniority of passengers in approaching boats. Although today it is normal for ships to be moored to piers and the use of hand-held radio communications between a ship and its boats has become common, the system of boat hails is still in use.

All boats approaching a ship at night should be hailed as soon as they are within hearing distance. The proper hail is "Boat ahoy!" The coxswain should answer as appropriate to indicate the rank of the senior passenger, as follows:

Senior Passenger	Hail
President or Vice President of the United States	"United States"
Secretary of Defense	"Defense"
Secretary of the Navy	"Navy"
Commander in Chief of the Fleet	"Fleet"
CO of a ship	"(ship name)"
Other commissioned officer	"Aye, aye"
Midshipman	"No, no"
Enlisted person	"Hello"
Passenger of any status in a boat not intending to come alongside	"Passing"

Boat Flags and Pennants. In addition to the national ensign, a boat should display the personal flag or pennant of an officer entitled to the boat, or when the officer is embarked for some other reason.

Boat Staff Insignia. Boats should display, on both staffs, insignia appropriate to the rank and position of the senior passenger. Figure 4-4 shows these insignia.

Boat Gongs. Boat gongs are used to announce the impending departure of a scheduled boat. Three gongs indicates ten minutes to departure, two gongs five minutes, and one gong one minute.

Display of the National Ensign

Marks of Respect. Title 4, USC, chap. 1 describes the required conduct with respect to the national ensign. The following excerpt outlines the appropriate actions during hoisting, lowering, or passing of the ensign:

> During the ceremony of hoisting or lowering the flag or when the flag is passing in a parade or in review, all persons present in uniform should render the military salute. Members of the Armed Forces and veterans who are present but not in uniform may render the military salute. All other persons present should face the flag and stand at attention with their right hand over the heart, or if applicable, remove their headdress with their right hand and hold it at the left shoulder, the hand being over the heart. Citizens of other countries present should stand at attention. All such conduct toward the flag in a moving column should be rendered at the moment the flag passes.

Display of the National Ensign and Union Jack Afloat. When not under way, ships display the national ensign and union jack from 0800 until sunset, from the flagstaff (at the stern of the ship) and the jackstaff (at the bow), respectively. The union jack must be the size of the union (the blue star-studded field) in the national ensign.

Ships under way must display the national ensign during daylight hours from the gaff under the following circumstances, unless otherwise directed by the senior officer present:

- Getting under way and coming to anchor
- Falling in with other ships
- Cruising near land
- During battle

Display of the National Ensign Ashore. Shore commands display the national ensign from 0800 to sunset near the headquarters building, or at the headquarters of the senior commander when the proximity of headquarters for two or more commands makes the display of separate ensigns inappropriate. This is another custom in which the services differ: Army and Air Force installations display the flag between reveille (normally 0630–0730), which marks the beginning of the workday, and retreat (1700), which marks the end of the workday.

Half-Masting the National Ensign and the Union Jack. The ensign is half-masted at the direction of higher authority to recognize the death of a senior officer or official. In half-masting the national ensign, it must, if not previously hoisted, first be hoisted to the truck or peak and then lowered to half-mast. Before lowering from half-mast, the ensign is hoisted to the truck or peak and then lowered.

When the national ensign is half-masted, the union jack is likewise half-masted.

Dipping the National Ensign. When any vessel, under the U.S. registry, or under the registry of a nation formally recognized by the government of the United States, salutes a ship of the Navy by dipping its ensign, the Navy ship answers dip for dip. If not already being displayed, the national ensign must be hoisted for the purpose of answering a dip. An ensign being displayed at half-mast is hoisted to the truck or peak before a dip is answered. No ship of the Navy should dip the national ensign unless in return for such compliment.

Morning and Evening Colors. All ships and shore commands follow the movements of the senior officer present afloat (SOPA) upon all occasions of hoisting, lowering, or half-masting the national ensign. The ship in which SOPA is embarked displays the "starboard" pennant from the inboard halyard of the starboard main yardarm for easy identification.

Ships in port observe certain ceremonies at colors. Each day, members of the duty section are detailed in the watch bill as the color guard. At 0755, in preparation for morning colors, a designated member of the duty section, who is in a position to observe the actions of SOPA, follows SOPA's lead and plays a recorded bugle call or announces "First call to colors." As first call is sounded, another member of the duty section (normally the duty signalman) hoists the "prep" pennant. At 0800, still following the movements of SOPA, the bugle call "Attention," or one blast on a whistle, is sounded and the duty signalman dips the "prep" pennant. This is followed by the playing of the national anthem, if music is available. At the beginning of the national anthem, members of the color guard simultaneously hoist the ensign and the jack smartly to the peak or truck. All Navy personnel face the ensign and render an appropriate salute as the ensign is hoisted. The salutes terminate, and the signalman hauls down the "prep" pennant, when the bugle call "Carry on" is played or three whistle blasts are sounded.

Ships observe the same ceremony during evening colors, beginning with first call at five minutes prior to sunset and evening colors at sunset when the ensign is lowered. Ships do not hold colors when under way. The procedure is similar on shore, except that the "prep" pennant is not hoisted, and bugle calls, music, and whistles are not always used.

During colors, a boat within sight or hearing of the ceremony must lie to (take all way off) or proceed at the minimum safe speed for navigation. The boat officer (or in his or her absence, the coxswain), must stand and salute, except when it is dangerous to do so. Other passengers remain seated and do not salute. Automobiles in the vicinity also stop, and the individuals riding in them do not salute but remain seated at attention during the ceremony.

The National Anthem. The same conduct prescribed for when the ensign is being hoisted, lowered, or passing is also followed when the national anthem is played, except that when the flag is not displayed, those present should face toward the music and act in the same manner they would if the flag were displayed there.

The national anthem of the United States, when played by a naval band, is played through without repetition of any part, except for those measures repeated to accommodate the words when the anthem is sung. It is prohibited to play the national anthem of the United States or of any other country as a part of a medley.

Commission Pennants and Other Distinctive Marks. Except when another distinctive mark is displayed as described in this section, commissioned ships display a commission pennant that is continuously flown from the after masthead.

When a flag officer eligible for command at sea is embarked, the ship hauls down the commission pennant and displays the flag officer's personal flag in the same manner. The personal flags of Navy officers are blue flags with white stars; Marine Corps officers have red flags with gold stars. A small boat displays a similar, smaller flag when a flag officer is aboard. A non-flag officer who is in command of a force, group, or squadron of ships or an aircraft wing is similarly entitled to display a broad command pennant. A burgee command pennant is displayed by officers in command of a division of ships or craft or a major subdivision of an aircraft wing. A ship may display only one distinctive mark at any one time.

Dress Ship/Full Dress Ship. Dress ship is prescribed for ships in port on all national holidays except Presidents' Day and the Fourth of July, and when directed by higher authority. For dress ship, the "holiday" ensign, the largest ensign with which the ship is furnished, is flown from the flagstaff and an appropriately sized jack from the jackstaff. In addition, except when as prescribed for a ship displaying a personal flag or command pennant, a national ensign is displayed from each masthead.

Full dress ship is prescribed for Presidents' Day, the Fourth of July, and special occasions when directed by higher authority. Full dress ship entails the same flag arrangements as in dress ship, with the addition of a rainbow of signal flags running from the foot of the jackstaff to the mastheads to the foot of the flagstaff. These signal flags are arranged in a specific prescribed order.

Dress ship and full dress ship are not displayed when under way.

Honors, Visits, and Calls

Honors, visits, and calls are important to military courtesy, and you must learn to carry them out meticulously. When acting as an OOD or otherwise involved in the preparations, you should carefully review all regulations concerning the events to take place. The CO, executive officer (XO), and command duty officer (CDO)

A Sailor polishes a bell aboard the ceremonial quarterdeck of the aircraft carrier USS *George H. W. Bush* (CVN 77).

will all be concerned with planning and preparing for these events and should be consulted if you have any questions, but the OOD is responsible for executing the required honors and must master all the details. Because advance notice is not always possible, you must always be prepared to render honors without the opportunity for extensive preparation.

The OOD is responsible for instructing the watchstanders in their responsibilities and for assembling, inspecting, and rehearsing the boatswain's mate and sideboys.

Quarterdeck Honors. Gongs are routinely used to announce the arrival and departure of the CO and embarked officers senior to the CO, as well as visiting officers in the pay grade of O-5 and senior; in special circumstances (such as to mark a retirement ceremony) gongs may be sounded for officers junior to pay grade O-5. The number of gongs corresponds to the number of sideboys appropriate to the officer's rank, although gongs are sounded even for informal visits when sideboys are not employed. Gongs are always sounded in pairs; the appropriate number of gongs for each pay grade is as follows:

Grade	Gongs
Officers in pay grades O-4 and below	2
Officers in pay grades O-5 and O-6	4
Officers in pay grade O-7 and O-8	6
Officers in pay grade O-9 and above	8

Immediately following the gongs, if the arriving officer is in command, his or her organization is announced followed by the word "arriving" or "departing." The chief of staff of an embarked commander is announced as "Staff," and all other officers are announced by their rank, as in "Commander, United States Navy." For the CO, or embarked chief of staff or flag officer, one final gong is sounded as the officer actually steps aboard or off the ship. Although several minutes or more may elapse between the announcement of the officer's imminent arrival or departure and the final gong, no intervening announcements may be made except in an emergency.

Sideboys are enlisted personnel paraded to render honors to a visiting dignitary. A dignitary rates the same number of sideboys as the number of gongs as listed above. Under the supervision and tutelage of a boatswain's mate, who pipes the side with a boatswain's pipe as the dignitary comes aboard, the sideboys line either side of the quarterdeck or other ceremonial area and render a salute to the visitor. Officers appropriate to the occasion must attend the side on the arrival and departure of officials and officers.

Ships do not normally parade sideboys on Sunday, or on other days between sunset and 0800, or during meal hours of the crew, general drills, or overhaul; and sideboys are paraded only for scheduled visits.

Passing Honors. Passing honors are those honors other than gun salutes that are rendered when ships (or boats with embarked officials or officers) pass, or are passed, close aboard. "Close aboard" is defined as within six hundred yards for ships, or four hundred yards for boats, although these rules are interpreted liberally to ensure passing honors are always rendered when appropriate. The "senior" ship or vessel is defined as the ship with the more senior CO or embarked officer. The signalmen maintain a publication containing a list of all of the ships and the relative seniority of their COs. Passing honors between ships of the Navy and Coast Guard consist of the following sequence of events:

- When the bows of the two ships cross (or the bow and stern, if in an overtaking situation), the junior vessel sounds "Attention" to starboard/port using one/two short blasts on a whistle, respectively. All personnel on the appropriate side of the junior vessel come to attention. The senior follows the action of the junior, calling "Attention" on its own port or starboard side, as appropriate.

- The junior vessel sounds one short whistle blast for "Hand salute." All personnel on the appropriate side of the ship render a salute to the senior vessel. The senior vessel returns the salute by sounding one whistle blast, and all personnel on the appropriate side of the senior vessel return the salute.

- The senior vessel sounds two short blasts on the whistle, signifying "Ready, two," and all personnel on the senior vessel drop their salutes. The junior vessel follows suit accordingly.

- The senior vessel sounds three short blasts on the whistle for "Carry on," and the junior vessel follows suit.

Ships do not exchange passing honors between sunset and 0800 except when required by international courtesy, nor are honors exchanged when ships are engaged in tactical evolutions outside port. The senior officer present may direct that passing honors be dispensed with in whole or in part.

Official Visits and Calls. An official visit is a formal courtesy requiring special honors and ceremonies; a call is an informal visit requiring no special ceremonies. Generally speaking, most official visits and calls are performed by the CO.

An officer assuming command at sea shall make an official visit to the senior to whom he or she is reporting for duty and to any successor of that senior.

Unless dispensed with by the senior, calls must be made by

- An officer assuming command ashore, on the senior to whom he or she is reporting for duty and on any successor of that senior.

- The commander of an arriving unit, on his or her immediate superior in the chain of command, if present; and, when circumstances permit, on the senior officer present

- An officer in command, on an immediate superior in the chain of command upon the arrival of the latter

- An officer who has been the senior officer present, on his or her successor

- The commander of a unit arriving at a naval base or station, on the commander of such base or station; except that when the former is senior, the latter shall make the call

- An officer reporting for duty, on the commanding officer

When visiting a foreign port, the CO may be required to make additional calls on senior officers and local officials and on U.S. diplomatic and consular representatives. A message sent to the ship prior to its arrival in port generally outlines specific requirements for these calls.

Entering and Leaving Port. When a ship departs from or returns to its home port, when it pays a visit to a foreign port, and on other special occasions at the discretion of the CO, the crew is mustered topside. There are two different procedures for this:

- Manning the rail. The crew members, dressed in the uniform of the day, line the rail. This procedure may be carried out on both sides of the ship, or on the side of the ship closest to the pier.

- Parade at quarters. Under this procedure, the crew members muster at their normal topside locations for quarters, normally in the uniform of the day.

The CO may dispense with the above procedures in foul weather.

Ceremonies

A ceremony is a formal series of acts carried out in a manner prescribed by authority or custom. *Navy Regulations* provides the details of formal ceremonies afloat, and informal ceremonies are governed by custom and tradition. This section covers a few of the more common Navy ceremonies.

Commissioning a Ship and Assuming Command. The ceremony for commissioning a ship is not prescribed specifically in *Navy Regulations*, but custom has established a relatively uniform procedure. The crew assembles on the quarterdeck, stern, or other open area, usually in two ranks facing inboard. Officers assemble in two ranks facing the ceremonial area. A band and guard form in or near the ceremonial area. Distinguished guests and principal participants are seated in a position to observe but not to be between the ceremonial area and the crew. If space is limited, guests may be seated on an adjacent ship or on the pier. The first watch, including the OOD, assembles on the quarterdeck. Sailors are stationed near the national ensign, jack, and commission pennant or personal flag halyards.

The officer making the transfer opens the ceremony by reading his or her orders for delivery of the ship. "Attention" is then sounded on the bugle, the national anthem is played, and the ensign, jack, and commission pennant or personal flag are hoisted simultaneously. The ship is officially commissioned with this act.

The officer effecting the transfer delivers the ship to the CO by saying, "I hereby deliver USS *Stethem.*" The officer ordered to command the ship reads his or her orders, then states, "I hereby assume command of USS *Stethem,*" and orders the XO to set the watch. The XO in turn directs the OOD to set the watch, and the ship's boatswain or senior boatswain's mate pipes the watch. The OOD and the other members of the watch take their stations.

The CO customarily makes a short speech, touching on the work of the building yard, the name of the ship, the history of any previous ships of the same name, and other items of interest. If appropriate, the state, city, or sponsor presents silver or other commemorative gift, and the CO makes an additional speech of appreciation. The ship's chaplain or a staff chaplain concludes the ceremony with a benediction.

It is customary, particularly in peacetime, for the CO to provide the officers and crew with formal invitations, which they may use to invite family and friends to the ceremony. Some COs prefer to have the officers and crew submit lists of guests and then have the ship's office do the addressing and mailing. After the ceremony, receptions are usually held simultaneously in the wardroom, chief petty officer mess, and crew's mess to entertain the guests.

Change of Command. Navy Regulations states, "a commanding officer about to be relieved will call all hands to muster, read the orders of detachment and turn over the command to his or her relief, who will read the orders of relief and assume command." This ceremony may be modified at shore commands.

A change-of-command ceremony is almost always quite formal, even though in smaller ships and shore commands it may be relatively simple. The turnover of command is the official passing of responsibility, authority, and accountability of command from one officer to another.

All hands are called to quarters for the ceremony, with the crew, officers, and guests in similar positions as for a commissioning ceremony. The main purpose of the ceremony is to turn over the responsibility from one officer to another, followed by a chance for the relieved CO to say goodbye to his or her officers and crew and for the new CO to greet the crew. The uniform is normally full dress with swords for principal participants and service dress for the crew and military guests.

When the XO reports that the crew is at quarters and the ceremony ready, the CO being relieved, the relieving CO, the chaplain, and any distinguished guests proceed to the ceremonial area. The XO normally acts as master of ceremonies. The chaplain delivers an invocation, and the offgoing CO delivers a speech, followed by the reading of his or her orders. If the CO has invited a guest to make brief remarks, he or she does so at this time. The offgoing CO then steps back and says to his or her relief, "Sir (Ma'am), I am ready to be relieved." The new CO steps forward, reads his or her orders, then faces the CO who is being relieved and says, "Sir (Ma'am), I relieve you." If the immediate superior in command is present, the new CO salutes him or her and says, "I report for duty." The new CO then makes a few brief remarks, usually confined to wishing the departing CO well and stating that all orders of his or her predecessor remain in effect. At the time of relief, a new commission pennant is broken. The old one is lowered and the command master chief presents it to the departing CO. After the chaplain offers a benediction, the new CO orders the XO to "pipe down." The ceremony is over and the official party retires. Usually the ship holds receptions simultaneously in the wardroom, the CPO mess, and the crew's mess.

Presentation of Awards. For this ceremony, the crew forms in approximately the same manner as for a change of command. Those receiving awards form in a single rank in front of the lectern. The XO calls each recipient forward by name, and the recipient then marches to a point one pace in front of the lectern and salutes the CO, who returns the salute. The CO reads the citation, makes a few personal remarks if he or she desires, and receives the medal from the XO or command master chief. The CO pins the medal on the recipient's uniform, shakes his or her hand, and steps back one pace. The recipient salutes and the CO returns the salute, and the recipient steps back one pace and reenters the ranks.

CHAPTER FIVE

TRADITIONS AND CUSTOMS OF THE NAVAL SERVICE

The value of tradition to the social body is immense. The veneration for practices, or for authority, consecrated by long acceptance, has a reserve of strength which cannot be obtained by any novel device. Respect for the old customs is planted deep in the hearts, as well as in the intelligence, of all inheritors of the English-speaking polity.

—Rear Admiral Alfred Thayer Mahan, *The Military Rule of Obedience*

Two hundred years of tradition uninterrupted by progress.

—Anonymous commentary on the U.S. Navy

The preceding chapter described courtesy, honors, and ceremonies. You should also become familiar with the many customs and traditions of the Naval Service.

This chapter will cover some of the better-known and most frequently practiced customs. The best comprehensive reference on the subject is the book *Naval Ceremonies, Customs and Traditions*.

Naval Customs and Traditions

Contrary to the anonymous quotation above, tradition is not a stale, meaningless ritual that takes the place of innovation and initiative. The body of naval tradition and customs has grown and evolved with modern circumstances, yet still permits modern Navy officers to honor the memories of those officers who served before us.

A custom may be defined as a course of action characteristically repeated under like circumstances, or a whole body of usages, practices, or conventions regulating social life. Much of our daily life is regulated by force of customs, many of which are so fully entrenched as to have become established as law.

There are many customs unique to the Naval Service. The origin of some of these is obscure, but Navy members conscientiously observe them nonetheless. Customs that have been incorporated into regulations have the force of law, and of those that have not, some are more stringently enforced than others. Nevertheless, the wisdom to recognize the unifying purpose behind even the most obscure of traditions and to observe them with enthusiasm will mark you as an officer who is likely to succeed.

Navy Customs Afloat

The Quarterdeck. The publication *Navy Regulations* states that the CO must "clearly define the limits of the quarterdeck." The sanctity of the quarterdeck should be firmly entrenched in the crew, and whether you are on watch or not, you should take pride in observing, and enforcing, proper decorum on the quarterdeck.

The following rules govern quarterdeck etiquette:

1. Never appear on the quarterdeck unless in the uniform of the day, except when crossing to arrive or depart.

2. Never stand around on the quarterdeck for any length of time unless conducting business there.

3. Salute the officer of the deck every time you come onto the quarterdeck.

4. Never smoke, eat, drink, or engage in horseplay on the quarterdeck.

5. Never walk in an area of the quarterdeck reserved for the flag officer or CO unless on official business or on invitation of those officers.

6. Never stand on the quarterdeck with your hands in your pockets. This pose is unmilitary in any area, but even more so on the quarterdeck.

Gangways. The gangway is the aperture in the side of a ship through which pass personnel and material. The ladders leading up to the gangway from the grating at the waterline are called accommodation ladders.

Larger ships may have two gangways: one a working gangway for enlisted members and the passage of supplies and material, and a more formal gangway for the use of officers and VIPs. If these gangways lead to separate areas of the ship, the area in which the officers' gangway terminates is the quarterdeck and manned by the OOD; the area in which the working gangway terminates is manned by another watchstander who may be given the title junior officer of the deck (JOOD).

Forms of Address and Introduction. You can find the proper form of address and introduction for very senior U.S. officials and foreign dignitaries in the *Social Usage and Protocol Handbook* (OPNAVINST 1710.7).

Navy Regulations states that every officer in the Naval Service is designated and addressed in official communications by the title of grade preceding his or her last name. In official spoken communications, officers are addressed by their ranks. Although no longer specified in *Navy Regulations*, in less formal spoken communications it is still common usage to address officers below the rank of commander by "Mr." or "Ms." instead of by their ranks. You may address officers of the medical and dental corps as "doctor," and officers of the chaplain corps as "chaplain." When addressing an officer whose grade includes a modifier (e.g., the "lieutenant," in "lieutenant commander") the modifier may be dropped. In written communication, indicate the name of the corps to which any staff officer belongs immediately after his or her name.

By custom, one person in any ship or organization is correctly addressed as "the captain," and that is the CO regardless of his or her actual rank. Likewise, the XO is referred to as "the commander." You should address other captains and commanders attached to the ship or station by their rank and name, for example, "Commander Jones."

Introduce officers using their rank, and always introduce the junior to the senior. When introducing military personnel to civilians, follow the civilian custom of introducing men to women and young people to their elders.

Address Marine Corps enlisted personnel by their titles, as in "Lance Corporal Smith." Introduce enlisted personnel, both Navy and Marine Corps, in the same manner as officers. A CPO is customarily addressed and introduced as "Chief Smith" or "Master Chief Green." Introduce a petty officer as "Petty Officer Brown" rather than as "Radioman Second Class Brown," particularly when the introduction is to a civilian. Introduce a nonrated Sailor as "Seaman (or Fireman, Airman, etc.) White," rather than "Seaman Apprentice White."

Relations with Seniors. When reporting to the office of a senior, first attempt to discreetly determine whether the senior is on the telephone or otherwise occupied. If not, knock on the door (even if it is open), announce yourself by name ("Ensign Gray reporting as ordered, sir [ma'am]"), and wait for permission to enter. In some cases, such as a busy office on board ship, you may be expected to enter without being told. Upon entering, proceed directly to the senior and, upon being recognized, state your business.

When conducting business with a senior, maintain a military bearing. Do not lounge against the desk or otherwise relax unless invited to stand easy or be seated. Unless on watch or wearing sidearms, always uncover when entering a room in which a senior is present.

It is customary to supplement your salute to a senior on the first meeting of the day with a brief greeting, such as "Good morning, Commander." Don't be too obtrusive with this greeting, particularly if the senior is engaged in conversation or otherwise occupied. Although you always salute the CO at every meeting, on board ship other seniors are normally saluted only at the first meeting of the day.

Never keep a senior waiting. When you are told that a senior wants to see you, you should assume that means right away. If the senior cannot see you immediately, he or she may tell you to return at a particular later time rather than keep you waiting. You should learn to use the same thoughtfulness when summoning your juniors.

When a senior says, "I desire," "I wish," or "Would you please," remember that the expressed desires and wishes of a senior, however tactfully presented, by custom and tradition are equivalent to an order. Even such statements as "I think it would be a good idea to . . . " should be construed as orders unless you obtain clarification to the contrary.

A senior presents "compliments" to a junior when the former is transmitting a message to the latter by a third person such as a messenger. A junior sends or pays his or her "respects" to a senior. In written correspondence a senior may "call" attention to certain matters, but the junior should "invite" attention. Similarly, a senior "requests" action of a junior, but a junior "respectfully requests" action of a senior. As discussed in chapter 8, in memoranda it is common practice for a senior to close with "Respectfully," but a junior closes with "Very respectfully."

When a senior orders you to perform a task, report back promptly when the task is complete. If you cannot complete the task right away, it is a good idea to give periodic reports on your progress. If you cannot complete the task as directed, report this fact back to your senior as soon as you are aware of it—don't wait until your deadline is imminent or has passed to report your inability to comply.

Learn to give accurate and brief responses to questions. If you don't know the answer to a question, don't guess! If your seniors can't rely on you to give them correct information, your credibility and reputation will suffer. A frank "I don't know, sir (ma'am), but I will find out and let you know" (followed by your actually finding out the answer and letting your superior know) is far better than an evasive or possibly incorrect reply. Chapter 8 discusses oral communications in more detail.

Phraseology. Certain standards of speech and address are in common use. The forms "Captain, I report . . . " and "Sir (Ma'am), I request . . . " are correct. At the end of the workday, enlisted personnel go on "liberty," but officers go on "shore leave." When preparing to leave your own ship, it is customary to check out with your immediate senior if he or she is still aboard. If appropriate, first brief your senior on the status of your work, and then say "Sir (Ma'am), request permission to leave the ship."

At the quarterdeck, say to the OOD, "Sir (Ma'am), I have permission to leave the ship." On your return, say, "Sir (Ma'am), I report my return aboard." When boarding a ship to which you are not attached, say to the OOD, "Sir (Ma'am), I request permission to come aboard," and show your identification. When departing, say, "Sir (Ma'am), I request permission to leave the ship."

When acknowledging an order, always respond with "Aye, aye, sir (ma'am)." The *only* proper use of the phrase "Very well" is by a senior to acknowledge a report by a junior.

Chain of Command. You will have a different chain of command under different circumstances: For routine division business you will report to your department head; for watch-qualification issues you will report to the senior watch officer; for watchstanding responsibilities you will report to the appropriate senior in the in-port duty section or underway watch; for some collateral duties you may report to the XO or a department head other than your own; and for certain operational matters it may be appropriate to report directly to the CO. It is important that you be clear on the rules governing each situation so that you do not inadvertently "go over the head" of someone in your chain of command. If it is necessary to report directly to an officer other than your department head, and time does not permit you to brief your department head ahead of time, it is important to back-brief him or her as soon as possible.

The Wardroom

Wardroom Mess. The term "mess" is applied to those in the Navy who, for convenience and sociability, eat together. It comes from the Latin word *mensa,* meaning table. Generally there are three messes on board a Navy ship: the general mess for the crew, the chiefs' mess, and the wardroom or officers' mess.

Wardroom Etiquette. In very large ships, the CO may have his or her own mess and the XO is president of the wardroom mess. Normally, however, the CO dines in the wardroom with the other officers and is president of the mess. Wardroom seating arrangements are no longer prescribed in *Navy Regulations,* but it remains customary for the president to sit at the head of the table, with the other officers seated in order of seniority on alternating sides of the table. Traditionally the mess treasurer occupies the seat at the foot of the table opposite the president. During the evening meal in port when a large number of mess members are ashore, the CDO may sit at the head of the table, with other officers present seated in order of seniority on alternating sides.

Wardroom protocol requires all members to arrive early for meals so that they may be seated at once when the president arrives and the meal is served. If you must join the mess late due to a watch or other responsibilities, before being seated you must approach the president and request permission to join the mess. Similarly, if you must leave the mess before the president, you must request permission to be excused. Proper uniforms are as designated by the mess president; coveralls, other nonuniform work attire, and civilian clothing are generally not permitted in the mess.

Wardroom Mess Fund. Every officers' mess has a fund from which it purchases food and other supplies. When reporting on board ship for duty, you will be required to buy a share of the mess—that is, to pay the mess fund an amount equal to your proportional share of the funds and supplies already on hand. When you detach from the ship, you will be refunded the appropriate current amount of a share of the mess. In addition, each member of the mess is required to contribute a monthly amount to the mess that may be based on a flat per-person rate or on the number of meals actually consumed. The mess fund is administered by the mess treasurer, who calculates bills and collects payments. Failure to promptly pay a mess bill is considered a serious breach of wardroom etiquette, and the president will likely counsel any officer who pays the bill habitually or significantly late.

Conduct in the Wardroom. Particularly while on deployment, the wardroom serves as the officers' home on board ship. Wardroom amenities may include a comfortable sofa and chairs, a television and DVD/Blu-ray player, stereo system, books, magazines, and games. You should feel comfortable spending time in the wardroom after working hours, relaxing and socializing with your fellow officers. During working hours, you may take brief breaks to have a cup of coffee in the wardroom, but it is not appropriate to "hang out" for long periods in the wardroom during the workday, or to do your paperwork there. As a rule, it is not appropriate to spend time in the wardroom wearing civilian clothes, although this rule may be relaxed at the CO's discretion.

Traditionally, during peacetime no business is transacted in the wardroom, and conversations during meals should not revolve around ship's business. Due to space limitations in small ships, the wardroom may be used for meetings and training lectures during working hours. Enlisted members (other than those mess specialists and food service assistants who work there) should never enter the wardroom unless specifically invited. Enlisted personnel should not conduct routine ship's business in the wardroom—if you have a need to confer with an enlisted member, it is appropriate to step outside the wardroom to do so.

The wardroom may upon occasion host a formal meal including one or more "guests of the mess." If such guests are invited by the mess at large, all members share equally in the associated costs as well as in their responsibilities to serve as hosts. It is polite to introduce yourself to all guests of the mess, and to help make them feel at home. Meal costs for guests of individual mess members are normally borne by the appropriate wardroom member, although the same rules of hospitality apply.

Wardroom Organization. The position of mess treasurer has already been mentioned; this officer is elected from among the members of the mess. It is not uncommon for a junior officer who arrives late to a meeting of the mess to find that he or she has been elected to serve as mess treasurer.

The duties of the mess treasurer include maintaining the accounts of the mess and forwarding required reports. The mess treasurer may not incur indebtedness that cannot be discharged by the funds appropriated by the mess, and must pay all bills before leaving port unless unusual circumstances exist.

The mess caterer is frequently a permanent collateral duty assigned to one of the ship's supply corps officers, although it may be assigned to any member of the mess. This officer's duties include supervising the preparation of the menu; providing variety and proper nutrition; supervising the wardroom culinary specialists and food service assistants in the performance of their duties, which include cleaning and maintenance of officer staterooms, as well as their duties in the wardroom.

Culinary specialists and food service assistants are not personal servants but have specific responsibilities to operate the wardroom. As with all enlisted personnel, they should be treated with appropriate courtesy and professionalism. If you have a complaint about the performance of one of the wardroom personnel, it is appropriate to discuss your concerns with the mess caterer.

Navy Social Life

The social requirements of Navy life are generally kept as simple and informal as possible. The days in which the off-duty schedules of officers and their spouses were overburdened with onerous "command performance" social functions are long past, particularly in the case of junior officers. However, at some point in your career you will likely be invited to, perhaps even tasked with organizing, a variety of events ranging from the casual to the traditional. A brief description of some customary Navy social functions follows.

Receptions and Cocktail Parties. These events may be given for a variety of reasons and may be held in a private home, at a command, or at an officers' club. A reception or cocktail party may be hosted by an organization. For example, if your command is sponsoring a visiting foreign navy ship, it is common practice to host a reception for the ship's officers on the first night of the visit. In turn, visiting ships often host cocktail parties on board to entertain local dignitaries and officers of the host ship and other area commands. Although alcohol is not normally permitted on board U.S. Navy ships, exceptions are occasionally granted for this purpose when a ship visits a foreign port.

When invited to a cocktail party or reception, your invitation may specify a particular period of time, for example 1800 to 2000. At very large gatherings there will frequently be more than one shift, with other guests invited for different blocks of time, so you should not overstay your invitation even if the party remains in full swing at the time scheduled for your departure.

Cocktail parties differ from receptions in that they are less formal, there is no receiving line and usually no guest of honor, and the time limits are not as strict. Both types of functions generally feature a buffet of light or heavy hors d'oeuvres, depending on the budget of the host(s), and some sort of beverage service ranging from a full bar at the high end to wine and nonalcoholic punch at more economical gatherings.

When visiting another port, your command may be issued a number of invitations to a variety of different social functions sponsored by local groups. You may be tapped to go to one of these functions and represent your command. These events will be some of your best opportunities to meet and socialize with local residents and officers of other navies. When attending, remember that you are a representative of your command as well as the U.S. Navy, and be a gracious and sociable guest.

Balls and Dances. If you are stationed in a major fleet concentration area, you will have many opportunities to participate in formal balls and dances. The largest of these are given on the occasion of the Navy Birthday and the Marine Corps Birthday, but many officer communities host their own events, such as the Supply Corps Ball and the Surface Warfare Ball. These events are usually quite formal, which may be reflected in the cost, but a sliding scale is frequently used to make tickets more affordable for junior officers and enlisted members. Attendance at these balls will give you and your spouse or significant other the opportunity to spend time with a large number of officers who share your professional interests, and it can prove both socially and professionally rewarding.

Dining In/Dining Out. These formal dinners represent a tradition dating back hundreds of years. These events, also sometimes referred to as "Mess Nights" have their roots in the customs of eighteenth-century European army regiments, where the officers would gather together for an evening of food, drink, and fellowship. The difference between a Dining In and a Dining Out is that the only members of the mess attend the former, whereas spouses, dates, and other guests are invited to the latter. (In the Marine Corps, the meaning of the two terms is reversed.) There are only two recognized officers of the mess: the president and vice president. "Mr. (or Ms.) Vice" is normally a junior officer selected for his or her engaging and entertaining personality as well as ability to hold the sometimes unruly members of the mess to some semblance of order.

The evening commences with a gathering for cocktails, during which members of the mess and their guests note their seat locations on the posted seating chart to avoid later embarrassment. After the cocktail hour, the president, assisted by Mr. or Ms. Vice, forms the members into the order in which they will be seated in the mess, normally in order of seniority. A bagpiper engaged for the occasion plays appropriate marching music and leads the president, members, and guests (if present) into the mess. The group parades around the mess in a full circle, each coming to a stop behind his or her assigned seat. When all members are in place, the music ceases, the president or designated member offers grace, and the president seats the mess with a rap of the gavel. Once the mess is seated, no one may join or be excused from the mess without first obtaining permission from the president. Mr. or Ms. Vice will then signal to the bagpiper to play "Roast Beef of Olde England" and lead the procession of food service personnel to the president's seat. The president will sample the beef and determine its quality. Once the president finds the beef acceptable, he or she will announce, "Ladies and Gentlemen, I pronounce this beef fit for human consumption."

Mr. or Ms. Vice sits alone at a small table opposite the president and head table. Prior to addressing the president, members of the mess must first obtain permission to do so from Mr. or Ms. Vice. Mr. or Ms. Vice may choose to deny a request in order to prevent frivolous business from interfering with the president's enjoyment of the meal. Failure to obtain prior permission to address the president is a serious breach of mess etiquette that the president normally allows Mr. or Ms. Vice to deal with as he or she sees fit. Other violations of the mess include:

- Untimely arrival at the proceedings
- Haggling over date of rank
- Leaving the dining area without permission from the president
- Loud and obtrusive remarks in a foreign language or in English
- Being caught with an uncharged glass
- Rising to applaud particularly witty, succinct, sarcastic, or irrelevant toasts unless following the example of the president
- Hog calling
- Inverted cummerbund
- A clip-on bow tie worn at an obvious list
- Foul language
- Carrying cocktails into the dining room
- Any other breach of proper decorum or etiquette

During the course of the meal, members may observe breaches of etiquette by other members of the mess, or recall such breaches from previous occasions, and feel compelled to bring these offenses to the attention of the president. After the member obtains permission from Mr. or Ms. Vice and relates the circumstances of the offense to the president, the president may choose to allow the accused offender the opportunity to present information in his or her defense. After this, the president will render judgment and, if necessary, determine a suitable penalty for the offender or allow Mr. or Ms. Vice to do so. Typical penalties include singing a song, reciting a poem, paying a fine, performing a service to the mess, wearing an appropriate article of attire, or other similar measures befitting the offense.

Following the meal, the president may choose to briefly excuse the members and guests to refresh themselves. As with the first entry into the mess, it is a serious breach of etiquette to be late rejoining the mess following this recess. When the mess is reassembled, preparations for formal toasting commence with the passing of the port. A bottle of port wine is passed from right to left ("to port"), with each member and guest filling his or her own glass and not allowing the bottle to touch the table until the last glass is filled. Nonalcoholic wine or cider may be substituted for the port to accommodate those who choose not to drink alcoholic beverages, but toasts may never be drunk with water. When the last glass is filled, the president rises, raps the gavel three times to require the attention of the members, and proposes a toast to the commander in chief: "Mr. (Ms.) Vice, the Commander in Chief of the United States." Mr. or Ms. Vice then rises and seconds the toast by repeating as follows: "Ladies and Gentlemen, the Commander in Chief," following which all members and guests rise, repeat "The Commander in Chief" in unison, and sip from their glasses. If a band or recorded music is available, "Hail to the Chief" is played. The president then raps the gavel to seat the members and guests.

Members of the mess offer additional formal toasts in the following order:

- United States Marine Corps
- Missing comrades
- Chief of Naval Operations

Additional toasts may be offered to the United States Army, Air Force, and Coast Guard, and to other appropriate organizations and dignitaries. Each toast that is not offered by the president is conducted in the following manner: the member rises, obtains permission from Mr. or Ms. Vice to offer a toast, and says, "Mr. (Madam) President, the United States Marine Corps" (or other toast as appropriate). The president rises and seconds the toast by saying "Ladies and Gentlemen, the United States Marine Corps," following which all members and guests rise, repeat the toast ("The United States Marine Corps"), and sip from their glasses. Mr. or Ms. Vice seconds all toasts offered by the president. Do not empty your glass until the final toast. If appropriate music is available, it will be played after each toast, following which the president reseats the mess with one rap of the gavel.

Following the formal toasting, the president introduces the guest of honor, if one is present, who briefly addresses the mess. Following this, the president invites informal toasting from members and guests. The procedures for informal toasting are the same as those for formal toasting; however, if the president fails to rise and second the toast it has not been accepted. Individuals are never toasted by name, only by title. Following the informal toasts, without rising, the president raps the gavel three times and proposes a final toast to the United States Navy. The president rises as Mr. or Ms. Vice seconds the toast, and all members and guests rise and repeat the toast, drain their glasses, and remain standing for the playing of "Anchors Aweigh." Following the final toast, the president invites the members and guests to join him or her at the bar. Attendees should remain at their places until the president and those seated at the head table have departed the mess, and they should not depart from the bar until the president and guest of honor have done so.

Cigar smoking, long a traditional feature of such events, is no longer standard practice due to health concerns and regulations. If smoking is permitted in the mess, it will be indicated by the president lighting a ceremonial "smoking lamp" following the toast to the commander in chief.

Wetting Down. It is traditional for an officer newly selected for promotion to share his or her good fortune with friends and fellow wardroom members with a Wetting Down party. Customarily, an officer is expected to spend the equivalent of his or her first month's pay increase on the event; it is not uncommon for more than one officer to share in hosting a Wetting Down.

Wetting Down parties are generally extremely informal and may consist of nothing more than modest beverages and finger foods. If a group of officers shares expenses, the event may be considerably more lavish.

Hail and Farewell. When new members join a wardroom, or old members depart, the wardroom will generally mark the occasion with a party called a Hail and Farewell. These events may be held at the home of the president of the mess or another member, or at an officers' club or restaurant. In any case, the costs of the event are equally borne by all members except those for whom the event is a farewell.

Although a Hail and Farewell is a relatively informal event, all wardroom members who are not on duty are expected to attend. It is considered extremely rude to miss a Hail and Farewell without good reason. If exceptional circumstances exist that would prevent your attendance, you should explain the situation to the XO in advance and request permission to be absent. Regardless of whether or not you attend, you will still be expected to contribute to the costs.

A Hail and Farewell generally consists of an informal cocktail party, which may include a buffet line or hors d'oeuvres. A more formal Hail and Farewell, such as for the CO, may include a sit-down dinner. After all members and their guests have had the opportunity to socialize, the CO addresses the gathering. The CO generally begins with a formal introduction and welcome for each of the new members being hailed and their spouses or significant others. Such introductions are normally made beginning with the most junior new member and ending with the most senior. Following this, the CO calls forward each of the members being bid farewell, beginning with the most junior, and provides a brief synopsis of their accomplishments and contributions to the command. The CO may open the floor to allow other mess members to make presentations or tell stories about the departing officer, after which the departing officer says a few words of farewell. Each farewell generally concludes with the presentation of some gift or memento from the mess.

Calls. The practice of junior officers paying formal at-home calls on the CO and other officers of the command has all but disappeared. Nevertheless, this practice still exists in some quarters, and upon reporting to a new command you should inquire of the XO whether this courtesy is expected of you. If you are advised that calls are expected, you should request a convenient time to call on the CO, the XO, and your department head, normally within two weeks of reporting aboard. If you are married, your spouse should accompany you if possible, and your calls should be brief (approximately twenty minutes).

You can expect your calls to be returned within two weeks. If you are a single officer, you may need to express a specific invitation to indicate your ability and willingness to host calls. When entertaining callers, you will not be expected to entertain lavishly. Simply offer your guests a choice of alcoholic or nonalcoholic beverages and simple snacks, and engage in pleasant, light conversation.

Officers' Clubs. Navy bases and other large shore stations normally have a Commissioned Officers' Mess (Open), commonly referred to as an officers' club. Such clubs in the Navy rarely require formal membership or dues but are open to all officers and their guests. Officers' clubs normally serve meals in a restaurant-type setting. Breakfasts and lunches may be informal, sometimes cafeteria-style, although the evening meal is usually somewhat more formal. Officers' clubs may also offer off-site catering and rooms for special events.

Never wear your cover inside an officers' club. By custom and tradition, any officer entering a club covered must buy a round of drinks for all those present. This is not an error you are likely to make twice.

CHAPTER SIX

MILITARY DUTIES OF THE NAVY OFFICER

An army formed with good officers moves like clockwork.

—George Washington, letter to the president of Congress

On the conduct of the officers alone depends the restoration of good order, discipline, and subordination in the Navy.

—Lord St. Vincent, letter to Admiral Dickson

Military leaders have long been interested in the practice of fixing responsibility. One of the best discourses on the subject came from Admiral Hyman G. Rickover, who said responsibility is "unique concept":

It can only reside and inhere in a single individual. You may share it with others, but your portion is not diminished. You may delegate it, but it is still with you. You may disdain it, but you cannot divest yourself of it. Even if you do not recognize it or admit its presence, you cannot escape it. If responsibility is rightfully yours, no evasion, or ignorance, no passing the blame, can shift the burden to someone else. Unless you can point your finger at the man who is responsible when something goes wrong, then you never really had anyone responsible.

These strong words demonstrate how sacred the concept of responsibility is in the Navy.

Basic Authority and Responsibility

Your authority and responsibility as a Navy officer began the day you accepted your commission and took the oath of office. The "special trust and confidence" placed in your "patriotism, fidelity, and abilities" should be an inspiration to you.

You swore to "support and defend the Constitution of the United States against all enemies, foreign and domestic; to bear true faith and allegiance to the same." This oath represents a solemn promise that no officer should enter into lightly.

On the day you accepted your commission and took this oath, you assumed certain basic responsibilities. *Navy Regulations* and other directives describe some of these; you should review these publications and become familiar with the extent and limits of your authority as a Navy officer.

Authority and Responsibility under Navy Regulations

Navy Regulations sets forth regulations concerning officers in chapter 10, "Precedence, Authority and Command." Art. 1130 gives the duties of officers with regard to laws, orders, and regulations and requires that all officers in the Naval Service acquaint themselves with, obey, and so far as their authority extends, perform these duties to the best of their ability in conformance with their solemn profession of the oath of office. In the absence of instructions, officers must act in conformity with policies and customs to protect the public interest.

Required Conduct. Art. 1110, "Standards of Conduct," states that all Department of the Navy personnel are expected to conduct themselves in accordance with the highest standards of personal and professional integrity and ethics. At a minimum, Navy personnel must comply with the standards of conduct and ethics directives issued by the Secretary of Defense and the Secretary of the Navy. Chapter 2 discusses these standards in greater detail.

Exercise of Authority. Art. 1020 of *Navy Regulations*, "Exercise of Authority," states that everyone in the Naval Service is at all times subject to naval authority. This article is somewhat convoluted, but in essence it says that any Navy officer, unless on the sick list, under custody or arrest, suspended from duty, under confinement, or otherwise incapable of discharging duties, *may* exercise authority.

Officers in the Navy not only *may* exercise authority when necessary—they *must* exercise it. Such action is not simply a right but also a duty under Navy custom. If, for example, you observe misconduct by a member of the Naval Service, whether or not you are in that member's chain of command, you are bound by custom to exercise your authority as a Navy officer and take corrective action.

Amplifying Directives Concerning the Authority and Responsibilities of Officers

Authority from Organizational Position. While the basic authority for all officers comes from *Navy Regulations,* your organizational position invests you with addi-

An ensign takes bearing readings on the bridge of the guided-missile destroyer USS *Laboon* (DDG 58).

tional authority and responsibilities described in the *Standard Organization and Regulations Manual (SORM)*. *SORM* art. 141 states that authority falls into two categories: the general authority necessary for all officers to carry out their duties and responsibilities, and the organizational authority necessary to fulfill the duties and responsibilities of specific billets. The command organizational structure is described in command, department, and division instructions, which set forth the positions, duties, and responsibilities of all persons in the command.

Limits on Authority: Lawful Orders

Injurious or Capricious Conduct. Officers' broad authority notwithstanding, there are limits to what they can do. Subordinates are not obliged to obey unlawful orders, and *Navy Regulations* prohibits those in authority from abusing their subordinates with tyrannical or capricious conduct or abusive language. There have been several recent incidences in which commanding officers were relieved of their commands for just such abuse.

Limits on Organizational Authority. SORM art. 141.7 points out that since authority is given only to fulfill duties and responsibilities, seniors may delegate only so much organizational authority as subordinates require to fulfill their responsibilities. This is limitation of authority by command.

Contradictory Orders. Navy Regulations art. 1024 covers the subject of contradictory and conflicting orders. If a superior officer contradicts the orders issued to you by another superior, he or she is required to report that fact immediately, preferably in writing, to the superior whose orders were contravened. If you receive such a contradictory order, you must explain the facts in writing to the officer who gave you the last order. If that officer insists upon the execution of his or her order; you must obey it; at the earliest opportunity you must then report the circumstances to the officer who issued you the original order.

Imposition of Nonjudicial Punishment. SORM art. 142.2 states that no one may impose punishment except under procedures outlined in the Uniform Code of Military Justice (UCMJ). It further states that UCMJ nonjudicial punishment is reserved for commanders, commanding officers, and officers in charge. Appendix B provides an overview of the military justice system.

Extra Military Instruction (EMI). Officers and petty officers may take nonpunitive measures to correct minor deficiencies not meriting punishment under UCMJ art. 15. These measures, called EMI, must be intended to correct deficiencies in a subordinate's performance of military duty, or to direct completion of work assignments that may extend beyond normal working hours.

SORM art. 142.2 establishes policy guidance for EMI. This article defines EMI as instruction in a phase of military duty in which an individual is deficient. This instruction, sanctioned by the *Manual for Courts-Martial (MCM)* para. v-1g (2008), is a training device to improve the efficiency of a command or unit and must not be used for punitive action that should have been taken under the *UCMJ*. *SORM* art. 142.2 describes how to implement this form of instruction and states that it may not be assigned for more than two hours a day, may be assigned at a reasonable time outside of working hours, must be no longer than necessary to correct the deficiency, and may not be assigned on a person's Sabbath. Further, any Navy member otherwise entitled to liberty may commence liberty on completion of EMI.

Any officer or petty officer may assign EMI during normal working hours. After working hours, EMI is assigned by the CO, whose authority may be delegated to other officers and petty officers in the chain of command. If the CO delegates authority to assign EMI, he or she must monitor the process to ensure it is not misused.

Withholding Privileges. The chain of command has the authority to withhold certain privileges temporarily, an act sanctioned by *MCM* para. v-1g. This procedure may be used to correct minor infractions of military regulations or performance deficiencies when stronger action is not required. Examples of privileges that may be withheld are special liberty, exchange of duty, special pay, special command programs, Internet access, libraries, and off-ship events on military bases. The authority to withhold a privilege rests with the individual empowered to grant the privilege. Withholding privileges from personnel in a liberty status is the prerogative of the CO. The CO may delegate this authority, but such withholding of privileges may not result in a deprivation of liberty itself.

Additional Work Assignments. SORM art. 142.2b states that deprivation of liberty as a punishment, except under the UCMJ, is illegal; no officer or petty officer may deny liberty as a punishment for any offense or unsatisfactory performance of duty. However, the article states that it is not a punishment to require a member to remain on board and perform work assignments that should have been completed during the normal workday, to perform additional essential work, or to maintain the required level of operational readiness.

Extending working hours for all hands or for certain selected personnel should be done only when absolutely necessary. When you recommend to your seniors that they extend working hours for your division, you should make every effort to ensure that your personnel understand the necessity for such action. If they understand it, they will carry out their duty readily and well. It may also be legitimate to extend working hours when work is not performed satisfactorily the first time or under circumstances of exceptional operational need.

Ordering and Assignment of Officers

Officer Distribution. The Chief of Naval Personnel has responsibility for assigning qualified officers to authorized billets. In determining an officer's next assignment, the distribution system considers the needs of the Navy, the effect of the assignment on the professional growth and development of the officer, the officer's record and qualifications, and the officer's personal preferences. The officer distribution system is described in more detail in chapter 17.

Assignment to Specific Billets. Officers are generally assigned to specific billets. These assignments may be indicated in the orders by listing the specific billet sequence code or by designating the officer as a "numerical relief for" another officer by name. In officer assignments, especially when ordered as a numerical relief, once you have arrived on board, the CO has broad latitude to reassign you based on your individual qualifications and the needs of the command. Junior officers can generally expect to rotate between several different assignments during a single shipboard tour.

Duties of Specific Assignments

When you arrive at a ship, squadron, or station and take position in the organization of that unit, you assume the authority and responsibility assigned to the billet by the ship's organization and regulations. These billet responsibilities are described in chapter 3 of the *SORM*.

Commanding Officer. Under *Navy Regulations*, the CO is charged with the absolute responsibility for the safety, well-being, and efficiency of his or her command

Executive Officer. The XO is second in command of the unit and is the alter ego of the CO. The XO takes precedence over all other officers of the command and has responsibility for the organization, performance of duty, good order, and discipline of the command. As the direct representative of the CO, the XO's orders have the same force and effect.

Boards and Committees. Many organizational functions lend themselves to administration by boards and committees. *SORM* art. 304 describes the composition and purpose of many such boards and committees. A board or committee is a group of persons organized under a chairman, president, or senior member to evaluate problems and make recommendations to proper authority for their solution. Boards and committees are generally policy-recommending groups, vice policymaking groups; recommendations concerning command policy or function must generally be forwarded through the chain of command for approval by the XO or CO. Enlisted personnel as well as officers may serve on boards.

Executive Assistants. A number of administrative assistants report directly to the XO. Many of these positions are collateral duties. The title of "officer" notwithstanding, senior enlisted members frequently perform many of these duties.

- Administration Assistant. The administration assistant is an aide to the XO, observing and reporting on the effectiveness of administrative policies, procedures, and regulations of the command. The administration assistant carries out those duties assigned by the XO, which may include screening and routing of incoming correspondence, assigning responsibility for replies, maintaining the tickler file, reviewing outgoing correspondence, and preparing the plan of the day (POD). He or she also exercises budgetary control over executive assistants.

- Automatic Data Processing (ADP) Security Officer. The ADP Security Officer is responsible for ensuring adequate security for ADP systems in the command, including software and hardware features. This officer oversees administrative, physical, and personnel security controls and conducts risk assessment, security tests, evaluations, and contingency planning.

- Chief Master-at-Arms (CMAA). The CMAA is responsible for the supervision, direction, and employment of the security department or division and for assisting the CO in maintaining the security, good order, and discipline of the ship.

- Command Career Counselor (CCC). The command career counselor is responsible for establishing a program to disseminate career information and for providing career counseling to the crew.

- Command Master Chief (CM/C). The CM/C is the senior enlisted adviser to the command on the formulation and implementation of policies pertinent to morale, welfare, job satisfaction, discipline, utilization, and training of all enlisted personnel. The CM/C has direct access to the CO and is senior in precedence to all other enlisted persons in the command.

- Drug/Alcohol Program Advisor (DAPA). The DAPA is responsible for the drug and alcohol abuse prevention and education program, administering onboard (Level I) drug- and alcohol-abuse rehabilitation programs and monitoring the progress of members who return to the command following completion of higher-level rehabilitation programs.

- Educational Services Officer (ESO). This officer administers educational programs, acts as a member of the planning board for training, and assists the training officer. He or she may be assigned other duties in the areas of education and training and usually administers examinations for advancement to pay grade E-3 and other examinations as required.

- Equal Opportunity Program Specialist. This individual serves as equal opportunity adviser to the command, provides briefings on equal opportunity matters, and facilitates formal command training team (CTT) and command assessment team (CAT) courses, seminars, and workshops.

- Health Benefits Advisor (HBA). The HBA provides awareness of health benefits to the crew and their dependents. Although not expected to be an expert in all aspects of health benefits, the HBA advises crew members and refers those requiring additional assistance.

- Legal Officer. The legal officer is an adviser and staff assistant to the CO and XO on all matters concerning the interpretation and application of the UCMJ and other military laws and regulations. The legal officer may be a member of the Judge Advocate General (JAG) corps, or may be a line officer serving in this capacity as a collateral duty. When a JAG officer is assigned as legal officer, he or she also serves as head of the legal department.

- Personnel Officer. The personnel officer is responsible for the placement of all enlisted personnel and for the administration and custody of all enlisted records.

- Postal Officer. This officer supervises the postal functions of the command.
- Public Affairs Officer (PAO). This officer carries out the command's public affairs program. In large commands, the PAO may be a member of the restricted line with a specialty in public affairs. In smaller commands, a line officer serving in a collateral duty capacity normally fills this position.
- Recreational Services Officer (RSO). The RSO exercises administrative and executive control and accountability for the recreational services program and may serve as custodian of the recreation fund if no other officer is assigned.
- Safety Officer. This officer carries out the command's safety program. The safety officer distributes safety information, conducts training, maintains safety records, and monitors the command's safety program. In some larger ships, this is a department head billet filled by an officer of the medical service corps.
- Security Manager. The security manager is responsible for the management of the command information and personnel security program. This position may be assigned as sole, principal, or collateral duty depending upon the scope of the unit's security responsibilities.
- Security Officer. The security officer is responsible for the supervision, direction, and employment of the assets of the Security Department/Division; for the security of the ship; and for assistance to the CO in maintaining good order and discipline. When no security officer is assigned, these duties are fulfilled by CMAA or an assigned officer assisted by the CMAA.
- Senior Watch Officer. The senior watch officer is responsible for the assignment and general supervision of all deck watchstanders, both under way and in port. This officer coordinates watchstander training, prepares underway and in-port watch bills, and schedules rotation of the unit's in-port duty sections.
- Ship's Secretary. The ship's secretary is responsible for administering ship's correspondence and directives, maintaining officer personnel records, preparing the CO's personal correspondence and officer fitness reports, and maintaining the ship's unclassified reference library.
- Navy Tactical Command Support System (NTCSS) Coordinator. This officer or petty officer coordinates the implementation, operation, and maintenance of the NTCSS.
- Training Officer. This officer, who is normally a department head, is adviser and assistant to the XO for training matters. The training officer is a mem-

ber of the planning board for training (PBFT) and prepares and monitors training plans and schedules.

- 3M Coordinator. This officer is responsible for administering the ship's maintenance, material, and management (3M) system.
- Lay Reader. The CO may appoint one or more lay readers to meet the religious needs of particular faith groups. Although no civilian credential or approval corresponds to this appointment, the CO consults with the command chaplain or chaplain attached to a higher-echelon commander to select lay readers with high moral character, motivation, and religious interest.
- Management Control Program Coordinator (MCPC). This officer is responsible for coordinating a Management Control Program to fulfill the requirements of the Federal Managers Financial Integrity Act (FMFIA) of 1982 (31 USC 3512), SECNAVINST 5200.35D, OPNAVINST 5200.25C, and associated directives.
- Navy Reserve Coordinator. The reserve coordinator assists the XO in the proper administration of Navy reserve personnel assigned for training or to fill mobilization billets within the command. The reserve coordinator integrates Navy reserve personnel into the command organization and assists in their training and readiness.

Collateral Duties. Other collateral duties are assigned to officers and senior petty officers. In assigning these duties, the XO and CO take care to ensure that those assigned are qualified, there is no conflict of interest, and no individual is overburdened. These duties include:

- Athletic officer
- Brig officer
- Command fitness coordinator
- Communications security material (CMS) custodian
- Controlled substances bulk custodian
- Crypto-security officer
- Custodian of cleaning alcohol
- Diving officer
- Electrical safety officer
- Library officer
- Ship's maintenance management officer
- Mess treasurer
- Mess caterer
- Naval warfare publications custodian

- Nuclear weapons handling supervisor
- Nuclear weapons radiological controls officer
- Nuclear weapons safety officer
- Photographic officer
- Radiation health officer
- Recreation fund custodian
- Security officer
- Top secret control officer
- Wartime information security program officer
- Witnessing official

Department Heads

In addition to the specific duties and responsibilities assigned to a department head by virtue of his or her billet, each department head also has certain general duties. A department head represents the CO in all matters pertaining to the department and must conform to the CO's orders and policies. All personnel in a department are subordinate to the department head. A department head normally reports to the XO, but may confer directly with the CO whenever he or she believes such action is necessary. In such cases, the department head must back-brief the XO promptly. The department head is responsible for maintaining the general condition of the equipment in that department and for promptly reporting any problems to the XO and CO, particularly conditions relating to the safety or operation of equipment. A department head may not disable equipment without the permission of the CO.

A department head is responsible for organizing and training the department for battle, preparing and writing bills and orders for the department, and assigning, training, and administering all personnel of the department. *SORM* art. 310 contains a detailed description of the duties and responsibilities of a department head.

A department head in a large ship may have an assistant department head and an administrative assistant. At a minimum, a department head will have a department training assistant and one or more division officers.

Operations Officer. The operations officer is responsible for the collection, evaluation, and dissemination of combat and operational information required by the mission of the ship. This information covers the areas of air, surface, and subsurface search; control of aircraft; collection, display, analysis, and dissemination of intelligence; preparation of operating plans and schedules; meteorological and oceanographic information; and repair of electronic equipment.

The following officers, if assigned, report to the operations officer: administrative and training assistant, air operations, combat information/direction center (CIC/CDC) officer, communications officer (when not a department head), electronics material officer (EMO; except when the ship has a combat systems department), electronics warfare (EW) officer, intelligence officer, oceanography officer, photographic officer, strike operations officer, first lieutenant (when the ship has a combat systems department but does not have a deck department), and cryptologic officer. As indicated, in large ships some of these officers may be heads of separate departments.

Navigator. The navigator is head of the navigation department. He or she is responsible under the CO for the safe navigation and piloting of the ship. The navigator will normally be senior to all watch and division officers.

Communication Officer. In ships with a communication department, the communication officer is head of that department. This officer is responsible for visual and electronic exterior communication systems and the administration of the interior systems supporting them. Assistants to the communication officer include the radio officer, signal officer, custodian of CMS distributed material, crypto-security officer, and a message center officer. In ships without a communication department, the communication officer reports to the operations officer.

Weapons Officer. In ships that have a weapons department, this officer is the department head and is also responsible for the ordnance equipment. In ships without a deck department, the weapons officer is also responsible for equipment associated with deck seamanship. Assistants to the weapons officer may include the first lieutenant (in ships without a deck department), anti-submarine warfare (ASW) officer, missile officer, gunnery officer, ordnance officer, Marine detachment officer, fire-control officer, and department training assistant.

Combat Systems Officer. On ships with a combat systems department, the duties of the combat systems officer include the duties otherwise specified for the weapons officer. Assistants to the combat systems officer may include the system test officer, weapons/weapons control officer, electronics material/electronic warfare officer, ASW officer, strike officer, fire-control officer, ordnance officer, and gunnery officer.

Deep Submergence Officer. On ships so equipped, the deep submergence officer is responsible for the supervision and direction of the launch and recovery operations and for the servicing and handling of the deep submergence vehicle.

Air Officer. In ships with an air department, the air officer is assigned as head of the department and is responsible for the supervision and direction of the launching and landing operations and for the servicing and handling of aircraft. The air officer is also responsible for salvage, firefighting, aviation fuels, aviation lubricants, and safety precautions. Assistants to the air officer include a flight deck officer, catapult officer, arresting-gear officer, hangar deck officer, aviation fuels officer, aircraft handling officer, and training assistant.

Aviation Officer. In air-capable ships (except LPD-class ships) with a Navy helicopter detachment embarked but without a permanent air officer assigned, the officer in charge of the helicopter detachment is the department head of the aviation department. This officer is responsible for the specific missions of the embarked aircraft. On LPD-class ships where an aviation officer is permanently assigned, that officer will retain the duties as air department head.

Embarked Air Wing Commander. An officer of the rank of captain commands an air wing and reports to the battle group commander. When the air wing embarks aboard a carrier, the air wing commander also reports to the CO as a department head. This officer, commonly referred to as CAG (for Carrier Air Group), has responsibility for the readiness and tactical operation of the air wing. A deputy CAG is generally assigned to supervise the tactical training and indoctrination of the air wing and the coordination and supervision of the various squadrons and detachments of the wing.

Aircraft Intermediate Maintenance Officer. In ships with an aircraft intermediate maintenance department, this officer will be responsible for the supervision and direction of the intermediate maintenance effort of aircraft embarked or assigned to the ship.

Aircraft Maintenance Officer. In aviation units that have an aircraft maintenance department, this officer is responsible for supervising and directing that department's support of unit aircraft.

First Lieutenant. In ships with a deck department, the first lieutenant is the department head responsible for supervising the use of deck seamanship equipment; and, in ships without a weapons or combat systems department, he or she is also responsible for the ordnance equipment. Assistants to the first lieutenant may include the ship's boatswain, weapons officer, gunnery officer, cargo officer, boat group commander, and department training officer.

Engineering Officer. This officer, commonly referred to as the chief engineer, or "cheng," is responsible for the operation, safety, and maintenance of all propulsion, electrical, and auxiliary machinery. As the ship's damage control officer, the engineering officer is also responsible for overseeing the damage control organization. The following assistants may be assigned to the engineering officer: the main propulsion assistant (MPA), auxiliaries officer, electrical officer, damage-control assistant (DCA), reactor control assistant, and department training officer.

Maintenance Management Officer. In CVNs, this officer is responsible for coordinating the planning and execution of ship maintenance and the documentation of ship maintenance requirements at the depot, intermediate, and organization levels.

Reactor Officer. In ships that have a reactor department, the reactor officer is responsible for the operation, care, maintenance, and safety of the reactor plants and their auxiliaries. This officer receives all orders concerning these responsibilities directly from the CO and makes all corresponding reports directly to the CO, but reports to the XO for administrative matters.

There is special responsibility attached to the operation of reactor plants: the reactor officer and the engineer officer must cooperate closely in matters pertaining to the propulsion plant. Assistants to the reactor officer may include the reactor-control assistant, the reactor mechanical assistant, a chemistry/radiological assistant, and a reactor training assistant.

Repair Officer. In ships with a repair department, this officer is responsible for repairs and alterations on designated ships and aircraft. The repair officer conducts timely planning, scheduling, accomplishment, and inspection of work to ensure its satisfactory completion in accordance with prescribed methods and standards.

Research Officer. In units with a research operations department, the head of that department will be designated the research officer. The research officer will be responsible for the operations, maintenance, and security of specified research, special-purpose communications, and associated equipment.

He or she will be the technical assistant to the CO on certain research operations.

Safety Officer. On ships with a safety department, the head is designated the safety officer. The safety officer is responsible for managing the safety program, participating in mishap investigations, and acting as hazardous material/hazardous waste coordinator.

Supply Officer. The supply officer is responsible for procuring, receiving, storing, issuing, transferring, selling, accounting for, and maintaining all stores and equipment in the ship. The supply officer oversees the operation of the ship's galleys and messes, resale operations, laundry, post office, and disbursing office. In all but the smallest ships, the supply officer will be an officer of the supply corps. Assistants to the supply officer may include the assistant supply officer and disbursing officer.

Medical Officer. In ships with one or more officers of the medical corps assigned, the most senior such officer will be head of the medical department. The medical officer is responsible for maintaining the health of the crew and for ship's sanitation and hygiene. This officer may be assisted by one or more assistant medical officers, physician's assistants, or officers of the medical service corps. In smaller ships without an assigned medical corps officer, a physician's assistant or senior corpsman who is qualified for independent duty may fill this position.

Legal Officer. On ships with a legal department, the head of department shall be a JAG officer designated the legal officer. The legal officer functions as the principal adviser and staff assistant to the CO and XO in matters concerning laws and regulations; maintenance of good order, discipline, efficiency, and economy of command; and administration of justice within the command.

Command Chaplain. When assigned, the head of the chaplain department is an officer of the chaplain corps, responsible for providing and facilitating religious ministries for all personnel and for advising the CO on all matters related to religious, moral, and spiritual need.

Dental Officer. In ships with one or more officers of the dental corps assigned, the senior such officer will be head of the dental department. This officer is responsible for overseeing the dental health of the crew and may have additional responsibilities to care for the crews of other ships. In ships without a dental department, maintenance of dental records and arrangements for dental care at shore facilities are the responsibilities of the medical officer or senior corpsman.

Division Officers

The next level below the department head is the division officer. Although such officers are normally junior officers, in some cases senior enlisted members may serve in division officer billets. The division officer is assisted in his or her duties by a leading petty officer (LPO) or leading chief petty officer (LCPO), one or more work center supervisors (WCS), and various special assistants as illustrated in figure 6-1. The *Division Officer's Guide* is an excellent handbook for division officers and describes their duties in detail.

Watchstanding

In addition to duties related to officers' specific billet assignments, the ship's watch organization assigns other authority and responsibilities.

Under the XO, the senior watch officer is responsible for the assignment and general supervision of all deck watch officers and enlisted watchstanders in port and under way. This officer maintains records concerning the qualifications of all watchstanders, coordinates their training, and prepares appropriate watch bills.

The Watch Officer's Guide is a good source of information and guidance on deck watchstanding. It covers deck watches, log writing, shiphandling, rules of the nautical road, and other safety-at-sea issues. It also covers the duties of the OOD in port.

Chapter 9 of this book describes the ship's watch bill.

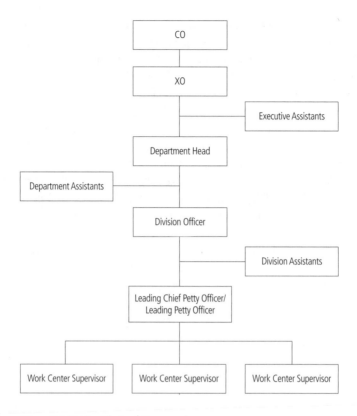

Figure 6-1 Division Chain of Command

Training Responsibilities

All officers are responsible for training their assigned personnel.

Executive Officer. The XO is responsible, under the CO, for forming a PBFT and for ensuring that the board produces a training plan with necessary subsidiary plans. The XO is responsible for monitoring the execution of the training plan and testing its effectiveness by scheduling drills, exercises, inspections, and critiques.

Department Heads. Department heads are responsible for executing that part of the training plan pertaining to their departments and for supervising their division officers' training efforts.

Division Officers. Division officers prepare the personnel of their divisions for the responsibilities relating to their ratings, administrative assignments, and battle station and watch qualifications. They must monitor their battle bills, watch bills, and emergency bill assignments to ensure their divisions can fulfill their obligations. In addition, division officers are responsible for the individual training, counseling, and education of their personnel.

Planning Board for Training (PBFT). PBFT is normally conducted at least monthly and is attended by all of the department heads and key executive assistants. This board, headed by the XO, establishes and monitors the command's training program.

The *SORM* sets forth in detail the requirements of a training program. The process begins with the establishment of a long-range program covering the period of a year. A short-range plan, quarterly plan, monthly plan, and a weekly training schedule are developed from the long-range plan. Many other subsidiary "General Military Training" (GMT) programs are included, such as drug- and alcohol-abuse prevention programs, career-benefits counseling, sexual-harassment prevention, and safe-driving programs.

Training Records. Each division officer must keep comprehensive records of the training accomplished by divisional personnel, both as individuals and as teams.

CHAPTER SEVEN

THE AMERICAN SAILOR

*The American Bluejacket can do anything, anytime, anywhere,
provided he is led by an equally capable officer.*

—Fleet Admiral Chester Nimitz

*The task of leadership is not to put greatness into humanity, but to
elicit it, for the greatness is already there.*

—John Buchnan

T he most important task that will be entrusted to you is the safety of your
ship or unit and the personnel in your charge. The next most important task, and the one that will occupy most of your time, is leading the
American Sailor. In order to effectively provide guidance and counseling to your
enlisted personnel to help them achieve their own career milestones, it is essential
to understand the history, demographics, and career opportunities of these men
and women.

Demography of the Navy

Despite an intense pace of operations, the size of the Navy has been reduced by
nearly 20 percent over the past decade. Navy enlisted force strength figures for
December 2009 showed the following:

Grade	Numbers
E-9	2,613
E-8	6,172
E-7	22,285
E-6	48,049
E-5	67,751
E-4	51,062
E-1–E-3	75,516
Total	273,448

Approximately 33 percent of the Navy's enlisted members are minorities, and over 18 percent are women. Enlisted members come from all states of the union and from backgrounds across the entire social and economic spectrum. Of new accessions, 94 percent are high school graduates, many have some college background, and 73 percent score above average in aptitude on the standardized entrance examination.

The men and women in your charge will be willing to accept the hardships that come with service in the Navy and to work hard and long hours if they understand the reasons for their sacrifices. Rear Admiral Richard Fontaine, a service group commander, said at a change of command ceremony for one of his COs, "Treat the American bluejacket well, with proper leadership and guidance, and there is nothing they can't or won't do for you and they will do it well." Chapter 18 offers some additional thoughts on leadership.

Enlistment and Basic Training

In order to enlist in the Navy, men and women must be between the ages of eighteen (seventeen with parental consent) and thirty-four. They must be citizens of the United States or immigrant aliens with a permanent resident visa or a green card. Enlistees must pass both an armed forces physical examination and the Armed Services Vocational Aptitude Battery (ASVAB) test, and, as a general rule, must be high school graduates or the equivalent. Most terms of initial enlistment range from four to six years of active duty. After enlisting at a Military Entrance Processing Station (MEPS), most enlistees are placed on delayed entry until the beginning of boot camp at Recruit Training Command (RTC), Great Lakes, Illinois.

Boot camp is a challenging eight-week introduction into Navy life consisting of classroom instruction, physical-readiness training, military drill, and field instruction in areas such as ship familiarization, deck seamanship, and military customs and courtesies. Following recruit training, many enlisted personnel go directly to "A" schools for training in particular enlisted ratings, or to apprenticeship training programs intended to prepare them for their first assignments.

The Enlisted Rating System

Pay Grades. The term "rank" is not properly used in reference to an enlisted member; the correct term for an enlisted member's level of seniority is "pay grade." Pay grades range from E-1 for a new recruit to E-9 for a master chief petty officer (E-10 for the one enlisted member holding the position of Master Chief Petty Officer of the Navy, or MCPON).

A Sailor steers the USS *George H. W. Bush* (CVN 77) from aft steering during a general quarters drill.

Ratings and Rates. The term used to identify an enlisted member's specialty is "rating." All petty officers (i.e., members in pay grade E-4 and above) have a rating. Examples of ratings are quartermaster, yeoman, and machinist's mate. Each rating has its own insignia that, when combined with pay grade insignia, forms a rating badge worn on the enlisted uniform. The combination of pay grade and rating (e.g., engineman second class) is called the member's *rate.*

General Rates and Designated Strikers. Members in pay grades E-1 to E-3 are categorized into one of five general rates, also called general apprenticeships:

seaman, fireman, airman, constructionman, and hospitalman. Each general rate is associated with a broad career field (e.g., firemen are in the engineering field), and each feeds into a distinct set of ratings. Members in pay grades E-1 through E-3 who already are assigned a rating are called designated strikers. Enlisted members may become designated strikers through successful completion of "A" school, by passing an advancement exam but not being selected for advancement, or as a result of on-the-job training.

Navy Enlisted Classification (NEC) Codes. NEC codes augment the rating system to identify and manage additional skill/knowledge/aptitude/qualification characteristics of both people and billets. NECs are divided into three groups: principal, component, and related. Principal NECs are stand-alone skills that generally encompass a group of component NECs. Related NECs are similar to principal NECs but are not prerequisites for them.

Enlisted Detailing and Assignment Policy

Detailing. The detailing system used for enlisted personnel is virtually identical to the officer system discussed in chapter 17. Each rating or group of related ratings has a detailer, and each command has an enlisted placement officer overseeing the assignment of enlisted personnel to that command. In addition, each rating has a community manager, who maintains control over manning and makes decisions affecting assignment policy and career progression in that rating.

Sea-Shore Rotation. Each rating has a sea-shore rotation, designating the normal length of sea and shore tours for Sailors in that rating. This notional rotation reflects the rating's relative proportions of billets afloat and ashore. Some shore-intensive ratings substitute overseas tours for sea tours.

Pay and Allowances. There are some subtle differences in the administration of pay and allowances for enlisted personnel compared with that of similar entitlements for officers. Although all officers and enlisted members with dependents are entitled to receive housing allowance, single enlisted members in the most junior pay grades who are serving on board ship are not entitled to this allowance and are expected to reside on board. Single Sailors on shore duty may also be required to reside in bachelor quarters on base if adequate quarters are available. While officers are always entitled to basic allowance for subsistence (BAS) regardless of their assignment, enlisted members may be required to receive subsistence in-kind at a government messing facility.

Members Married to Members. Enlisted detailers make every effort to co-locate married service couples in the same geographic area, consistent with the needs of the service. Due to the difficulties involved in spouse co-location, fulfilling duty preferences for geographic location or type of duty/unit may not always be possible.

Reenlistment, Retention, and Career Management

Unlike many private enterprises that have the luxury of being able to recruit journeymen skilled workers and middle-level managers from outside the organization, the Navy is wholly dependent on its ability to produce and retain an experienced "home-grown" workforce. For this reason, it is absolutely essential that significant numbers of the most promising petty officers make the decision to reenlist when eligible, and to stay for a full career. Unfortunately for the Navy, in many cases the most valuable enlisted members are the same individuals whose experience, skills, and knowledge make them attractive to employers outside the Navy. Job satisfaction can be the factor that tips the balance for these Sailors, and as a division officer, you will be in a position to assist the Navy to retain these key individuals. Your knowledge about such subjects as reenlistment bonuses and special reenlistment programs, described later in this chapter, can help your Sailors progress in their careers.

Selective Reenlistment Bonus (SRB). In order to remain competitive with the outside job market, the Navy has devised a system of reenlistment bonuses for petty officers in the most critical skills. The amounts of SRBs, which vary with rating and pay grade, are adjusted twice each year based on available funding and reenlistment patterns. In 2009, SRB could be awarded in amounts up to $90,000. Sailors eligible to reenlist with SRB must submit their reenlistment applications to NPC between 35–120 days prior to their reenlistment dates, and Sailors can reenlist for SRB no more than 90 days prior to their end of active obligated service (EAOS). Fifty percent of the SRB award amount is paid at the time of reenlistment, and the remainder is paid in equal annual installments over the contract period.

Perform to Serve (PTS). PTS is a centralized reservation system that helps the Navy to manage reenlistments of all E-3 through E-6 Sailors with less than fourteen years of service. While most Sailors are permitted to reenlist in their current rating, Sailors in overmanned ratings may be offered reenlistment in an undermanned rating, and those with a poor performance history may be denied permission to reenlist.

Extension of Enlistment. Under some circumstances, Sailors approaching the end of their current enlistments may extend their enlistments from one month to forty-eight months, in one-month increments. Authorized reasons for extensions include to complete a cruise or deployment, to have sufficient obligated service remaining to execute a set of orders or attend formal training, to match the EAOS with the end of a tour (called projected rotation date, or PRD), or to await advancement examination results.

A Sailor calculates chart measurements on the bridge of the guided-missile cruiser USS *Bunker Hill* (CG 52).

Rating Entry for General Apprentices (REGA). The primary method of entry into a rating for general apprentices who enter the Navy without guarantee of an "A" school is through on-the-job training followed by successful participation in an advancement examination. In order to provide an appropriate distribution of enlisted skills, the REGA program divides ratings into those that are open (meaning an undesignated general apprentice in the appropriate pipeline may take the appropriate advancement exam and compete for advancement to third class petty officer in that rating) and those that are closed. A Sailor can generally only enter a closed rating following completion of the appropriate "A" school. Commanding officers can request "A" school quotas for promising Sailors desiring to enter these ratings.

Voluntary Conversions. In order to improve their opportunities for upward mobility, or to pursue areas of personal interest, enlisted personnel may request to change their ratings. Approval of a lateral conversion from one rating to another is contingent upon the member's release from his or her current detailer and acceptance by the detailer and community manager of the new rating. Normally, Sailors may only convert from ratings in career reenlistment objective (CREO) 2 or 3 categories—meaning, those categories that are either manned to desired levels, or overmanned—to ratings in the CREO 1, or undermanned, category. Although conversions are possible up to the E-6 level, first class petty officers should be cautioned that they will be expected to carry out their duties in their new rating with little or no training.

Selective Conversion and Reenlistment (SCORE) Program and Selective Training and Reenlistment (STAR) Program. Under the SCORE program, a Sailor may change his or her rating at reenlistment and be guaranteed attendance at "A" or "C" (advanced training) school in the new rating. This program is reserved for superior performers who are within one year of their EAOS. In some cases, an eligible recipient may be automatically advanced to E-4 or E-5 following completion of training. The STAR program provides similar benefits for members reenlisting to remain in their present ratings.

Forced Conversion. Personnel who are no longer qualified to serve in their current ratings, because of security considerations, medical concerns, inaptitude, or other reasons, may be involuntarily converted to other ratings. Forced conversion is not a disciplinary tool but may be required in cases where a significant disciplinary infraction has resulted in the loss of a member's security clearance. In addition, a Sailor or CO may request a no-fault conversion to a former rating when the Sailor fails to succeed in a new rating through no fault of his or her own.

Reenlistment Ceremonies. Reenlistment is a major event in a Sailor's career and should be accorded an appropriate and meaningful ceremony to mark the occasion. The officers and senior petty officers in the Sailor's chain of command, as well as his or her family, friends, and shipmates, normally attend. An officer of the reenlistee's choosing administers the oath. Most commands provide photographic coverage and forward press releases to base newspapers as well as to the Sailor's hometown newspapers, and provide other recognition such as refreshments, a period of special liberty, and other selected privileges and benefits.

Education, Training, and Qualification

Enlisted Warfare Qualifications. Warfare qualification is a formal system of recognizing the initiative, technical competence, and broadened expertise of enlisted personnel serving in different types of combatant commands. Figure 7-1 illustrates the different types of enlisted warfare qualifications. In both the surface and aviation forces, all Sailors in pay grades E-5 or above must be actively working toward attaining their primary warfare device. Attainment of a warfare qualification is a recognized milestone in the professional development of any Sailor. In practice, attainment of a warfare qualification is nearly a prerequisite for selection to any competitive program.

United Services Military Apprenticeship Program (USMAP). USMAP is a formal military training program that provides active-duty Coast Guard, Marine Corps, and

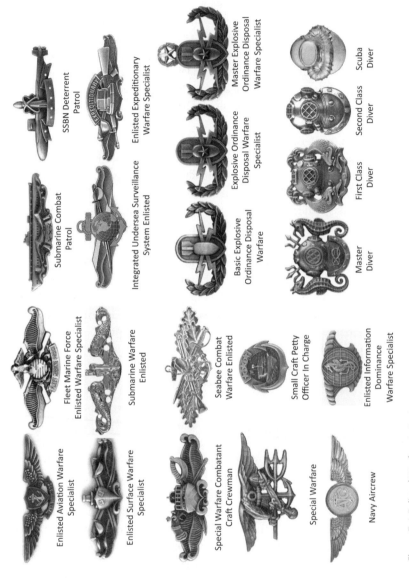

Enlisted Aviation Warfare Specialist

Enlisted Surface Warfare Specialist

Fleet Marine Force Enlisted Warfare Specialist

Submarine Warfare Enlisted

Special Warfare Combatant Craft Crewman

Seabee Combat Warfare Enlisted

Small Craft Petty Officer In Charge

Special Warfare

Enlisted Information Dominance Warfare Specialist

Navy Aircrew

SSBN Deterrent Patrol

Submarine Combat Patrol

Enlisted Expeditionary Warfare Specialist

Integrated Undersea Surveillance System Enlisted

Master Explosive Ordinance Disposal Warfare Specialist

Explosive Ordinance Disposal Warfare Specialist

Basic Explosive Ordinance Disposal Warfare

Scuba Diver

Second Class Diver

First Class Diver

Master Diver

Figure 7-1 Enlisted Warfare Insignia

Navy members the opportunity to complete their civilian apprenticeship requirements while they are on active duty, and earn a Certificate of Completion in their trade from the U.S. Department of Labor. Each apprenticeship requires from two thousand to ten thousand work hours to complete, but requires no off-duty work.

Credentialing Opportunities Online (COOL). COOL identifies civilian credentials that best map to a Sailor's rating and training and lays out a path for a Sailor to achieve industry-recognized, professional certification and licensure.

Learning and Development Roadmap (LaDR). LaDR provides Sailors with a tool to manage their personal and professional training goals, providing a well-defined path to advancement.

Off-Duty Voluntary Education (VOLED). Like officers, enlisted members are encouraged to continue their formal education, and are eligible to participate in tuition assistance (TA) or the Navy College Program for Advanced College Education (NCPACE). To use these programs, Sailors must be recommended for advancement and must have taken and passed their most recent advancement exam. They must have passed or been medically waived from their most recent physical readiness test (PRT), and Sailors with fewer than twenty years of service must have at least one year remaining on their current enlistment.

Enlisted Advancement and Development

Unlike officers, who are "promoted" to the next rank, the proper term for an enlisted career progression is "advancement." The Navy manages its enlisted advancements through the Navy Enlisted Advancement System (NEAS).

Requirements for Advancement. Requirements for enlisted members to be advanced between pay grades vary, although an absolute requirement is a favorable recommendation by the member's CO. Other requirements generally include serving a minimum time in the previous pay grade, completing applicable correspondence courses and practical qualifications, and achieving a passing score on a standardized advancement examination. Selectees for advancements to pay grades E-4 through E-6 are determined numerically, based on computation of a "final multiple" score that takes into account evaluation grades, advancement exam score, personal awards, tours in a combat zone, time in grade, and other factors. Members who pass the advancement exam but are not selected for advancement are called "passed, not advanced," or PNA. Although eligibility to be considered for selection to E-7 is determined by an advancement exam, selectees for advancements to pay grades E-7 through E-9 are determined by selection boards that carefully review the members' overall records in much the same manner as do officer promotion boards.

Command Advancement Program (CAP). Commanding officers of ships and selected shore commands are authorized to advance a small number of enlisted personnel to pay grades E-4 through E-6 outside of the normal advancement process. Sailors who advance under this program must meet most of the normal requirements for advancement in rate, although they need not have passed the advancement examination.

Career Milestones. The two most significant milestones in the career of an enlisted person are advancement to petty officer third class at the E-4 level and advancement to chief petty officer at the E-7 level. The first marks a member's initial entry into leadership, as petty officer third class is the level at which an enlisted member first becomes entrusted with overseeing others. Advancement to chief petty officer is an even more significant milestone and is marked by an elaborate initiation ceremony conducted by the chiefs' mess under the supervision of the command master chief.

Professional Development Board (PDB). Each command has established a PDB that augments a Sailor's chain of command to provide a visibly fair and impartial opportunity for enlisted personnel to attain positions of greater responsibility. The PDB periodically reviews each Sailor's record to provide expertise and counseling on career progress. In addition, the PDB reviews applications and requests for striker designations, rating conversion, commissioning programs, and other avenues for professional growth. Normally the command master chief chairs the PDB, and other members of the board include the command career counselor, leading chief petty officer of the member appearing before the board, and the educational services officer.

Commissioning Programs

Many Sailors dream of becoming commissioned officers, and there are programs designed specifically to help enlisted personnel achieve this goal.

Limited Duty Officer (LDO) and Chief Warrant Officer (CWO) Programs. These programs are targeted toward senior enlisted members who already possess unique experience in technical fields. Unlike most other commissioning programs, Sailors do not need a college degree for application, but exceptional evaluation and FITREP marks are a necessity.

Applicants to the LDO program must be in pay grades E-6 through E-8, with between eight and sixteen years of service. Applicants to the CWO program must be in pay grades E-7 or above, or E-6s who have been selected for E-7, with between twelve and twenty-four years of service.

Upon commissioning, LDOs and CWOs are assigned to duties that utilize their specific expertise.

Seaman to Admiral-21 (STA-21). STA-21 combined a number of older commissioning programs, streamlining what had previously been a cumbersome and confusing administrative process. STA-21 provides a path for outstanding active-duty Sailors to further their educations and become commissioned officers in the Unrestricted Line; Restricted Line in Human Resources; Special Duty Officer in Information Professional, Intelligence, Warfare, and Oceanography; or Staff Corps in Civil Engineering, Medical Corps, Nurse Corps, or Supply Corps. While attending school, STA-21 participants remain on active duty at their current enlisted pay grade and receive pay, allowances, benefits, and privileges. In addition, they are provided up to $10,000 per year to cover tuition, books, and fees.

Naval ROTC, U.S. Naval Academy and Officer Candidate School (OCS). Enlisted members are eligible to apply directly to Naval ROTC and the U.S. Naval Academy in the same manner as their civilian counterparts, although some age waivers are available for current or former active-duty members. Enlisted members who have previously completed their college degrees may apply to attend OCS.

Separations and Retirement

Unlike officers, who serve at the pleasure of the President and who may request to resign, Sailors enlist for specific periods of time and under normal circumstances may elect to be separated only upon completion of an enlistment period.

Administrative Separations. Enlisted members may be administratively separated prior to completing the end of an enlistment for reasons including the following: conscientious objection, certain designated physical or mental conditions, parenthood, pregnancy, hardship, personality disorder, a desire to further their education, status as a surviving family member, weight-control failure, and defective enlistments and inductions. Separations may be voluntary or involuntary. Appendix B discusses involuntary administrative separations.

High-Year Tenure (HYT). As with officers, who are generally separated from the Navy after twice failing to select for promotion, enlisted members are separated if they fail to reach the next pay grade prior to reaching a certain number of years of service. HYT limits for each pay grade are as follows:

Grade	Year
E-1–E-2	6 years
E-3	6 years (8 years if PNA'd the advancement exam)
E-4	8 years
E-5	14 years
E-6	20 years
E-7	24 years
E-8	26 years
E-9	30 years

Waivers to remain on active duty past HYT limits are considered for members in support of urgent, immediate operational requirements, members who are in CREO undermanned ratings, and those members under certain other limited circumstances. Waivers are not authorized to await advancement examination results.

Fleet Reserve and Retirement. Enlisted members with twenty years of active service may request to be transferred to the fleet reserve. In most respects fleet-reserve status is identical to retired status and entitles the members to retirement pay and benefits. At the end of thirty years of service, to include time in the fleet reserve, enlisted members may be retired. This transition occurs automatically for members in the fleet reserve.

CHAPTER EIGHT

ORAL AND WRITTEN COMMUNICATION

Make everything as simple as possible, but not simpler.

—Albert Einstein

Captain, I have a vessel on my . . . Oh, we missed 'em!

—Former unnamed Navy officer

A s a junior officer, it is unlikely that you will become known as an especially skilled orator or as a gifted writer; however, it is not necessary to attain this level of accomplishment at this stage of your career. What is critically important is to be reasonably competent in both skills in order to effectively communicate with other members of your command and to prepare messages and correspondence to assist the commanding officer (CO) in interaction with outside commands and agencies.

Oral Communication

No doubt you have already had numerous opportunities to observe oral presentations by a variety of senior officers. Although not every senior officer is capable of rousing and inspiring oratory, virtually all are reasonably adept at speaking to a large group without evident discomfort, and of presenting a well-organized and informative lecture that is attuned to the needs of that particular audience. For some of these officers, this ability to speak comfortably in public may have been a gift that required little practice to master, but for most it is a skill that they honed over many years of experience.

Although as a junior officer, the thought of addressing a large group of people in a formal setting may still fill you with dread, be assured that you will almost certainly be afforded frequent opportunities to employ your skills as a speaker in more mundane settings before being thrust into the spotlight. Your earliest such opportunities will be holding morning quarters with your own division, but as you grow in seniority and experience your comfort level will increase, and you will gradually be tasked with giving increasingly complex presentations to larger groups.

Voice Qualities. The human voice has several qualities that distinguish it. The most important are pitch, resonance, projection, and a less definable attribute that we will call tension. You are born with these physical traits, but to some extent you can improve upon or control them.

Pitch is the average frequency of tones produced by the vocal cords. A low-pitched voice is more pleasing to the ear than a high-pitched voice, even though the latter carries farther. Nervousness or stress tend to increase the pitch of your voice, but you can counteract this by mastery of proper breathing techniques. Watch an opera singer closely. You will see that her chest does not move appreciably, because she uses her lower abdomen for breathing. This technique is not what most of us are used to, particularly if we have engaged in sports, so it will take some time to learn but is well worth the effort. Try to speak using your diaphragm and lower abdomen muscles for breathing. At the same time, consciously relax your chest muscles. You will find that you can learn to speak with a minimum use of the muscles of your upper chest and that your throat and voice can be made to relax in the process. This will lower the pitch of your voice and increase resonance and projection. Most important, it will decrease the discernible tension in your voice.

Resonance is the ability of your voice-producing apparatus to vibrate the vocal cords to produce tones and overtones. Greater resonance makes a voice sound richer and more pleasant in the same way that an orchestra produces richer and more pleasant sounds than does a single violin. Good resonance is a function of the internal cavities and shape of the throat, sinuses, and skull. You can improve your resonance by use of the opera-singer exercise described above.

Projection is the property of a voice that helps it carry over long distances. Clearly, the ability to project your voice in a noisy situation can be an important tactical skill, as with the conning officer giving directions to the helm in an emergency situation in a crowded and turbulent pilothouse. In addition, the ability to project your voice well will benefit your ability to make yourself heard to a large group without tiring or straining your vocal cords. The opera-singer exercise will help here, too, as will keeping your mouth pointed in the direction you wish your voice to be projected and opening it as wide as possible to maximize the sound waves you produce.

Tension is a combination of pitch and resonance and is directly affected by stress. The voice of a relaxed speaker is more pleasing to the audience and carries far more authority than the wavering voice of a nervous, tense speaker. In addition to this quality of the voice itself, nervous speakers tend to speak faster, as if to rush through the presentation and get it over with as quickly as possible. This rapid-fire delivery also tends to antagonize an audience.

To help avoid the "jitters" that can lead to this vocal tension, before you make a presentation practice the breathing exercises described earlier in this section and try to focus on something else during the hour or so immediately preceding your talk. Some speakers find it eases their nervousness to pick out one person in the back of the room and talk directly to him or her. Too much caffeine, as from coffee or caffeinated soft drinks, can accentuate your nervousness and should probably be avoided immediately before your presentation.

Grammar, Diction, and Delivery. The most vibrant, beautiful voice can easily be marred by a myriad of hindering factors. These can include a delivery comprising poor grammar, limited vocabulary, poor pronunciation, a regional accent so pronounced as to make the speaker unintelligible to the average listener, repeated use of stock phrases ("you know," and "like" being among the worst offenders), or other verbal idiosyncrasies that detract from the speaker's message.

The rules of grammar are considerably relaxed in verbal communications; you may augment your spoken words with nonverbal gestures and take other liberties to emphasize thoughts or accommodate the mood of the conversation. Nevertheless, a speaker's utter lack of knowledge of or regard for appropriate grammar will become apparent in the course of a conversation or presentation and may have a subtle or overt effect on the listeners' trust. Similarly, verbal eccentricities such as the use of obscure words or undue reliance on profanity or other offensive language to make a point can interfere with your ability to communicate effectively.

The most important rule to remember in verbal communications is that your aim is to share your thoughts with your listeners as clearly and simply as possible, to make it easy for them to understand what you want them to know. This doesn't mean you should "talk down" to your listeners, but you also shouldn't try to impress them with your intellect or your worldliness—such a goal is almost certain to backfire.

Communications with Seniors. A good rule when giving a report to your boss is to remember the guideline taught to all beginning journalists: start with the important facts first, the "who, what, when, where, why, and how" of the situation. Save the lengthy explanations for after you have communicated your main points, and try to ensure that your report does not raise more questions in your boss's mind than it answers. This is often referred to as presenting the "bottom line up front" (BLUF, for short).

Many superiors take a dim view of a junior who begins every report with a lengthy preface, particularly when they recognize a pattern in which this preface takes the form of a series of excuses leading up to the ultimate bad news. Putting the bad news first can prevent the buildup of anxiety in your listeners as they wait to find out what you are trying to say, and it will often make them more willing to hear you out without interruption. Conversely, when the news is exceedingly bad, such as the report of an accident involving members of the crew, a superior is likely to appreciate hearing early on a sentence such as "No one was seriously injured."

Another good rule is to never bring the boss a problem without also suggesting (and demonstrating your ability to implement) an appropriate solution. Inexperienced officers may find it difficult to apply this rule consistently, particularly in an emergency situation, but the report "I have a surface contact on a collision course" is incomplete without following it with "Recommend altering course 30 degrees to starboard to open the closest point of approach to two thousand yards." Such reports demonstrate your decision-making ability and enhance your superiors' view of your competence.

Communications with Juniors. When giving orders to juniors, in order to develop their own decision-making ability, it is a good idea to tell them *what* you want done without specifying exactly *how* you want it done. At the same time, you should ensure that you are making clear exactly what results you expect from their efforts. Once you become familiar with your subordinates' individual personalities and abilities and they become familiar with your expectations, you may be able to use a kind of verbal shorthand that eliminates much of the explicit detail in such orders.

It is important to get into the habit of giving frequent feedback to your subordinates on their day-to-day performance. You can easily work this kind of communication into your daily routine, and it will pay big dividends for you and your organization over the long run. Telling your chief, "Overall I was happy with the work you did on the performance evaluations, but I noticed some format errors that had to be corrected—here, let me show you what I mean . . . ," is better than saying nothing about the errors and losing your temper the next time the chief makes the same mistake.

A time-honored rule of communicating with subordinates is to "Praise in public, reprimand in private." When one of your sailors does a good job, mention it at quarters in front of the whole division. The average sailor may pretend not to care or may even be embarrassed by such attention, but in reality your public praise will serve as a reward for the kind of performance you want to encourage in your subordinates. On the other hand, when you have a criticism of subordinates, you will do better to take them aside to privately express your concerns to avoid embarrassing them in front of others. Public reprimands are rarely effective in correcting poor performance and can frequently aggravate a troublesome situation.

An exception to the above rule applies when safety or imminent operational need demands immediate correction of a subordinate's—or superior's—misstep. Good leaders not only use these occasions as learning experiences for their people, but empower subordinates to correct their own errors.

Although seniors are not obliged to give subordinates justification for their orders, the best leaders typically explain their reasons to subordinates when time permits. Subordinates who understand the reasons for an order not only appreciate that the senior took the time to explain, but are much more likely to carry out the order enthusiastically and thoroughly.

Making a Speech. As you increase in seniority, you will find yourself invited to give talks to groups of people who want to hear about your experiences or who have a particular interest in one of your areas of expertise. For the novice speaker, the best method to ensure you give a relaxed, professional delivery is to rehearse extensively. After you write your speech, practice into a recording device, in front of a mirror, or with a friend. This exercise will serve several functions. If you use a recorder or practice with a particularly honest friend, your rehearsal will provide insight into how your delivery is coming across and will allow you to improve the mechanics of your technique. In addition, the added familiarity you gain with the subject matter of the speech will allow you to be more comfortable, and the partial memorization that results will ensure your ability to make more eye contact with your audience and refer less frequently to your notes.

If your speech will be followed by a question-and-answer period, try to anticipate the questions you are likely to be asked and rough out some notes to use in answer to each. Even if you are not asked the particular questions you anticipate, you will likely find that the notes you made will come in handy in your answers to other questions.

Once you have given a few speeches from prepared texts, try to take the next step by leaving the copy of the verbatim text at home and instead relying on a series of file cards with short notes on them. If you can develop the ability to briefly glance at your notes to refresh your memory as to your next point and then look up from your notes while you are speaking, it will prevent those panicked moments when you lose your place in the text, and it will also allow you look directly at your audience, greatly enhancing your credibility as a speaker. In addition to the intangible benefits of being able to make more eye contact with your audience, your voice will project better because you will be speaking out into the room, rather than down toward the podium.

If you will be using an unfamiliar sound system, you should try to acclimate yourself with its use beforehand. With a stationary microphone, you must adjust it so that you don't have to hunch over to maintain an appropriate distance (normally no more than several inches) from the microphone, and you must take care to maintain a constant distance between your mouth and the microphone to avoid creating distracting fluctuations in the sound level. Lapel microphones are considerably more flexible and easier to use.

Giving a Training Lecture or Briefing. A training lecture is generally given to a group of subordinates or peers, while a briefing generally is given to a senior or group of seniors. These two types of presentation have much in common; in both cases you are the recognized subject-matter expert and are being tasked with sharing your expertise with a group, and in both cases you are likely to make use of such presentation tools as PowerPoint slides, videos, or other audiovisual aids.

Ideally, substantial effort should go into your preparations for a training lecture or briefing. First, you need to prepare an outline of the important points you plan to cover, with amplifying data for each point. Translating these points into good PowerPoint slides is an art form. You should strive to include sufficient information that reinforces your verbal message with visual cues and also jogs the memory of your audience if they review the presentation at a later time; however, you don't want so much detail that your audience has to choose between reading the slides and listening to you. If you use paper handouts, you should plan to include sufficient "white space" for your listeners to take notes directly on those pages.

In your preparations, make sure you are gearing your presentation to the appropriate knowledge level for your audience. You don't want to bore them by reviewing information with which they are already very familiar, but you also don't want to lose them by assuming knowledge that they do not have. As with your preparations for a speech, it is a good idea to try to anticipate the questions the audience will ask and to prepare answers for these questions in advance. Experienced briefers often prepare "backup slides," with amplifying information to be used if the audience requests additional information in a particular area. Such foresight generally reflects very favorably on the briefer.

It has been said that a good training lecture or brief has the following format: tell them what you are going to tell them, tell them, then tell them what you told them. The introductory portion ("tell them what you are going to tell them") should preview for the audience the major points you plan to cover so that they don't stop to wonder during your presentation where you are going with a particular thought. During the body of your presentation ("tell them"), it can be useful to hold your audience's attention by saying something like "I plan to show five advantages to this new technique" or "We will discuss the four basic types of fires," and then tick off each point in some manner as you cover it. It is a good habit to close your training lecture or brief ("tell them what you told them") with a short recap of the important points you have covered to reinforce your key ideas.

Listening Skills. Equally important to the skill of speaking is the skill of listening. Learn to give your full attention to a subordinate's report, without allowing your attention to be diverted by your email or a ringing telephone (unless, of course, it represents an emergency). Although you may find it necessary to ask questions to help coax the information out of the speaker, you should try to avoid excessive interruptions, which may cause the speaker to lose his or her train of thought or become flustered. When a superior is providing oral direction, it is good practice to take notes so that you will later be able to remember exactly what you have been told to do. Many officers carry a small "wheelbook" in their back pockets for just this purpose.

Televised Presentations. With the growing use of videoconferencing and digital media, it is no longer only the most senior officers who must concern themselves with television appearances. The same general presentation guidelines apply for televised appearances as for "in-person" presentations, with a few additional rules.

As is true with still photographs, the camera tends to accentuate the negative aspects of your appearance. If your shirt isn't tucked in properly or your hair is unkempt, it will be painfully noticeable, and your unfortunate grooming lapse will not only distract your immediate audience, but may live on in electronic format for a very long time, so you would be well advised to take extra pains with your appearance as you prepare for the presentation. Many experienced officers state that the best method of addressing the camera is to make eye contact with it just as if you were speaking to one individual.

If you are asked to give an interview for a non-Navy broadcast, make sure that your appearance is cleared with the appropriate public affairs office. Be aware that the content of your talk will not likely be used in its entirety on the air. An otherwise good interview can be ruined by one sentence that gives false information or the wrong impression when taken out of context.

Written Communication

All officers will spend a considerable amount of time writing documents, messages, emails, and correspondence, and as they become more senior, proofreading the written efforts of others. With the wide availability of spell-checking tools, there is little excuse for sloppily edited work.

All officers, except for the most senior, spend considerable time on the computer, which requires a familiarity with the appropriate software as well as a good understanding of the fundamentals of Navy correspondence, records, and documents. This section will not make you an expert on these rules, but it will provide you with a general overview of the different types of commonly used written communications.

The primary reference for most forms of written correspondence is the SECNAVINST 5216.5 series instruction. SECNAVINST 5215.1 series governs instructions and notices. The Naval Institute book *Guide to Naval Writing; A Practical Manual* is another excellent reference.

Navy Writing Standards

It is a common misperception that Navy writing is supposed to be bureaucratic, bloated, difficult to comprehend, and couched in impenetrable technical jargon. Nothing could be further from the truth. In fact, for a number of years the Navy has been actively working to encourage a style of writing that is simple, direct, and easily understood. A few general rules will help you to develop this style in your own work.

Be Organized. As in oral communications, remember the "who, what, when, where, why, and how" of journalism. Get to the key issues quickly to avoid wasting your readers' time; if you believe amplifying details may be required, include them *after* your main points. A chronological record of events is rarely the most effective method of communicating your information.

Be Brief. Don't write a long paragraph if you can get the same ideas across in a short one. Avoid swelling your prose with legalese (e.g., "pursuant," "notwithstanding," and "aforesaid"), unnecessary stock phrases (e.g., "in order to," "be advised," or "in the event of"), and don't use long words (e.g., "utilize" or "procure") when short ones will do (e.g., "use" or "buy," respectively). Don't be afraid to use contractions.

Take the Active Voice. Nothing makes writing appear bureaucratic and overblown faster than using the passive voice. Don't say "It is believed by the investigating officer that the casualty resulted from lack of oversight on the part of the watch supervisor." Instead say "I believe the watch supervisor's lack of oversight caused the casualty." It is highly appropriate to use the personal pronoun in most such situations.

Navy Correspondence and Documents

Letters. A Navy letter is an official piece of correspondence, in most cases from the CO or commander of one unit to that of another unit. Letters may be signed by the CO or by another member of the command to whom the CO has delegated "by direction" authority. Typically a number of officers in a command have "by direction" signature authority for routine correspondence in their areas of responsibility. With this authority goes the understanding that the officer signing "by direction" speaks directly for the CO.

Navy letters are generally printed on command letterhead stationery and follow a strict format as illustrated in figure 8-1, from SECNAVINST 5216.5D. The

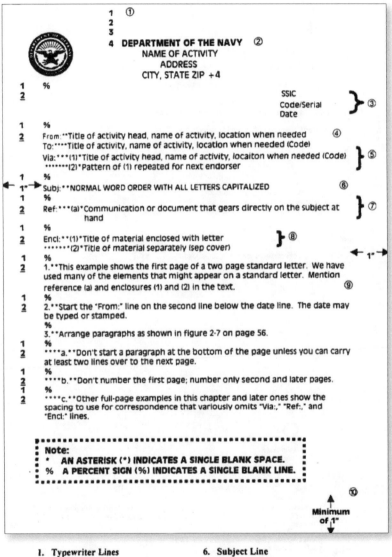

```
                    1   ①
                    2
                    3
                    4   DEPARTMENT OF THE NAVY  ②
                        NAME OF ACTIVITY
                        ADDRESS
                        CITY, STATE ZIP +4
     1    %
     2                                                      SSIC        ⎫
                                                            Code/Serial  ⎬ ③
                                                            Date        ⎭

     1    %
     2    From:**Title of activity head, name of activity, location when needed  ④
          To:****Title of activity, name of activity, location when needed (Code)
          Via:***(1)*Title of activity head, name of activity, locaiton when needed (Code)  ⎫
          *******(2)*Pattern of (1) repeated for next endorser                              ⎬ ⑤
     1    %                                                                                  ⎭
     1"→ Subj:**NORMAL WORD ORDER WITH ALL LETTERS CAPITALIZED         ⑥
     1    %
     2    Ref:***(a)*Communication or document that gears directly on the subject at  ⎫ ⑦
               hand                                                                    ⎭
     1    %
     2    Encl:**(1)*Title of material enclosed with letter           ⎫ ⑧
          *******(2)*Title of material separately (sep cover)          ⎭
     1    %                                                                    ←1"→
     2    1.**This example shows the first page of a two page standard letter.  We have
          used many of the elements that might appear on a standard letter.  Mention
          reference (a) and enclosures (1) and (2) in the text.                ⑨
     1    %
     2    2.**Start the "From:" line on the second line below the date line.  The date may
          be typed or stamped.
               %
          3.**Arrange paragraphs as shown in figure 2-7 on page 56.
     1    %
     2    ****a.**Don't start a paragraph at the bottom of the page unless you can carry
          at least two lines over to the next page.
     1    %
     2    ****b.**Don't number the first page; number only second and later pages.
     1    %
     2    ****c.**Other full-page examples in this chapter and later ones show the
          spacing to use for correspondence that variously omits "Via:," "Ref:," and
          "Encl:" lines.
```

Note:
* AN ASTERISK (*) INDICATES A SINGLE BLANK SPACE.
% A PERCENT SIGN (%) INDICATES A SINGLE BLANK LINE.

⑩

Minimum of 1"

1. Typewriter Lines
2. Letterhead Format
3. Identification Symbols
4. From Line
5. To & Via Lines
6. Subject Line
7. Reference Line
8. Enclosure Line
9. Text
10. Margins

Figure 8-1 Navy Letter

1
2 (1)
3
4
5
6 (2) SUBJECT BLOCK
1 %
2 ****d.**Second and succeeding pages of a standard letter may look like this:
1 %
2 ********(1)*Start typing on the sixth line. Repeat the subject line.
1 %
2 ********(2)*Start the text on the second line below the date or subject line.
%
4.***Copy to:" addressees appear on all copies. "Blind copy to:" addresses as well as
◄ 1" ► the identity of the writer and typist appear on internal copies only.
%
5.**A standard letter uses no complimentary close.
1 %
2 %
3 %
4

                                        NAME OF SIGNER } (3)   ◄ 1" ►
                                        By direction
1 %
2 Copy to:
SNDL number and/or short title of information addressee
SNDL number and/or short title of 2nd information addressee } (4)
1 %
2 Blind Copy to:
List blind copy addressees } (5)
1 %
2 Writer: Name, organization, room # or telephone # } (6)
Typist: Name, date, word processing symbols

7

                (7) ↑   (8)
                Minimum
                of 1"   2

                ↓

1.   Typewriter Lines   6.   Drafter's Identification Block.
2.   Subject Line   Appears on internal copies
3.   Signature Block   only
4.   Copy-to Block   7.   Margins
5.   Blind Copy-to Block. Appears only on 8. Page number
     internal copies

Figure 8-1 Navy Letter *(continued)*

SSIC, or standard subject identification code, listed in the upper right-hand corner, is a code that permits correspondence to be routed and filed as appropriate for the subject matter. SECNAVINST 5210.11 instruction series contains a complete listing of these four- and five-digit codes. Underneath the SSIC is a line containing a locally assigned numerical code corresponding to the drafter of the correspondence and the serial number corresponding to the letter. Serial numbers are not required on unclassified correspondence, but are normally used to assist in correspondence management. If used, serial numbers are assigned sequentially, beginning with the number 001 on the first day of each new year. Beneath this line is the date the letter has been signed.

To ensure routing to the appropriate individual within the command on the receiving end of a letter, the specific office code may be designated in parenthesis in the address line. A "via" command is an intermediate level in the chain of command; the format for such a command's endorsement of a letter is discussed below. "References" are other documents that pertain to the subject matter; these are designated by letters and are not included with the correspondence. "Enclosures" are supporting documents that are included in the correspondence; these are designated by number. All listed references and enclosures are discussed, in order, in the body of the letter.

The only exception to the rule that letters are from COs is for letters from individuals on personal or career matters. Examples of such official personal letters include correspondence with selection boards or detailers or requests for augmentation. For identification purposes, the "From" line in such a personal letter always lists the officer's rank, full name, and social security number/designator, and unless otherwise directed such letters are normally sent via the drafter's CO and other intermediates in the chain of command.

Intermediate activities (designated as "via" addressees in the letter) endorse correspondence and forward it to the next "via" addressee or to the ultimate addressee as appropriate. Normally the first word of the first paragraph of an endorsement is "Forwarded." (This may be expanded into a phrase such as "Forwarded, recommending approval," or other appropriate remark.) Figure 8-2 shows the format for an endorsement.

When corresponding with a civilian business or other non-DoD activity, use standard business letter format in place of Navy letter format. Figure 8-3 shows an example of such correspondence.

Memoranda. A memorandum is a less formal means of communication used between individuals in the same command or different commands. With a few exceptions, the signer of a memorandum speaks only for himself or herself rather than as an official representative of the CO. The general format of a memorandum is similar to that of a Navy letter, except that a memorandum is normally

DEPARTMENT OF THE NAVY
NAVAL AIR STATION
CECIL FIELD, FL 32215-5000

5216
Ser 11/273
9 Jul 98

From: Commanding Officer, Naval Air Station, Cecil Field
To: Commander in Chief, U.S. Atlantic Fleet
Via: (1) Commander, Sea Based ASW Wings, Atlantic
        (2) Commander, Naval Air Force, U.S. Atlantic Fleet

Subj: HOW TO PREPARE ENDORSEMENTS

Encl: (1) Example of New-Page Endorsement

1. An endorsement may be added to the bottom of a basic letter, like this one, or to a previous endorsement if: (a) All of the endorsement will fit on the page, and (b) It is sure to be signed without revision.

                                        C. WORTHY

_____

                                        Ser 019/870
                                        17 Jul 98

FIRST ENDORSEMENT

From: Commander, Sea Based ASW Wings, Atlantic
To: Commander in Chief, U.S. Atlantic Fleet
Via: Commander, Naval Air Force, U.S. Atlantic Fleet

1. A same-page endorsement may omit the SSIC, subject, and the basic letter's identification if the entire page will be photocopied. But these elements are required on all new-page endorsements, such as the one on the next page.

                                        M. R. SAILORS

Copy to: NAS Cecil Field (Code 11)

Figure 8-2 Endorsement

written on plain paper or preprinted forms rather than on letterhead, and the word "MEMORANDUM" is typed or printed at the top of the page. Memoranda are generally typed, although very informal ones may be handwritten.

The "From" and "To" lines in a memorandum identify the sender and recipient by name or position. The signature block of a memorandum does not list the signer's organizational title, although his or her name may be typed underneath for clarity. Although it is technically incorrect to use a complimentary closing in a memorandum, it is still common (and in many commands, expected) for a junior to close a memorandum to a senior with "Very respectfully" and a senior to close a memorandum to a junior with "Respectfully." In very informal correspondence these complimentary closes may be abbreviated as "V/r," and "R."

Figure 8-4 illustrates a simple informal memorandum. SECNAVINST 5216.5 discusses in detail more formal and specialized memorandum formats used for particular purposes, such as a memorandum for the record or a memorandum of agreement.

Point Papers. The point paper (and its close relative, the discussion paper or talking paper) is a document produced by staff members to provide condensed briefing information on key issues to busy flag officers and other senior officials. A point paper should be short (no more than one page long) and should list in bullet format the background, discussion, and drafter's recommendation(s) pertaining to the issue in the subject line. Figure 8-5 illustrates the format for a point paper.

Instructions and Notices. An instruction is a directive containing information of continuous reference value or information that requires continuous action; it remains in effect until canceled or superseded. A notice is a directive that contains information that is of value for one time or for a brief duration (not more than one year); a notice is always self-canceling after a specified date. Both instructions and notices are organized according to the same SSICs as are Navy letters.

Any commander or CO may issue instructions and notices as necessary in the administration of his or her responsibilities. Instructions issued by the Secretary of the Navy (SECNAVINSTs), Chief of Naval Operations (OPNAVINSTs), and other high-ranking officials are termed "general instructions" and carry the force of law. Every command maintains a file of all the instructions and notices that govern its operation. Such files are normally distributed and maintained electronically. Formal correspondence is frequently converted from Microsoft Word format (i.e., .docx) to Adobe Acrobat format (i.e., .pdf) when the document is finalized. This conversion prevents unauthorized tampering or revision and also permits the signature to be preserved.

Navy Messages. The Navy message is the primary means of rapid, official communications between Navy commands. A message is transmitted electronically, permitting almost immediate and highly secure communications between ships

DEPARTMENT OF THE NAVY
USS CUSHING (DD 985)
FPO AP 96662-1223

5216
Ser DD 985/28   ①
January 5, 1996

② { 1
    2 } Mr. A. B. Seay
         Vice President, Accounting
         Widgets Unlimited, Inc.   ③
         1234 Any Street
         Baltimore, MD 21085-1234

    1
    2 Dear Mr. Seay: ④
    1

    2 SUBJECT: PREPARATION OF A BUSINESS LETTER ⑤   ← 1" →
    1

    2   This example shows the first page of a two page business letter. A
         "subject" line is optional and may replace the salutation.   Phrase the
         "subject" line in normal word order. Make it very brief, to the point, and
         not longer than one line. Capitalize every letter in the subject line.

    1"   Refer to previous communications and enclosures in the body of the
         letter only, without calling them references or enclosures. Do not number
         main paragraphs. Subparagraphs are numbered and lettered the same as a
         standard letter.

               Prior to typing a business letter, try to estimate the length of the
         letter. Set your margins to obtain maximum balance. Never use less than
         a 1-inch margin.   ⑥

               Start a paragraph near the end of a page only if that page has room
         for two lines or more. Continue a paragraph on the following page only if
         two lines or more can be carried over. A signature page must have at least
         two lines of text.

               Do not number the first page of a single page letter or multiple page
         letter. The first page is assumed to be page 1. Center page numbers ½ inch
         from the bottom edge, starting with the number 2. No punctuation
         accompanies a page number.

                                        Minimum   ⑦
                                         of 1"

1. Identification Symbols	5. Subject Line
2. Typewriter Lines	6. Body of Letter
3. Inside Address	7. Margins
4. Salutation Line	

Figure 8-3 Business Letter

```
                          1
                          2
                          3
                          4
                          5
                          6                              8 Jul 99
      1
      2      MEMORANDUM
      1
      2      From:  Head, DON Records Management Branch (N161)
             To:    Head, Technical Library Branch (N21)
                    Head, Mail and Files Branch (N13)
             Via:   Head, Office Services Division (N1))
      1
      2      Subj:  PLAIN-PAPER MEMORANDUM
      1
      2      1.   The plain-paper "from-to" memorandum may be used within your activity.  It is
             no more formal than the memorandum form, but it is more flexible when there are
             multiple addressees, via addressees, or both.
      1
      2      2.   The only identification symbol you need is the date, unless local practice calls
             for more.  Start typing the date on the sixth line, flush with the right margin.

             3.   Prepare a plain-paper memorandum on white bond.
      1
      2
      3
      4                            J. C. JAY
```

Figure 8-4 Memorandum

at sea, shore commands, DoD activities, and other government agencies, and even foreign military units.

To ensure proper handling and routing to their destinations, Navy messages must be very carefully formatted. Rules that are more specific apply to certain types of messages, such as those used to report emergencies. Before you are tasked with drafting such messages, you will receive more detailed instructions.

SECRET (#)

CLASSIFICATION (Typed here
and stamped top and bottom
of page)

Rank and Name
Office Code/Telephone #
Date of Preparation

Subj: SAMPLE POINT (TALKING) PAPER FORMAT (*) (Unclassified if possible)

BACKGROUND (*)

(*) Why you are writing this paper. Brevity, clarity, and graphic representation are
key ingredients of point papers. Use cascading indentation to organize subordinate
points.

DISCUSSION (*)

- (*) To prepare a "Talking Paper" substitute those words for "Point Paper."

- (*) Might contain problems pros and cons, present status, and outlook for
  future.

- (*) Other points which will aid in your preparation of point papers:

  -- Point papers should be concisely written in bulletized format. Indent
     subordinate points in cascading style. Continuation lines start directly
     under the first word of the paragraph.

  -- Point papers should not exceed one page.

  -- Who has been involved and concurs or non-concurs.

- (*) Type on 8 ½ X 11 paper with a 1-inch margin all around. Increase
  left margin if binding is anticipated.

RECOMMENDATION (*)

(*) State what recommended approach should be. State whether recommendation
concerns discussion of plans and policies that have not been approved by
higher authority.

**(CLASSIFIED MARKINGS FOR
ILLUSTRATION PURPOSES ONLY)**

Derived from_____
Declassify on _____

SECRET (#)

Figure 8-5 Point Paper

Email. Email provides a much more rapid means of communication than traditional paper correspondence. However, its ease can be deceptive—every email sent or received has an associated time cost, for the sender and receiver, and written communication always has greater potential to be misunderstood and misinterpreted than face-to-face communications. Be responsible, respectful, and brief in your email correspondence. Address it to only those who need to answer or be aware of its content—use global or group addresses only when the email is relevant to the entire group. Acknowledge and return emails sent to you in a timely manner, and use the same level of formality (e.g., use of first names) as the sender. Whenever possible avoid sending bad news via email. Get to the point quickly—if you find yourself in a lengthy "back and forth" email chain, you may be able to clear up misunderstandings more quickly with a phone call than with another email.

Classification Markings. Information that requires protection against unauthorized disclosure is classified as Top Secret, Secret, or Confidential based on its potential for damage to national security. Additional designations, including Sensitive but Unclassified (SBU) and Not Releasable to Foreign Nationals (NOFORN) may be used in conjunction with classification markings but are not themselves considered classifications. OPNAVINST 5510.1 series, *Department of the Navy (DON) Information Security Program Instruction*, contains detailed guidance for the assignment of classifications and marking of documents.

Classified information may be disclosed only to individuals with the appropriate clearance and "need to know" (also called "access"), meaning that the individual must have the information to do his or her job. No one has a right to classified material based solely on rank, position, or security clearance.

Only those commands with facilities adequate to safeguard classified material are authorized to maintain it. In general, all classified material must be held in such a manner as to prevent unauthorized access by personnel without the appropriate clearance or need to know, usually by means of safes or other secure storage areas. Any person in possession of classified material is responsible for preventing its unauthorized disclosure and for returning the material to the appropriate secure storage.

Classified instructions, correspondence, messages, and other material are required to be appropriately marked in a manner that ensures proper safeguarding of the information. These markings must leave no doubt as to the level of classification, which parts contain classified information, how long the material must remain classified, and any additional protective measures required.

The overall classification of a document is marked at the top and bottom center of the front and back covers, the title page, and the front and back pages. Each internal page of the document may be marked with the overall classification of the entire document, or the highest classification of the information on that particular page. Classification markings must be highly visible—generally larger than the capital letters used in the text and, whenever possible, marked in red. In addition to page markings, each section, part, paragraph, or other portion of a classified document is marked with the appropriate symbol to indicate the highest classification of the information in that portion: TS (for Top Secret), S (for Secret), C (for Confidential), or U (for Unclassified).

CHAPTER NINE

Ship's Organization and Regulations

Generally, management of the many is the same as the management of the few. It is a matter of organization.

—Sun Tzu, *The Art of War*

Organizations and regulations are necessary to cover ninety percent of what happens on a ship. If this much is taken care of automatically, the other ten percent can be given the full attention it should have.

—Admiral Robert L. Dennison

A n efficient ship with a happy crew is organized so that all crew members know what their duties are, how they relate to the routines of others, and what can and cannot be done in the daily routine of living. A ship lacking organization, on the other hand, is lax and unsure, and its crew is indifferent.

General Principles of Organization

Planning an Organization. Chapters 2, 3, and 4 of OPNAVINST 3120.32, *Standard Organization and Regulations Manual (SORM)* describe some of the basic principles of Navy organization. Although you should take time to read these chapters, this section covers most of the basic principles discussed in the *SORM*.

The *SORM* defines organization as "the element of administration which entails the orderly arrangement of materials and personnel by functions in order to attain the objective of the unit." It further states that standardizing organizational systems and procedures in writing fosters the use of best practices, provides for uniformity of operations, and provides a clear understanding of duties, responsibility, and authority.

Definitions. SORM gives definitions of several basic terms you should be familiar with.

- *Accountability* is the obligation of the individual to render an account of the discharge of his or her responsibilities to a superior. An individual assigned both authority and responsibility also accepts a commensurate accountability, which means answering for his or her success or failure.

- *Authority* is the power to command, enforce laws, exact obedience, determine, or judge.

- *Delegating* is tasking another, by a person in authority, to act on his or her behalf. Authority may be delegated; responsibility may never be delegated.

- *Duties* are the tasks that an individual is required to perform.

- *Responsibility* is the obligation to carry forward an assigned task to a successful conclusion.

There is nothing new about these terms, nor are they unique to the Navy. The same terms and the same elements of organization apply in any organizational setting.

Setting up an Organization. Chapter 1 of the *SORM* lists the steps necessary to establish an organization. Your ship, unless newly commissioned, will already have one, but you may wish to modify the organization of your own division. If so, you will need to do the following:

- Prepare a statement of objectives or missions and tasks.
- Familiarize yourself with the principles of organization.
- Group functions logically so that they can be assigned to appropriate segments of the organization.
- Prepare manuals, charts, and functional guides.
- Establish policies and procedures.
- Inform key personnel of their individual and group responsibilities.
- Set up controls to ensure achievement of objectives.

Chapter 1 of the *SORM* discusses three principles of organization: unity of command, span of control, and delegation of authority.

Unity of Command. One person should report to only one superior. One person should have control over one segment of the organization. Lines of authority should be clear-cut, simple, and understood by all.

Span of Control. Ideally a supervisor should be responsible for a group of three to seven individuals. Organizations should be structured so that at higher levels of the organization, a supervisor who is responsible for overseeing a large group directly oversees three to seven supervisors, each supervising three to seven lower-level supervisors, and so on.

Delegation of Authority. Authority delegated to a subordinate should be commensurate with his or her ability and should be delegated to the lowest level of competence. Regardless of delegation, officers remain ultimately responsible for the performance of their subordinates.

Organizational Authority and Directives

Organizational Authority. Navy Regulations arts. 1020–1039 are the source of authority for Navy personnel. Exact limits and kinds of authority stem from guidance promulgated by ship, department, division, and other manuals and regulations accompanying the corresponding organization.

Organizational Directives. The basic directive for the organization of Navy ships is in *Navy Regulations* art. 0804, which states that all commands are to be organized and administered in accordance with law (as set forth in *Navy Regulations*) and with the orders of competent authority, and that all orders and instructions of the CO are to conform to these directives.

Art. 0826 requires COs to take action as appropriate to prevent unauthorized access to their equipment and installations and to safeguard their personnel and facilities against espionage, sabotage, damage, theft, acts of terrorism, and natural disasters.

The *SORM* is the next echelon of directive. This volume is inclusive, covering shipboard organization in detail.

The authority on the organization for each particular type of command is the type commander (TYCOM), who is the force provider in support of operational commands. Since 2001 there has been a single type commander assigned for each traditional warfare area of surface, subsurface, and air: Commander Naval Surface Forces is in charge of surface ships, Commander Submarine Force is in charge of submarines, and Commander Naval Air Forces is in charge of aviation units, including aircraft carriers. Naval Expeditionary Combat Command (NECC), established in 2006, is the force provider for expeditionary units, and Naval Network Warfare Command (NNWC), established in 2002, delivers cyber mission capabilities. Type commanders may promulgate standard organization and regulations manuals for their subordinate units.

Finally, there is the ship's own organization. It must conform to the *SORM* as well as to applicable type commander directives.

Each ship has its own organizational directive, regulations, and standing orders; a battle bill including a condition watch system; watch, quarter, and station bills; safety program; training program; and necessary boards and committees. The *SORM* includes miscellaneous bills and committees, not all of which are required on every ship.

Administrative Organization

While a ship's primary mission is to fight, it remains a fact that a far larger proportion of a crew's time, even during wartime, is spent on routine and administrative matters. Administration requires an organization of its own, known as the ship's organization plan. Chapters 2 and 3 of the *SORM* describe in great detail the form of the standard organization of any ship. Each ship refines this organization to provide for the functions, duties, responsibilities, and authority of each officer and petty officer on board. Responsibilities of specific positions are described in chapter 6 of this book.

The normal administrative chain of command is from the CO through the XO through the department heads, division officers, and work center supervisors to the individual Sailors. Larger ships may have additional levels in the chain of command.

An ensign stands bridge watch aboard USS *Bunker Hill* (CG 52).

Organization for Battle

A combatant ship is built to fight, and a ship's allowance of officers and enlisted personnel is based on the manning level required to fulfill that duty. A crew member's position in the battle organization, and the qualifications required to fulfill that position, should be a source of pride. Many a ship's cook or barber has become a gun-mount captain or key person in a missile-loading system.

Conditions of Readiness. Each ship must have a watch organization for each of the conditions of readiness appropriate to that ship. The conditions of readiness are:

Condition I	General Quarters. All hands at battle stations, all armaments and sensors fully operational and loaded
Condition I AS	Variation of Condition I to meet ASW threat
Condition IE	Relaxed Condition I to feed crew
Condition II	Special watch for gunfire support
Condition III	Normal wartime cruising. Approximately one third of the crew on watch; armament manned to match threat.
Condition IV	Normal peacetime cruising. Figure 9-1 illustrates a typical Condition IV watch organization.
Condition V	Normal peacetime in port, with enough personnel on board to cover emergencies and get under way. Figure 9-2 illustrates a typical condition V watch organization.

Watch Organization

Chapter 4 of the *SORM* covers the watch organization, both in port and under way, in great detail. The *SORM* describes the watches required for the safety and operation of the ship. Two watches, the OOD and engineering officer of the watch (EOOW), are required to be continuous except as specified.

Development of a Watch Organization. The standard, required watch organization is provided in the *SORM*. The CO may eliminate those functions that do not apply to that particular ship. Each ship generates written guidelines to delineate the responsibilities of each watchstander, as well as the corresponding system to qualify personnel for those positions.

Certain departments are responsible for manning specified watch stations; for example, engineering department personnel normally man all engineering watches. The senior watch officer is responsible for all watches that are not the responsibility of a particular department, such as quarterdeck watches in port. The senior watch officer maintains duty-section assignments and records of individual watch-station qualifications, and periodically publishes watch assignments in watch bills and in the plan of the day.

The standard daily watch schedule is as follows:

0000–0400	Mid watch
0400–0800	Morning watch
0800–1200	Forenoon watch
1200–1600	Afternoon watch
1600–1800	First dog watch
1800–2000	Second dog watch
2000–0000	Evening watch

Commanding officers may prescribe longer or shorter watch rotations as required by the conditions under which the watches are stood and the number of qualified personnel available.

When a ship is in port, duty personnel are normally assigned a day's duty from 0800 to 0800 on the following day. Duty personnel must remain on board for the duration of the duty day, except as required in the performance of their duties, and may be assigned specific watches or other duty section responsibilities for that day.

Relieving the Watch. Watches are customarily relieved at fifteen minutes prior to the hour; for example, the 1200–1600 watch comes on duty at 1145. Prior to relieving a watch, the oncoming watchstander inspects all appropriate spaces and equipment and is on station in sufficient time to be familiarized with the overall situation and equipment status and obtain a thorough turnover from the offgoing watchstander prior to the designated time for relieving the watch. In the case of an underway OOD, this can require the oncoming watchstander to begin the turnover process as much as a half hour prior to the beginning of the watch. The senior watchstander at each station is not relieved until all subordinate watches have been relieved.

The standard procedure for relieving a watch is as follows:

- The oncoming watchstander performs any required tours or inspections and, when applicable, receives permission from the appropriate individual (e.g., watch supervisor, OOD) to relieve the watch.
- Relief reports to the offgoing watchstander, "I am ready to relieve you."
- Offgoing watchstander replies, "I am ready to be relieved."
- The oncoming and offgoing watchstanders tour the watch station and review the tactical and equipment situation, including any orders to the watch and unexecuted signals.

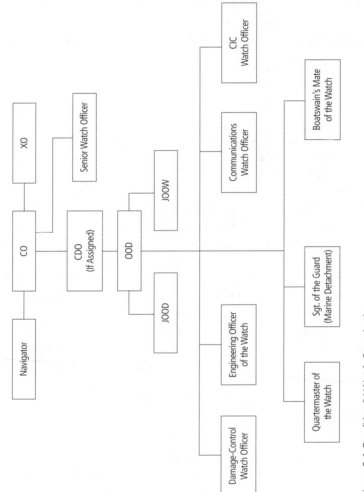

Figure 9-1 Condition IV Watch Organization

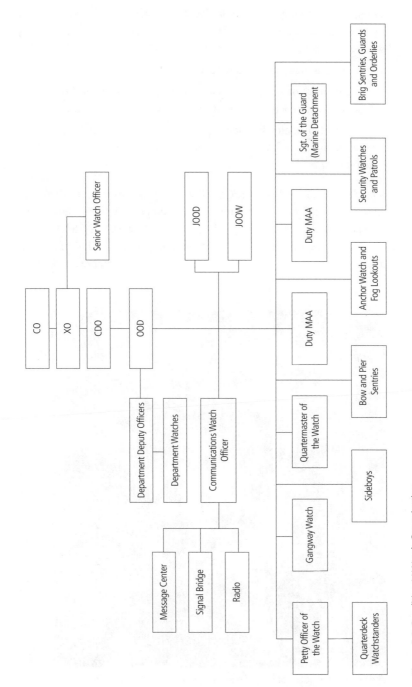

Figure 9-2 Condition V Watch Organization

- When the oncoming watchstander is satisfied that he or she is completely informed regarding the status of the watch, he or she relieves the watch by saying, "I relieve you."
- The offgoing watchstander states, "I stand relieved."
- The oncoming or offgoing watchstanders report the watch relief to the individual from whom permission was received to relieve the watch.
- On stations that maintain a log, the log is annotated to indicate relief of the watch, and the offgoing watchstander signs the log prior to leaving the watch station.

Personnel Qualification System (PQS). The PQS program requires that individuals obtain certification of a minimum level of competency before they can be qualified to perform specific duties or stand particular watches. A PQS book for a duty or watch station specifies the minimum knowledge and skills that an individual must demonstrate in order to ensure the safety, security, or proper operation of

The officer of the deck of USS *Norfolk* (SSN 714) performs a periscope inspection of the surface.

a ship, aircraft, or support system. The objective of PQS is to standardize and facilitate these qualifications. Job qualification requirements (JQRs) are similar to PQS, but are locally produced; JQRs should be forwarded to the appropriate TYCOM for incorporation into the PQS program. Commands are required to maintain a list of all personnel who are qualified in each applicable PQS and JQR watch station or duty as well as a list of those individuals authorized to "sign off" each type of PQS and JQR.

Unit Bills

A unit bill sets forth policy and directions for assigning personnel to duties or stations for specific purposes or functions. The *SORM* requires that each bill have a preface stating its purpose, assigning responsibility for its maintenance, and giving background information. A bill should set forth a procedure for interpreting the responsibilities of each person with regard to the functions discussed in the bill. Chapter 6 of the *SORM* contains bills for every possible contingency or evolution. The bills in the *SORM* are intended as a guide for type commanders and COs.

There are four types of bills: administrative, operational, emergency, and special. Examples of administrative bills are those for cleaning, formation and parade, and berthing and locker assignments. Examples of operational bills include special sea and anchor detail (set when entering or leaving port, or maneuvering in restricted waters), underway replenishment (UNREP), and helicopter operations. Emergency bills include bills for aircraft crash and rescue, man-overboard recovery, and emergency steering. Special bills include those for anti-swimmer attack, evacuation of civilians, and handling of prisoners of war.

Watch, Quarter, and Station Bill (WQSB)

The WQSB is the division officer's summary of the allocation of personnel, listed by billet number, to duties and assignments; as its title suggests, it is your way to keep track of the watches, berthing assignments, and bill assignments for each person in your division. A Sailor's billet number consists of either four numbers, or a letter and three numbers; the first number or letter corresponds to the division, the second number indicates the watch section, and the last two numbers indicate the Sailor's relative seniority. Keep it up to date, accounting for personnel who have transferred in or out of your division as changes occur.

Organization Communications

No organization can function unless the will of the CO is known to those who must carry it out. No less important is the flow of information up the chain of command, to provide the CO with the information required to make sound decisions.

Methods of Communication. Every ship has several methods of communication, in addition to the familiar means of oral and written communications discussed in detail in chapter 8.

One method of communication is the intercommunications voice (MC) system, which links major areas with multistation transmitter-receivers. This method ensures receipt of messages as long as someone is present in the area and can approach the transmitter-receiver. Other MC systems, such as the 1MC, or general announcing system, are one-way systems that announce orders or information to various areas or to the entire ship. This system is degraded by battle noise, needs electrical power, and has no way of ensuring the receipt of orders.

Ships also have a ship's service telephone system linking stations throughout the ship. Theoretically this is an administrative system, not designed to issue operational orders, but it can be so used in an emergency.

The most reliable internal communications system on board is the sound-powered phone system (J circuits). As the name implies, this system requires no electrical power to operate and so is ideally suited for use in emergency situations. Its components are rugged and less susceptible to casualty than other communications systems, and headphones worn by sound-powered telephone operators provide some protection against distracting external noise. Numerous individual J circuits exist, connecting watch stations that need to communicate with each other; when required, circuits can be cross-connected. Some circuits in this system are manned during normal underway watches; others are manned for special evolutions such as general quarters, refueling, flight operations, special sea and anchor detail, and so forth. The primary disadvantage of this system is that it requires training and discipline on the part of the phone talkers. Strict "repeat-back" procedures are required to ensure that transmissions are not garbled as they are passed from one station to another.

Many ships augment the sound-powered phone system with portable walkie-talkie–type radios for emergency internal communications. Although such radios are less cumbersome to use than the sound-powered phone system, their range below decks can be compromised by the metal hull partitions, and therefore it can be risky to rely on them in an emergency. Radios are also commonly used for short-range external communications, such as with the crew of a small boat or with a line-handling detail.

When no other means of communication between stations exists, runners may be used to pass messages between them. In damage-control situations, preprinted message pads facilitate passing information between the scene of the casualty and damage-control central.

The general, chemical and collision alarms sound over the 1MC system; each has a distinctive sound that should be familiar to everyone in the crew. Additional specialized alarm systems, such as high-temperature alarms and flooding alarms, are monitored by particular watch stations.

STAFF ORGANIZATION
AND FUNCTIONS

*No military or naval force, in war, can accomplish anything
worthwhile unless there is back of it the work of an efficient, loyal, and
devoted staff.*

—Lieutenant General Hunter Liggett

*And so, while the great ones depart to their dinner, the secretariat
works—and gets thinner and thinner.*

—British military jingle

Staffs are assigned to flag officers or other senior officers who are in command of a group of subordinate commands. A commander who is not a flag officer normally has the title Commodore.

Staffs are absolutely essential for the smooth functioning of a military organization. No commander acting alone, however versatile and intelligent, can hope to gather and collate all of the information available, make a reasoned and correct decision, organize assigned personnel and forces, and then issue detailed orders for the execution of the decision. A staff is the organization that exists to assist the commander in all of these functions.

Because military operations are increasingly employed in joint or federal interagency settings under reactive or contingency circumstances, staff composition and organization have adapted accordingly. In practice, depending on their function, staffs may be organized differently from the notional staff organization described in this chapter.

Staffs vary widely in size, from the handful of officers and dozen enlisted personnel on the staff of a destroyer squadron commander to the hundreds of personnel assisting the Chairman of the Joint Chiefs of Staff (JCS). A staff may have a largely administrative function if assigned to a commander in the administrative chain of command, or an operational function if assigned to an operational commander, or both if assigned to a commander who has a role in both chains of command.

General Staff Functions

A staff exists for one purpose: to assist the commander in carrying out the functions of command for which he or she is responsible. These include operational functions and supporting functions. Operational functions are the missions assigned to the command: making decisions, evaluating intelligence, and formulating plans for executing missions. Supporting functions provide for the welfare of assigned personnel, for training, for personnel management, and for supply and allocation of resources.

The magnitude of these functions will vary with the commander's mission. For example, an administrative commander is concerned mainly with support to the fleet: personnel administration, basic-phase training, and maintenance and repair of ships and aircraft. These support tasks form the basis for operational functions. An operational commander is more concerned with advanced training for combat and with planning, supervising, and evaluating the execution of combat operations. Regardless of the mission and size of a staff organization, some basic functions are common to all staffs.

Effective staff organization ensures the staff's ability to furnish maximum assistance to the commander. In addition, efficient staff work, which relies on a good organizational structure, is essential to the accomplishment of the commander's mission. For this reason, staff organizations follow a standardized plan for dividing the work of the staff, for assigning personnel to positions on the staff, and for delegating authority and assigning duties within the staff organization.

Liaison with Other Commands. The following discussion of duties applies to all types of staffs.

Coordinated teamwork is the essence of not only successful military operations but also efficient staff functioning. The operations of a naval task force or strike group, often involving all the elements of the armed forces of the United States and of allied powers, require extensive liaison between members of the staff and commanders as well as with staff members of other armed forces. Staff officers must conduct liaison in a courteous and cooperative manner, keeping the commander fully informed, as tentative agreements reached at staff levels are not binding on the commander. The vast scope of naval and joint operations, particularly in amphibious operations, and the complex interrelation of forces and types make good staff work essential.

Completed Staff Work. It is not sufficient for a staff officer to bring a problem to the commander's attention and wait for guidance on how to resolve it. When a staff officer presents an issue to the commander for decision, it should normally be in the format of a smooth point paper (never a rough draft) as discussed in chapter 8. Staff officers are responsible for researching all aspects of issues in their areas and for providing detailed but succinct information to the commander, including the pros and cons of various options and thoughtful recommendations for action. A good staff officer never asks the commander "What do you want to do?" or "How should we handle this?" He or she should be flexible enough to accommodate changes in plans, if the commander overrules his or her recommended action.

Providing Advice to the Commander. A staff officer must be willing to tell the commander that a planned action would be a mistake. As Major General Orland Ward, USA, said in 1934, "A yes man on a staff is a menace to the commander. One with the courage to express his convictions is an asset." However, once you have made your objections clear, you are obligated to carry out your commander's orders to the best of your ability.

Navy Staff Organization

A staff's organization will depend on its mission and size. While staffs are generally organized by standard operational functions for consistency and to facilitate external liaison with other organizations and patterned after the joint staff, there are many variations on the pattern described below. In addition, as threats and technology evolve, staff organizations change to optimize their effectiveness, as evidenced by the ongoing process of reorganization within the Office of the Chief of Naval Operations (OPNAV) staff itself.

Although the division heads, sometimes called assistant chiefs of staff or deputy chiefs of staff, are all on the same level organizationally, they may be of widely disparate ranks. The chain of staff authority extends from the commander to the chief of staff (or chief staff officer) and on down through each division, but does not cross from one division to another.

Navy Staff Functions

Chief of Staff. The chief of staff (COS) is the senior officer on an admiral's staff. Instead of a chief of staff, the officer assigned to coordinate the activities of a commodore's staff is called a chief staff officer (CSO). The COS or CSO functions much as an XO does. He or she keeps the commander informed of the condition and situation of the command, of subordinate commands and other commands in the theater of operations; advises the commander on administrative matters; supervises administrative work; and coordinates staff activities. The COS or CSO signs routine correspondence for the commander, except those concerning policy or legal action; and acts for the commander on issues for which the commander's policy is known, such as requests for repairs and maintenance, endorsements of routine correspondence, and orders to subordinate officers other than flag officers. If the admiral delegates this authority, his or her COS may exercise nonjudicial-punishment authority for the admiral.

Flag Secretary. The flag secretary is a personal aide who, on many staffs, acts as assistant COS for administration. He or she is responsible for routing, filing, and managing incoming and outgoing correspondence and message traffic; for managing the commander's directives and instructions; for administering the flag office; and for supervising the preparation of evaluations and fitness reports.

Flag Lieutenant. The personal aide to a flag officer (flag lieutenant) looks out for such matters as honors, presentations of awards, official calls, uniforms, entertainment, invitations, and liaisons with other organizations. He or she schedules the commander's calls; maintains the commander's schedule; arranges transportation; and keeps the COS, staff duty officer, OOD of the flagship, and other interested persons advised as to the commander's prospective movements.

In addition, the flag lieutenant tends the side upon the arrival and departure of the commander, visiting flag and general officers, and other dignitaries, and serves as flag signal officer. In this latter capacity, the flag aide is responsible to the staff communications officer and, on many flagships, is responsible for all visual signaling to and from the flagship and the performance of all signal personnel, whether assigned to the ship or staff.

Principal Assistants and Deputies. Assignments and titles of staff division heads depend in large measure on the mission of the staff. Administrative staffs have different primary functions than do operational staffs, and their organization reflects that difference. Although no staff will have an assistant or deputy COS in every one of the positions described below, the following numbering system is fairly standard throughout the Navy.

- *N1, Administration and Personnel.* The officer heading the administration division is often also the flag secretary. In addition to the duties already discussed for the flag secretary, he or she advises the commander on the formulation of command administrative policies and handles all administrative matters for assigned staff personnel. N1 also supervises training for enlisted staff members.

- *N2, Intelligence.* The head of the intelligence division formulates and implements policies pertaining to combat intelligence, counterintelligence, information operations, and public information. The intelligence officer also keeps the commander and staff informed as to the capabilities of present and potential enemies by the collection, evaluation, interpretation, and dissemination of information regarding the enemy, hydrography, terrain, and weather. Through liaison with subordinate, parallel, and higher commands, and by use of all existing sources of intelligence, including aviation, satellite, and submarine visual and photographic reconnaissance, he or she strives to maintain accurate and current intelligence on all actual and potential enemies. The Navy staff was recently reorganized to combine N2 and N6, as well as other information capabilities, into a single organization (N2/N6) under the Deputy Chief of Naval Operations for Information Dominance.

- *N3, Operations.* The operations division is the primary executive element of the staff. The operations officer is responsible for the functions that relate to organization and command: training, preparing and issuing directives for combat operations and training exercises, and managing related reports. He or she also prepares operation orders, prepares the command employment schedule, issues the necessary movement orders, keeps track of the location and movement of ships and units assigned to the command, and advises the commander on the assignment of ships and other units to task groups to perform specific tasks. On the Navy staff, N3 and N5 are combined as N3/N5, Deputy Chief of Naval Operations for Information, Plans and Strategy.

- *N4, Logistics.* The logistics division is responsible for advising the commander on all matters relating to logistics and material. Logistics is essential to strategy and the execution of operations and is emphasized throughout the planning process. The assistant chief of staff for logistics prepares studies for proposed operations and the logistics annex for all operational orders and plans. He or she maintains full liaison with subordinate, parallel, and senior commands.

- *N5, Plans.* This officer prepares and develops operation plans, monitors force levels and structure, and makes plans to carry out all assigned missions of the commander under peacetime, limited-war, or general-war conditions. As previously described, on the OPNAV staff, N3 and N5 are combined into a single division.

- *N6, Communications.* This officer is responsible for providing adequate, rapid communication within the command and with other commands, and for operation of the message center. Normally, cyberwarfare falls under the N6 umbrella, as do information warfare activities that don't fall within the purview of N2. As previously described, on the OPNAV staff, N2 and N6 are combined.

- *N7, Readiness and Training.* This officer conducts readiness inspections, reviews inspection reports, and oversees training of individuals, ships, units, and special task organizations.

- *N8, Resources and Assessment.* This officer is the commander's representative in the development of primary mission assessment and procurement.

- *Other Staff Officers.* In addition to the positions described above, staffs may include a chaplain, medical officer, staff JAG officer, PAO, meteorologist, and other specialists. These officers are typically assigned three-digit numerical codes beginning with the number 01.

Staff Duty Officers. The COS designates certain staff officers to take turns being staff duty officer on watch at sea and to perform a day's duty in port. In port, the staff duty officer receives routine reports and acts on routine matters as necessary in the absence of other staff officers. He or she regulates the use of staff boats and tends the side on all occasions of ceremony or when officers of command or flag rank are visiting; sees all message traffic; and takes prompt action on those messages requiring immediate attention. In the absence of the flag secretary, the staff duty officer examines incoming mail and takes appropriate action as required.

The duties of the staff duty officer assume special importance when, in the absence of the commander and COS, he or she is called upon to make decisions in an emergency or other urgent situation. For this reason it is imperative that officers on duty keep informed as to the status quo, the policies of the commander, and the appropriate actions in various situations. In port, in an emergency, and in the absence of the admiral and COS, the staff duty officer may refer the situation to the senior unit CO present.

When the flagship is under way, the staff duty officer represents the admiral in much the same way as the OOD represents the CO. He or she must remain abreast of the formation and location of ships and units, of the navigational situation, and of any significant scheduled events. The staff duty officer makes reports to the admiral and COS as required.

Relationships between Staff and Flagship Personnel

Officers serving in a flagship or on the staff of an embarked commander are involved daily in relationships between members of the staff and flagship crew.

Relationship between Flag and Flagship Officers. A flagship crew plays a dual role. The CO is at all times responsible for the safety of the ship and its performance, but the CO and the ship are answerable to the embarked commander. While under way, the flagship maneuvers as directed by the signals from the officer in tactical command (OTC). When the embarked commander is OTC, he or she may verbally direct the flagship to maneuver, in which case the flagship must notify other ships in company.

The embarked commander takes over responsibility for the operation of all communications of the flagship, absorbing into his or her organization the members of the flagship communication unit. This unit is then responsible to the flagship for all communications.

Staff Officers' Responsibilities. Staff officers embarked in a ship must always be careful to respect the flagship's unity of command. When making requests to the ship in the name of the admiral, staff officers should always make requests directly to the CO or XO, and preface them with "The admiral desires that you . . .".

All officers and enlisted personnel who serve in a ship, except for the commander, are subject to the authority of the CO and to his or her discipline and punishment. Staff officers have no authority of their own; all of their authority comes from the admiral.

Shore leave and liberty for staff members should conform as closely as possible to that of the flagship. Flag watch, quarter, and station bills should be kept up to date, and flag personnel, unless excused by proper authority, should observe calls to general drills promptly. Staff compartments, lockers, berthing, and messing areas should be kept in a condition on par with or better than that of similar ship facilities.

CHAPTER ELEVEN

THE ARMED FORCES OF THE UNITED STATES

We live in a world in which strength on the part of peace-loving nations is still the greatest deterrent to aggression. World stability can be destroyed when nations with great responsibilities neglect to maintain the means of discharging those responsibilities.

—President Harry Truman

It's not the strength of our arms or the power of our technology that gives the United States our military dominance—it's our people.

—President Barack Obama

Organization for National Security

The *Commander in Chief.* The President of the United States is, by provision of the Constitution, commander in chief of the armed forces. The National Security Council (NSC), the President's Intelligence Advisory Board and Intelligence Oversight Board, and the White House Military Office (WHMO) are among the government entities within the Executive Office of the President.

The National Command Authorities (NCA). The NCA consists of the President and the Secretary of Defense, who have the sole authority for making certain types of defense-related decisions. The combatant commanders (COCOMs) of the operational forces report to the NCA.

The National Security Council (NSC). Established by the National Security Act of 1947 and modified by the Goldwater-Nichols Department of Defense Reorganization Act of 1986, the NSC is chaired by the President and has as statutory members the Vice President, Secretary of State, and Secretary of Defense. Other regular attendees include the Secretary of the Treasury, the Assistant to the President for National Security Affairs, the Chief of Staff to the President, Counsel to the President, and the Assistant to the President for Economic Policy. The Director of National Intelligence (DNI) and Chairman of the Joint Chiefs of Staff

(JCS) are statutory advisers to the NSC. The National Security Act provides that the secretaries and undersecretaries of the other executive departments and of the military departments may serve as members of the NSC, when appointed by the President with the advice and consent of the Senate. A civilian executive secretary, appointed by the President, heads the NSC staff. The staff includes officers and civilian officials from the departments of State and Defense and the four military services. The secretariat conducts the routine business of the NSC.

The NSC advises the President on domestic, foreign, and military policies and on problems relating to national security, so as to enable the military services and other departments and agencies of the government to cooperate more effectively in matters involving national security. The duties of the NSC are to assess and appraise the objectives, commitments, and risks of the United States in relation to the actual and potential military power of the nation, to consider policies of common interest to departments and agencies of the government concerned with national security, and to make recommendations to the President on subjects that may affect the national policy of the government.

The Office of the Director of National Intelligence (ODNI). The Intelligence Reform and Terrorism Prevention Act of 2004 established this office to oversee the U.S. intelligence community (IC), which consists of the Central Intelligence Agency (CIA), Defense Intelligence Agency (DIA), Federal Bureau of Investigation (FBI), National Geospatial-Intelligence Agency (NGA), National Reconnaissance Office (NRO), National Security Agency (NSA); offices in the departments of Justice, Energy, Homeland Security, State, and Treasury; and the service components of the Air Force, Army, Coast Guard, Marine Corps, and Navy. A Director of National Intelligence (DNI), appointed by the President with the advice and consent of the Senate, administers the office.

The DNI coordinates intelligence activities of the government. The DNI advises the NSC concerning the intelligence activities of the government that relate to national security; makes recommendations to the NSC for coordination of these intelligence activities; correlates and evaluates intelligence; disseminates such intelligence within the government, using existing agencies where appropriate; and performs additional intelligence services that the NSC determines.

The Department of Defense

Mission. The Department of Defense (DoD) was established following World War II to unify the military departments under a single cabinet-level secretary. The National Security Act of 1947 marked the beginning of the modern military organization. The act created the National Military Establishment (renamed DoD by a 1949 amendment) and established civilian secretaries for the departments of the Navy, Army, and newly created Air Force. The DoD is responsible for providing the military forces needed to deter war and protect the security of the United States. The organization of the DoD is shown in figure 11-1.

The Secretary of Defense (SECDEF). The SECDEF is the principal assistant to the President in all matters relating to the DoD. The Secretary is a civilian appointed by the President with the advice and consent of the Senate. Under the President, and subject to the provisions of the National Security Act, the Secretary exercises control over the department.

The Goldwater-Nichols Department of Defense Reorganization Act of 1986 clarified the Secretary's position in the operational chain of command, which runs from the President (as commander in chief) through the Secretary directly to the combatant commanders.

Office of the Secretary of Defense (OSD). Various agencies, offices, and positions created under the National Security Act, together with certain other agencies that assist the Secretary of Defense, are referred to as OSD. They constitute the primary staff of the Secretary. The principal members of this staff serve as advisers to the Secretary and Deputy Secretary in the areas described below.

- The Deputy Secretary of Defense acts on all matters in the Secretary's absence.

- The Under Secretary of Defense for Acquisition, Technology and Logistics is responsible for all matters involving acquisition, research and development, advanced technology, developmental test and evaluation, production, logistics, installation management, military construction, procurement, environment security, and nuclear, chemical, and biological matters. The Under Secretary is assisted by a Principal Deputy Under Secretary of Defense; the Deputy Under Secretary of Defense for Installations and Environment; Assistant Secretaries of Defense (ASDs) for Acquisition, Logistics and Materiel Readiness, and Nuclear, Chemical and Biological Defense Programs; the Executive Director, Defense Science Board; and Directors of Acquisition Resources and Analysis, Corrosion Policy and Oversight, Defense Procurement and Acquisition Policy, Defense Research and Engineering, International Cooperation, Operational Test and Evaluation, and Test Resources Management Center.

- The Under Secretary of Defense (Comptroller)/Chief Financial Officer (CFO), assisted by a Principal Deputy Under Secretary of Defense is responsible for budgetary and fiscal matters, DoD program analysis and evaluation, and general management improvement programs.

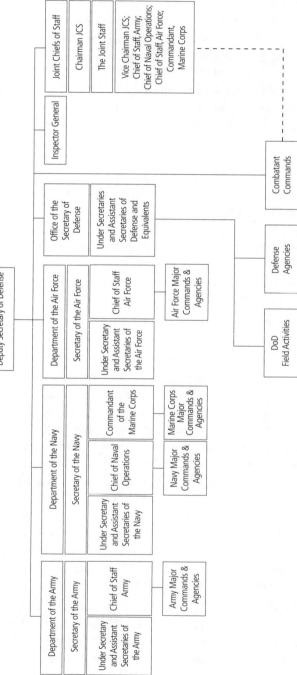

Figure 11-1 Department of Defense

- The Under Secretary of Defense for Personnel and Readiness oversees readiness, National Guard and Reserve component affairs, health affairs, training, and personnel requirements and management, including equal opportunity, morale, welfare, recreation, dependents' education, and quality-of-life programs. The Under Secretary is assisted by a Principal Deputy Under Secretary of Defense; Deputy Under Secretaries of Defense for Civilian Personnel Policy, Military Community and Family Policy, Military Personnel Policy, Wounded Warrior Care and Transition Policy, and Readiness; Assistant Secretaries of Defense for Health Affairs and Reserve Affairs; and Directors of Defense Human Resources Activity and Requirements and Strategic Integration.

- The Under Secretary of Defense for Policy is responsible for the formulation of national security and defense policy and the integration and oversight of DoD policy and plans to achieve national security objectives. The Under Secretary is assisted by Deputy Under Secretaries of Defense for Policy Integration and Strategy, Plans and Forces; and Assistant Secretaries of Defense for International Security Affairs, Asian and Pacific Security Affairs, Homeland Defense and Americas' Security Affairs, Global Strategic Affairs, and Special Operations and Low Intensity Conflict and Interdependent Capabilities.

- The Under Secretary of Defense for Intelligence is responsible for achieving and maintaining information superiority through the collection, processing, and dissemination of information, while exploiting or denying an adversary's ability to do the same.

- The Assistant Secretary of Defense (Legislative Affairs) is responsible for overseeing DoD relations with the members of Congress.

- The Assistant Secretary of Defense (Public Affairs) handles public information, internal information, community relations, information training, and audiovisual matters.

- The General Counsel to the Department of Defense serves as chief legal officer of the Department of Defense.

- The Assistant to the Secretary of Defense (Intelligence Oversight) is responsible for the independent oversight of all intelligence and counterintelligence activities in the Department of Defense.

- The Deputy Chief Management Officer is the principal staff assistant and adviser to the Secretary and Deputy Secretary of Defense for matters relating to the management and improvement of DoD business operations.

- The Director of Administration and Management is responsible for DoD-wide organizational and administrative management matters.
- The Director of Net Assessment develops and coordinates assessments to identify emerging or future threats or opportunities for the United States.

Defense Agencies. The following DoD agencies operate under the control of the Secretary of Defense:

- Missile Defense Agency (MDA)
- Defense Advanced Research Projects Agency (DARPA)
- Defense Commissary Agency (DeCA)
- Defense Contract Audit Agency (DCAA)
- Defense Contract Management Agency (DCMA)
- Defense Finance and Accounting Service (DFAS)
- Defense Information Systems Agency (DISA)
- Defense Intelligence Agency (DIA)
- Defense Legal Services Agency (DLSA)
- Defense Logistics Agency (DLA)
- Defense Security Cooperation Agency (DSCA)
- Defense Security Service (DSS)
- Defense Threat Reduction Agency (DTRA)
- National Imagery and Mapping Agency (NIMA)
- National Security Agency/Central Security Service (NSA)

The National Security Act. The National Security Act of 1947, incorporated into Title 50 of the United States Code and amended several times in subsequent years, is the basic military legislation of the United States.

The policy section of the act reads, "It is the intent of Congress to provide a comprehensive program for the future security of the United States; to provide for the establishment of integrated policies and procedures for the departments, agencies and functions of the Government relating to national security." In so doing, the act provides for

- three military departments, separately administered, for the operation and administration of the Army, the Navy (including the Marine Corps), and the Air Force, with their assigned combatant and service components
- coordination and direction of the three military departments and four services under the Secretary of Defense

- strategic direction of the armed forces, for their operation under unified control, and for the integration of the services into an efficient team of land, naval, and air forces

Unification was accomplished by giving the Secretary of Defense the authority, direction, and virtual military control over the four services. The Secretary also has authority to eliminate duplication in procurement, supply, transportation, storage, health, and research.

At the same time, the law established that there would not be a single uniformed chief of staff over all the armed forces and the general staff, reinforcing the concept of civilian control of the military.

Administrative vs. Operational Chain of Command

Within the organization of the United States military is drawn an important distinction between the administrative and operational chains of command.

Administrative Chain of Command. The administrative chain of command is assigned to recruit, organize, supply, equip, train, service, mobilize, demobilize, administer, and maintain its respective forces. This organization is responsible for providing fully trained and equipped combatant units to the operational commanders. The administrative chain of command, which includes the Secretaries of the Army, Navy, and Air Force as well as the Chiefs of Staff of the Army and Air Force, the Chief of Naval Operations, and the Commandant of the Marine Corps, is not directly involved in the employment of combatant forces.

Operational Chain of Command. This organization is responsible for the employment of forces provided by the administrative chain of command, in order to carry out missions in support of the national defense. The operational chain was further clarified by the Goldwater-Nichols DoD Reorganization Act of 1986, which specified that the operational chain of command runs from the President, through the Secretary of Defense, directly to the COCOMs.

The Joint Chiefs of Staff

History. The authority of the President as commander in chief of the Army and Navy was formerly exercised through the Secretaries of War and Navy. During World War II, the President felt a need for more personal control, and wanted direct access to his military advisers as well as improved coordination between the Army and Navy. He ordered the organization of the JCS, with Admiral William D. Leahy as Chief of Staff to the President. Admiral Leahy became the senior member and presiding officer of the JCS. The first members of the JCS were General George C. Marshall, Chief of Staff of the Army, and Admiral Ernest J. King, Chief of Naval Operations (CNO). Lieutenant General H. H. Arnold, Chief of the Army Air Corps, was added as a third member. These four officers, later promoted to five-star rank, conducted U.S. global efforts in World War II.

The original National Security Act of 1947 established the Joint Chiefs of Staff as planners and advisers but excluded them from the operational chain of command. Nevertheless, members of the JCS were allowed to also serve as executive agents for unified commands, in which capacity they were in the operational chain of command. A 1953 amendment to the act withdrew this authority from members of the JCS, and today, as clarified by the Goldwater-Nichols DoD Reorganization Act, the members are clearly outside of the operational chain of command although they do act as advisers to the President and Secretary of Defense.

Composition and Functions. The composition and functions of the Joint Chiefs of Staff are outlined in Title 10 of the United States Code. The Joint Chiefs of Staff are headed by the Chairman, who serves as the principal military adviser to the President, the National Security Council, and the Secretary of Defense. In presenting advice, the Chairman consults with the other members of the JCS and presents the full range of military advice and opinions, unless doing so would cause undue delay. The Chairman may transmit communications to the commanders of the combatant commands from the President and Secretary of Defense but does not exercise military command over any combatant forces.

The Goldwater-Nichols DoD Reorganization Act of 1986 created the position of Vice Chairman of the Joint Chiefs of Staff, who performs such duties as the Chairman may prescribe. By law, the Vice Chairman is the second ranking member of the Armed Forces and replaces the Chairman in his or her absence or disability. Although not originally included as a member of the JCS, the National Defense Authorization Act of 1992 made the Vice Chairman a full voting member.

In addition to the Chairman and Vice Chairman, the other members of the JCS are:

- Chief of Staff of the Army
- Chief of Naval Operations
- Chief of Staff of the Air Force
- Commandant of the Marine Corps

The other members of the Joint Chiefs of Staff also serve as military advisers to the President, the National Security Council, and the Secretary of Defense and may present their advice individually or collectively. After first informing the Secretary of Defense, any member of the JCS may make such recommendations to Congress relating to the Department of Defense as are considered appropriate.

The military service chiefs are often said to "wear two hats." As members of the Joint Chiefs of Staff, they offer operational advice to the President, the Secretary of Defense, and the NSC. Under the administrative chain of command, as chiefs of military services they are responsible to the secretaries of their respective departments. Responsibilities as members of the Joint Chiefs of Staff take precedence over their duties as chiefs of military services.

The JCS is supported by the Joint Staff, composed of approximately equal numbers of officers from the Army, the Navy–Marine Corps team, and the Air Force. In practice, the Marines make up about 20 percent of the number of officers allocated to the Department of the Navy. The Joint Staff has no direct operational authority over combatant forces. The Chairman of the Joint Chiefs of Staff, after consultation with other JCS members and with the approval of the Secretary of Defense, selects the Director, Joint Staff, to assist in managing the Joint Staff. By law, the direction of the Joint Staff rests exclusively with the Chairman of the Joint Chiefs of Staff. As the Chairman directs, the Joint Staff also may assist the other JCS members in carrying out their responsibilities.

In the joint arena, a body of senior flag or general officers assists in resolving matters that do not require JCS attention. Each service chief appoints an operations deputy who works with the Director, Joint Staff, to form the subsidiary body known as the Operations Deputies. They meet in sessions chaired by the Director, Joint Staff, to consider issues of lesser importance or to review major issues before they reach the JCS. With the exception of the Director, this body is not part of the Joint Staff. There is also a subsidiary body known as the Deputy Operations Deputies, composed of the Vice Director, Joint Staff, and a two-star flag or general officer appointed by each Service Chief. Issues come before the Deputy Operations Deputies to be settled at their level or forwarded to the Operations Deputies. The Director, Joint Staff, is authorized to review and approve issues when there is no dispute between the services, when the issue does not warrant JCS attention, when the proposed action is in conformance with CJCS policy, or when the issue has not been raised by a member of the Joint Chiefs of Staff. Except for the Vice Director, Joint Staff, the Deputy Operations Deputies are not part of the Joint Staff.

Strategic Planning. As principal military adviser to the President, SECDEF, and NSC, the Chairman is responsible for providing strategic planning, direction, and advice on requirements, programs, and budget priorities These statutory requirements are fulfilled using the Joint Strategic Planning System (JSPS), Joint Requirements Oversight Council (JROC), Joint Capability Board (JCB), and Functional Capability Boards (FCBs).

The JSPS is the means by which the Chairman, in coordination with the other members of the Joint Chiefs of Staff and the combatant commanders, reviews the national security environment and U.S. national security objectives and provides military advice and strategic guidance. Products of the JSPS include the National Military Strategy, Joint Planning Document, Joint Strategic Capabilities Plan, and Chairman's Program Assessment.

Title 10 directs SECDEF to establish the JROC. The Chairman leads the JROC and the Vice Chairman oversees operations. The JROC identifies, assesses, and prioritizes joint military capabilities to define interoperable joint capabilities that best meet future needs.

The JCB is composed of general or flag officers from each of the services, designated by their respective JROC permanent member and chaired by the Joint Staff, J-8, Director of Force Structure, Resources, and Assessment. The JCB assists the JROC by reviewing and, if appropriate, endorsing proposals prior to their submission to the JROC.

FCBs are established according to functional areas to assist the JCB and JROC. The JROC determines which FCBs will be established, which areas are assigned to each FCB, and the sponsoring organization(s). Chaired by a general or flag officer, FCBs provide assessments and recommendations that enhance capabilities integration, examine joint priorities among existing and future programs, assess program alternatives, minimize duplication of effort, and provide oversight in the management of materiel and non-materiel changes. Currently there are eight FCBs: command and control, battlespace awareness, net-centric operations, force application, focused logistics, protection, force management, and joint training.

Combatant Commands

Structure. Combatant commands (COCOMs) are composed of forces from across the services, have a broad or continuing mission, and are organized on a geographical basis or by mission. The number of COCOMs is not fixed by law or regulation and so may vary. Figure 11-2 shows the area of responsibility (AOR) for each geographic COCOM.

The ten current COCOMs are:

- U.S. Northern Command (NORTHCOM), established in 2002, provides command and control of homeland defense efforts and coordinates defense support of civil authorities. Located at Peterson Air Force Base, Colorado Springs, Colorado, NORTHCOM's area of responsibility includes the continental United States, Alaska, Canada, Mexico, and the water surrounding these nations, out to approximately five hundred nautical miles, as well as the Gulf of Mexico, the Straits of Florida, and portions of the Caribbean including the Bahamas, Puerto Rico, and the U.S. Virgin Islands. Component commands are:

— Joint Force Headquarters National Capital Region
— Joint Task Force, Alaska
— Joint Task Force, Civil Support
— Joint Task Force, North
— Standing Joint Force Headquarters
— Army North
— Air Force North
— U.S. Fleet Forces Command

- U.S. Pacific Command (PACOM) is the oldest of the unified commands, established in 1947 as an outgrowth of the command structure used during World War II. Located at Camp H. M. Smith, Hawaii, PACOM is responsible for U.S. military activities in an area that reaches from the west coast of United States mainland to the east coast of Africa, and from the Arctic to Antarctic, including the states of Alaska and Hawaii. Subordinate commands include:

— U.S. Pacific Fleet
— U.S. Pacific Air Forces
— U.S. Army, Pacific
— U.S. Marine Corps Forces, Pacific
— U.S. Forces, Korea
— U.S. Forces, Japan
— Alaska Command
— Special Operations Command, Pacific
— Center for Excellence in Disaster Management and
  Humanitarian Assistance
— Joint Intelligence Operations Center
— Joint POW/MIA Accounting Command
— Asia Pacific Center for Security Studies
— Standing Joint Force Headquarters, Pacific
— Joint Interagency Task Force, West

- U.S. Central Command (CENTCOM) is located at MacDill Air Force Base, Tampa, Florida. Established in 1983, CENTCOM's area of responsibility includes twenty countries in the Middle East and Central and South Asia. Component commands include:

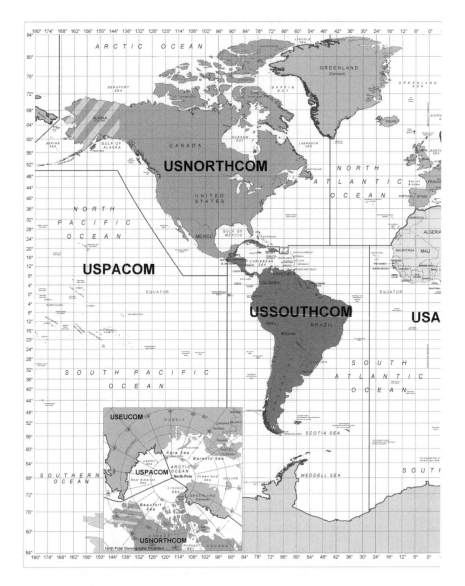

Figure 11-2 Geographic Combatant Commanders

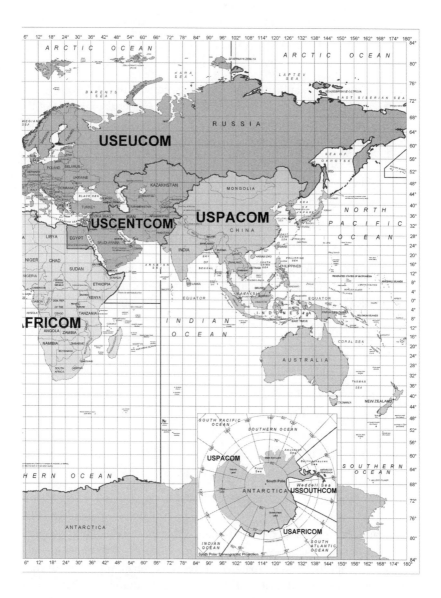

— U.S. Army Forces, Central Command
— U.S. Central Command Air Forces
— U.S. Naval Forces, Central Command/U.S. Fifth Fleet
— U.S. Marine Corps Forces, Central Command
— U.S. Special Operations Command, Central

- U.S. European Command (EUCOM), located in Stuttgart, Germany, was established in 1952. EUCOM exercises joint operational command of the U.S. forces in the European theater and serves as NATO's Supreme Allied Commander, Europe. Component commands are:

— U.S. Army Forces, Europe
— U.S. Air Forces in Europe
— U.S. Naval Forces, Europe/U.S. Sixth Fleet
— U.S. Marine Corps Forces, Europe
— U.S. Special Operations Command, Europe

- U.S. Africa Command (AFRICOM). Established in 2008 and currently assigned to an interim location at Kelley Barracks in Stuttgart, Germany, AFRICOM's mission is focused on war prevention rather than warfighting. AFRICOM is responsible for U.S. military relations with fifty-three African countries, including the Islands of Cape Verde, Equatorial Guinea, and Sao Tome and Principe, and the Indian Ocean islands of Comoros, Madagascar, Mauritius, and Seychelles. Component commands include:

— Combined Joint Task Force, Horn of Africa
— U.S. Army, Africa
— U.S. Air Forces, Africa
— U.S. Marine Corps Forces, Africa
— U.S. Naval Forces, Africa/U.S. Sixth Fleet

- U.S. Southern Command (SOUTHCOM), headquartered in Miami, Florida, is responsible for all U.S. military activities in Central America, South America, and the Caribbean, with emphasis on drug suppression, counterinsurgency, nation assistance, military professionalism, and treaty implementation programs. Three task forces with specific missions are under SOUTHCOM: Joint Task Force, Bravo; Joint Task Force, Guantanamo; and Joint Interagency Task Force, South. SOUTHCOM component commands are:

— U.S. Army, South
— 12th U.S. Air Force (Air Forces Southern)

— U.S. Naval Forces, Southern Command/ U.S. Fourth Fleet
— U.S. Marine Forces, South
— Special Operations Command, South

- U.S. Strategic Command (STRATCOM) was established in 1992 to unify U.S. strategic forces under a single commander. Located at Offutt Air Force Base in Nebraska, STRATCOM is responsible for overseeing nuclear command and control mission with responsibility for space operations; global strike; Defense Department information operations; global missile defense; and global command, control, communications, computers, intelligence, surveillance, and reconnaissance (C4ISR). STRATCOM is also responsible for combating weapons of mass destruction. Subordinate and component commands include:
  — U.S. Cyber Command
  — U.S. Army Forces Strategic Command
  — Fleet Forces Command
  — U.S. Marine Corps Forces, U.S. Strategic Command
  — Air Force Space Command

- U.S. Special Operations Command (SOCOM) was activated in 1987 to provide command, control, and training for all special operations forces. SOCOM is located at MacDill Air Force Base, Tampa, Florida. SOCOM's component commands include:
  — U.S. Army Special Operations Command
  — U.S. Air Force Special Operations Command
  — U.S. Naval Special Warfare Command
  — Marine Corps Forces, Special Operations Command
  — Joint Special Operations Command
  — John F. Kennedy Special Warfare Center and School
  — U.S. Air Force Special Operations School
  — U.S. Naval Special Warfare Center

- U.S. Joint Forces Command (JFCOM),* headquartered in Norfolk, Virginia, oversees joint concept development and experimentation, joint training, and joint capabilities development and acts as a joint force provider for forces within the continental United States. Component commands are:
  — Army Forces Command
  — Marine Forces Command

*The Secretary of Defense has proposed closing JFCOM; the closure could happen as early as 2011.

- — U.S. Fleet Forces Command
- — Air Combat Command
- U.S. Transportation Command (TRANSCOM), located at Scott Air Force Base, Illinois, is responsible for rapidly moving U.S. troops, equipment, and supplies by land, sea, or air to or from any place in the world whenever necessary. Component commands are:
  - — U.S. Air Force Air Mobility Command
  - — U. S. Army Military Surface Deployment and Distribution Command
  - — U.S. Navy Military Sealift Command

The Department of the Army

Mission. The Department of the Army is charged with providing support for national and international policy and the security of the United States by planning, directing, and reviewing the military and civil operations of the Army establishment.

The U.S. Army includes land-combat and service forces; of the four services, the Army has a primary interest in all operations on land.

Functions of the Department of the Army. The functions of the Army, as set forth in DoD Directive 5100.1 of 1 August 2002, are as follows:

(1) The Army, within the Department of the Army, includes land combat and service forces and any organic aviation, space forces, and water transport assigned. The Army is responsible for the preparation of land forces necessary for the effective prosecution of war and military operations short of war, except as otherwise assigned and, in accordance with integrated joint mobilization plans, for the expansion of the peacetime components of the Army to meet the needs of war.

(2) The primary functions of the Army are:

    (a) To organize, train, and equip forces for the conduct of prompt and sustained combat operations on land—specifically, forces to defeat enemy land forces and to seize, occupy, and defend land areas.

    (b) To organize, train, equip, and provide forces for appropriate air and missile defense and space operations unique to the Army, including the provision of forces as required for the strategic defense of the United States, in accordance with joint doctrines.

    (c) To organize, equip, and provide Army forces, in coordination with the other Military Services, for joint amphibious, airborne, and space operations and to provide for the training of such forces, in accordance with joint doctrines. Specifically, the Army shall:

1. Develop, in coordination with the other Military Services, doctrines, tactics, techniques, and equipment of interest to the Army for amphibious operations and not provided for elsewhere.

2. Develop, in coordination with the other Military Services, the doctrines, procedures, and equipment employed by Army and Marine Corps forces in airborne operations. The Army shall have primary responsibility for developing those airborne doctrines, procedures, and equipment that are of common interest to the Army and the Marine Corps.

3. Develop, in coordination with the other Military Services, Army doctrines, procedures, and equipment employed by Army forces in the conduct of space operations.

(d) To organize, train, equip, and provide forces for the support and conduct of special operations.

(e) To provide equipment, forces, procedures, and doctrine necessary for the effective prosecution of operations and, as directed, support of other forces.

A squad of soldiers work in a computer lab at an NCO Academy Warrior Leaders Course.

(f)   To organize, train, equip, and provide forces for the support and conduct of psychological operations.

(g)   To provide forces for the occupation of territories abroad, including initial establishment of military government pending transfer of this responsibility to other authority.

(h)   To develop doctrines and procedures, in coordination with the other Military Services, for organizing, equipping, training, and employing forces operating on land, except that the development of doctrines and procedures for organizing, equipping, training, and employing Marine Corps units for amphibious operations shall be a function of the Marine Corps coordinating, as required, with the other Military Services.

(i)   To organize, train, equip, and provide forces, as directed, to operate land lines of communication.

(j)   To conduct the following activities:

1.   Functions relating to the management and operation of the Panama Canal, as assigned by the Secretary or Deputy Secretary of Defense.

2.   The authorized civil works program, including projects for improvement of navigation, flood control, beach erosion control, and other water resource developments in the United States, its territories, and its possessions.

3.   Certain other civil activities prescribed by law.

(3)   A collateral function of the Army is to train forces to interdict enemy sea and air power and communications through operations on or from land.

(4)   Army responsibilities in support of space operations include the following:

(a)   To organize, train, equip, and provide Army forces to support space operations.

(b)   To develop, in coordination with the other Military Services, tactics, techniques, and equipment employed by Army forces for use in space operations.

(c)   To conduct individual and unit training of Army space operations forces.

(d)   To participate with other Services in joint space operations, training, and exercises as mutually agreed to by the Services concerned, or as directed by competent authority.

(e)   To provide forces for space support operations for the Department of Defense when directed.

(5) Other responsibilities of the Army. With respect to close air support of ground forces, the Army has specific responsibility for the following:

(a) To provide, in accordance with inter-Service agreements, communications, personnel, and equipment employed by Army forces.

(b) To conduct individual and unit training of Army forces.

(c) To develop equipment, tactics, and techniques employed by Army forces.

Department of the Army Structure. The Secretary of the Army is responsible to the Secretary of Defense for overseeing the administrative chain of command of the department (i.e., organizing, training, and equipping a strategic land combat force).

The Secretary of the Army is assisted by five assistant secretaries, as follows:

1. Assistant Secretary of the Army for Acquisition, Logistics and Technology serves as the Army Acquisition Executive, the Senior Procurement Executive, the Science Adviser to the Secretary, and as the senior research and development official for the Department of the Army.

2. Assistant Secretary of the Army for Civil Works supervises Army functions for conservation, development, and management of national water resources for flood control, navigation, and the environment, and directs the foreign activities of the Corps of Engineers.

3. Assistant Secretary of the Army for Financial Management and Comptroller directs and manages the department's financial management activities.

4. Assistant Secretary of the Army for Installations and Environment determines long-range strategic direction and policy for Army installations and oversees installations, logistics, environment, and safety programs.

5. Assistant Secretary of the Army for Manpower and Reserve Affairs exercises overall supervision of manpower within the Army and oversees all personnel policies.

The Chief of Staff of the Army, in addition to serving as a member of the JCS, is the primary military adviser to the Secretary of the Army and is responsible for planning, developing, executing, reviewing, and analyzing Army programs. The Chief of Staff is assisted by the following officers:

• Deputy Chief of Staff, Personnel (G1) manages and executes manpower and personnel plans, programs, and policies across all Army components.

• Deputy Chief of Staff, Intelligence (G2) is responsible for policy formulation, planning, programming, budgeting, management, staff supervision, evaluation, and oversight for intelligence activities for the Department of the Army.

- Deputy Chief of Staff, Operations, Plans and Training (G3/5/7) is responsible for training, operations and plans, and force development and modernization.
- Deputy Chief of Staff, Logistics (G4) provides and oversees integrated logistics policies, programs, and plans.
- Army Chief Information Officer (G6) is responsible for delivering timely, trusted, and shared information.
- Deputy Chief of Staff, Resource Management (G8) matches available resources to the defense strategy and the Army plan.

Organization of the Army. The Army is organized into four general communities: combat arms, combat support arms, combat service support arms, and special branches.

Combat arms are the branches of the Army that directly engage in combat. They are:

- Air defense artillery
- Armor
- Aviation
- Engineer
- Field artillery
- Infantry
- Special Forces

Combat support arms provides operational assistance to include:

- Chemical
- Civil affairs
- Military intelligence
- Military police
- Signal corps

Combat service support arms are not directly involved in combat. These branches provide logistics, personnel, and administrative functions and include:

- Adjutant general
- Finance
- Ordnance

- Quartermaster
- Transportation

Special branches include:

- Judge Advocate General's corps
- Chaplain corps
- Medical corps
- Dental corps
- Veterinary corps
- Army medical specialists
- Army nurse corps
- Medical service corps

General Structuring of Army Forces. In the field, the Army is divided into armies made up of corps and divisions, all of which contain a balance of combat arms, combat support arms, and combat service support arms to make them effective and independent. The units of the Army, from the lowest echelon up, are as follows:

- A squad/section is the lowest level of organization that acts independently. It consists of nine to twelve soldiers, led by a noncommissioned officer, normally a staff sergeant (E-6).
- A platoon consists of two to four squads (16–50 soldiers), led by a lieutenant (O-1/O-2).
- A company consists of three to five platoons (60–200 soldiers) and is normally led by a captain (O-3).
- A battalion consists of four to six companies (400–1,000 soldiers) and is led by a lieutenant colonel (O-5). A battalion is normally organized around a single major weapon system or capability. It is self-sufficient and capable of independent operations for twenty-four to thirty-six hours.
- A brigade consists of two to three battalions of different types (3,000–5,000 soldiers) and is commanded by a colonel (O-6). When organized for combat, a brigade includes artillery, engineers, and support units and is termed a Brigade Combat Team (BCT). A BCT can operate independently for ninety-six hours.
- A division consists of multiple brigades (10,000–18,000 soldiers) and is normally led by a major general (O-8). Divisions are numbered and assigned missions including infantry, airborne, air assault, light or mechanized infantry, or armored, based on their structure. Divisions can operate independently for extended periods.

- A corps consists of two or more divisions (30,000–100,000 soldiers) and is led by a lieutenant general (O-9). A corps is the lowest unit capable of conducting an independent ground campaign.
- An army consists of two or more corps (100,000+ soldiers) and is led by a lieutenant general (O-9) or general (O-10). An army may be a theater army, the army component of a unified command; a field army, constituted from existing assets and structured to meet specific operational requirements; or an army group, formed to control the operations of two or more armies.

Army Roles. The Army has over 255,000 soldiers and more than 18,500 civilians stationed in nearly eighty countries. Current Army roles include:

- Conduct counterinsurgency operations
- Conduct security force assistance to build the capacity of partner nations
- Provide support to civil authorities in the United States and abroad
- Deter and defeat hybrid threats and hostile state actors that threaten U.S. national security

Army Reserve and National Guard. There are two types of Army reserve forces: the Army Reserve and the Army National Guard. In recent years, the demand for Army forces in Iraq, Afghanistan, and other locations has exceeded the active Army's capabilities, demanding integration of the Army Reserve and Army National Guard into the operational force.

As of 2009 there were approximately 206,000 Army Reserve personnel, primarily concentrated in combat-support and combat service–support roles.

Each state and U.S. territory has its own National Guard unit, consisting of both active-duty and reserve members. As of 2009 there were approximately 358,000 National Guard personnel assigned to roles in combat (infantry, artillery, armor, aviation, air defense); combat support (engineer, chemical, military police, signal, military intelligence, civil affairs); and combat service support (finance, public affairs, personnel, supply, maintenance, and transportation).

Army Commissioning Programs. The Army relies on three separate programs to produce most of its officer accessions: ROTC, the U.S. Military Academy, and OCS. ROTC provides about 40 percent of the Army's officers and is offered at over one thousand colleges and universities nationwide. The U.S. Military Academy, in West Point, New York, was established in 1802 for the purpose of training commissioned officers. The academy's four-year curriculum combines military science and other subjects, and commissions 20 percent of the Army's new second lieutenants. OCS, at the U.S. Army Infantry Center, Fort Benning, Georgia, is a twelve-week program of intense instruction for previous college graduates that commissions 40 percent of the Army's new officers each year.

The Department of the Air Force

Mission. The Department of the Air Force and the U.S. Air Force were established in 1947 by the National Security Act, which severed the Air Force from the Army. The Air Force includes air combat, missile, and service forces. It is organized, trained, and equipped for prompt and sustained offensive and defensive combat operations in the air. The mission of the Air Force is to defend the United States through control and exploitation of air and space.

Functions of the Department of the Air Force. The functions of the Air Force, as set forth in DoD Directive 5100.1 of 25 September 1987 are as follows:

(1) The Air Force, within the Department of the Air Force, includes aviation and space forces, both combat and service, not otherwise assigned. The Air Force is responsible for the preparation of the air and space forces necessary for the effective prosecution of war and military operations short of war, except as otherwise assigned and, according to integrated joint mobilization plans, for the expansion of the peacetime components of the Air Force to meet the needs of war.

(2) The primary functions of the Air Force include the following:

   (a) To organize, train, equip, and provide forces for the conduct of prompt and sustained offensive and defensive combat operations in the air and space—specifically, forces to defend the United States against air and space attack in accordance with doctrines established by the JCS, gain and maintain general air and space supremacy, defeat enemy air and space forces, conduct space operations, control vital air areas, and establish local air and space superiority except as otherwise assigned herein.

   (b) To organize, train, equip, and provide forces for appropriate air and missile defense and space control operations, including the provision of forces as required for the strategic defense of the United States, in accordance with joint doctrines.

   (c) To organize, train, equip, and provide forces for strategic air and missile warfare.

   (d) To organize, equip, and provide forces for joint amphibious, space, and airborne operations, in coordination with the other Military Services, and to provide for their training in accordance with joint doctrines.

(e) To organize, train, equip, and provide forces for close air support and air logistic support to the Army and other forces, as directed, including airlift, air and space support, resupply of airborne operations, aerial photography, tactical air reconnaissance, and air interdiction of enemy land forces and communications.

(f) To organize, train, equip, and provide forces for air transport for the Armed Forces, except as otherwise assigned.

(g) To develop, in coordination with the other Services, doctrines, procedures, and equipment for air and space defense from land areas, including the United States.

(h) To organize, train, equip, and provide forces to furnish aerial imagery for use by the Army and other agencies as directed, including aerial imagery for cartographic purposes.

(i) To develop, in coordination with the other Services, tactics, techniques, and equipment of interest to the Air Force for amphibious operations and not provided for elsewhere.

(j) To develop, in coordination with the other Services, doctrines, procedures, and equipment employed by Air Force forces in airborne operations.

(k) To provide launch and space support for the Department of Defense, except as otherwise assigned.

(l) To develop, in coordination with the other Services, doctrines, procedures, and equipment employed by Air Force forces in the conduct of space operations.

(m) To organize, train, equip, and provide land-based tanker forces for the in-flight refueling support of strategic operations and deployments of aircraft of the Armed Forces and Air Force tactical operations, except as otherwise assigned.

(n) To organize, train, equip, and provide forces, as directed to operate air and space lines of communications.

(o) To organize, train, equip, and provide forces for the support and conduct of special operations.

(p) To organize, train, equip, and provide forces for the support and conduct of psychological operations.

(q) To provide equipment, forces, procedures, and doctrine necessary for the effective prosecution of electronic warfare operations and, as directed, support of other forces.

(3) Collateral functions of the Air Force include the following:

    (a) Surface sea surveillance and anti–surface ship warfare through air and space operations.

    (b) Antisubmarine warfare and anti–air warfare operations to protect sea lines of communications.

    (c) Aerial mine-laying operations.

    (d) Air-to-air refueling in support of naval campaigns.

(4) Other responsibilities of the Air Force include:

    (a) With respect to amphibious operations, the Air Force shall develop, in coordination with the other Services, tactics, techniques, and equipment of interest to the Air Force and not provided for by the Navy and Marine Corps.

    (b) With respect to airborne operations, the Air Force has specific responsibility:

        1. To provide Air Force forces for the air movement of troops, supplies, and equipment in joint airborne operations, including parachuted and aircraft landings.

        2. To develop tactics and techniques employed by Air Force forces in the air movement of troops, supplies, and equipment.

    (c) With respect to close air support of ground forces, the Air Force has specific responsibility for developing, in coordination with the other Services, doctrines and procedures, except as provided for in Navy responsibilities for amphibious operations and in responsibilities for the Marine Corps.

Department of the Air Force Structure. The Secretary of the Air Force is responsible to the Secretary of Defense for overseeing the administrative chain of command of the department.

Principal assistants to the Secretary of the Air Force are as follows:

- The Under Secretary of the Air Force is responsible for all actions of the Air Force on behalf of the Secretary of the Air Force and is acting Secretary in the Secretary's absence.

- The Assistant Secretary for Acquisition is responsible for all Air Force research, development and non-space acquisition activities and provides direction, guidance, and supervision of all matters pertaining to the formulation, review, approval, and execution of acquisition plans, policies, and programs.

- The Assistant Secretary for Manpower, Reserve Affairs, provides overall supervision of manpower, military and civilian personnel, Reserve component affairs, and readiness support for the Department of the Air Force.
- The Assistant Secretary for Installations, Environment, and Logistics is responsible for the management and policy of all matters pertaining to the formulation, review, and execution of plans and programs for Air Force military and civilian personnel, Air Force Reserve and Air National Guard forces, installations, and the environment.
- The Assistant Secretary for Financial Management and Comptroller serves as the Air Force's Chief Financial Officer and principal adviser to the Secretary of the Air Force on all financial matters.

The Office of the Secretary of the Air Force also includes a general counsel, auditor general, inspector general, administrative assistant, public affairs director, legislative liaison, director of small business programs, warfighting integration and chief information officer, and various statutory boards and committees.

The Chief of Staff, U.S. Air Force, is appointed by the President, with the consent of the Senate, from among Air Force general officers—normally for a four-year term. The Chief of Staff serves as a member of the JCS and the Armed Forces Policy Council. In the JCS capacity, the chief is one of the military advisers to the President, the National Security Council, and the Secretary of Defense as well as the principal adviser to the Secretary of the Air Force on Air Force activities.

The Chief of Staff presides over the Air Staff, transmits Air Staff plans and recommendations to the Secretary of the Air Force, and acts as the Secretary's agent in carrying them out. The Chief is responsible for the efficiency of the Air Force and the preparation of its forces for military operations; supervises the administration of Air Force personnel assigned to COCOMs; and supervises support of these forces assigned by the Air Force as directed by the SECDEF.

The Chief of Staff has the following principal assistants:

- Vice Chief of Staff
- Assistant Vice Chief of Staff
- Deputy Chief of Staff for Manpower and Personnel
- Deputy Chief of Staff for Operations, Plans, and Requirements
- Deputy Chief of Staff for Logistics, Installations, and Mission Support
- Deputy Chief of Staff for Strategic Plans and Programs
- Deputy Chief of Staff for Intelligence, Surveillance, and Reconnaissance
- Assistant Chief of Staff for Strategic Deterrence and Nuclear Integration

An Air Force crew chief prepares the cockpit of an F-16 before a flight.

Additional members of the Air Staff include the Chief Master Sergeant of the Air Force, Chief of Safety, Judge Advocate General, Director of Test and Evaluation, Surgeon General, Air Force Historian, Chief Scientist, Chief of the Air Force Reserve, Chief of the National Guard Bureau, Chief of Chaplain Service, and Director of Analyses, Assessments, and Lessons Learned.

Organization of the Air Force. The Air and Space Expeditionary Force (AEF) concept was designed to permit the Air Force to provide a source of ready operational and support forces for expeditionary operations. Deployed AEF forces fall in on existing in-theater command structures—normally, Numbered Air Forces (NAFs) to form Air and Space Expeditionary Task Forces (AETFs). AETFs are task-organized, integrated packages of varying sizes, providing a scalable, tailorable organization under the authority of a single commander. The AETF commander is called the Commander, Air Forces (COMAFFOR), whose rank ranges from lieutenant colonel to lieutenant general, depending on the size of the force.

In descending order of command, elements of the Air Force include major commands, numbered air forces, wings, groups, squadrons, and flights.

Air Force Major Commands. There are eleven major commands in the Air Force:

- The Air Combat Command organizes, trains, and equips nuclear capable forces for the U.S. Strategic Command and theater air combat forces for the geographic U.S. combatant commands.

- The Air Education and Training Command conducts recruiting and training programs, including basic military training, officer training, advanced training, and technical training.

- The Air Mobility Command provides forces for airlift and sustainment of U.S. armed forces, and for humanitarian missions.

- The Air Force Material Command conducts research and development of weapons systems (and was created by the merger of the Air Force Logistics Command and the Air Force Systems Command).

- Air Forces in Europe is the air component of U.S. European Command.

- Pacific Air Forces is the air component of U.S. Pacific Command.

- The Air Force Space Command utilizes space to provide support for combat forces and is responsible for the Air Force's ICBM forces.

- The Air Force Special Operations Command provides Air Force special operations forces for worldwide deployment and assignment to regional combatant commands.

- The Air Force Global Strike Command is responsible for ICBM forces and dual mission–capable bomber forces.

- The Air Force Reserve Command commands the reserve component of the Air Force. The Reserve Associate Program trains Reserve aircrews and maintenance personnel to fly and maintain more than three hundred active-duty aircraft, including the C-5, C-9, C-17, C-40, E-3A, F-16C, F-22, KC-10, T-1, T-37, T-38, and AT-38. The Air Force Reserve Command also supports space, flight test, special operations, aerial port operations, civil engineer, security forces, intelligence, military training, communications, mobility support, transportation, and services missions.

- The Air National Guard trains and equips units available for prompt mobilization during war and national emergencies (e.g., natural disasters or civil disturbances). During peacetime, the combat-ready units/support units are assigned to most Air Force major commands to carry out missions compatible with training, mobilization readiness, and contingency operations.

In addition to the major commands, twenty-one field operating agencies and four direct reporting units report to Headquarters, U.S. Air Force. Field agencies are assigned specialized missions such as modeling and simulation, logistics, communications, reserve administration, civil engineering, and personnel. Direct reporting units are the 11th Wing in Washington, D.C.; Headquarters Air Force Doctrine Center; Air Force Operational Test and Evaluation Center; and the U.S. Air Force Academy.

Core Competencies. Air Force Basic Doctrine identifies three core competencies:

- Developing Airmen. Recognizing that the ultimate source of Air Force combat capability is its professional airmen and civilian workforce, the Air Force is committed to providing them with quality education, training, and professional development.

- Technology-to-Warfighting. The competency includes innovation to guide research; development; and fielding of air and space; and intelligence, surveillance, and reconnaissance technologies.

- Integrating Operations. This third competency employs innovative operational concepts and the efficient integration of all military systems—air, land, maritime, space, and information—to ensure maximum flexibility in the delivery of desired effects across the spectrum of conflict.

Distinctive Capabilities. Air Force Basic Doctrine identifies the following functions that are best accomplished by air and space forces, or that achieve the most benefit when performed by air and space forces:

- Air and space superiority to secure freedom of action for friendly forces provides freedom to attack as well as freedom from attack.

- Information superiority is the ability to collect, control, exploit, and defend information while denying an adversary the ability to do the same.

- Global attack is the ability to attack rapidly and persistently with a wide range of munitions anywhere on the globe at any time.

- Precision engagement is the ability to command, control, and employ forces to cause specific strategic, operational, or tactical effects.

- Rapid global mobility is the timely movement, positioning, and sustainment of military forces and capabilities through air and space, across the range of military operations.

- Agile combat support provides responsive maintenance, supply, transportation, communications, services, engineering, security, health services, finance, legal services, and chaplain services for deployed units.

Air Force Commissioning Programs. The Air Force trains future officers in Air Force ROTC programs at nearly 144 colleges and universities, at the U.S. Air Force Academy in Colorado Springs, Colorado, and in a twelve-week course of instruction at Officer Training School (OTS) located at Maxwell Air Force Base in Montgomery, Alabama.

CHAPTER TWELVE

THE NAVAL SERVICE

Ninety percent of the world's commerce travels by sea; the vast majority of the world's population lives within a few hundred miles of the oceans; nearly three quarters of the planet is covered by water. Seapower protects the American way of life.

—*A Cooperative Strategy for 21st Century Seapower*

Every danger of a military character to which the United States is exposed can be met best outside her own territory—at sea.

—Rear Admiral Alfred Thayer Mahan

In 2007 the U.S. Coast Guard, Marine Corps, and Navy issued *A Cooperative Strategy for 21st Century Seapower,* representing the first time the three services jointly crafted a maritime strategy. The document stresses the naval services' mutual commitment to protecting the homeland and winning and preventing wars.

Proliferation of weapons and information technology to transnational threats and rogue states poses an increasing range of threats to U.S. security interests. In addition to threats from kinetic weapons, hybrid warfare threats (e.g., financial, cyber) pose new challenges for the sea services, demanding a coordinated strategy and response. To better understand how responsibility for security in the maritime domain is shared among the sea services, this chapter describes organization, mission, and capabilities of each.

The Department of the Navy

The Department of the Navy (DON) is to "be organized, trained, and equipped primarily for prompt and sustained combat incident to operations at sea" (*Navy Regulations* art. 0202). The National Security Act of 1947, as amended in 1949, governs the role of the Navy in national defense. The Goldwater-Nichols Department of Defense Reorganization Act of 1986 streamlined the operational chain of command and provided detailed descriptions of the roles of the Secretary of the Navy, the CNO, and the Commandant of the Marine Corps (CMC).

Composition of the Department of the Navy. The composition of DON, as set forth in Title 10, U.S. Code (USC), includes the following:

- The Office of the Secretary of the Navy
- The Office of the Chief of Naval Operations
- The Headquarters, Marine Corps
- The entire operating forces, including naval aviation, of the Navy and of the Marine Corps, and the reserve components of those operating forces
- All field activities, headquarters, forces, bases, installations, activities, and functions under the control or supervision of the Secretary of the Navy
- The Coast Guard when it is operating as a service in the Navy

Composition and Functions of the Navy. As defined in Title 10, USC:

(a) The Navy, within the Department of the Navy, includes, in general, naval combat and service forces and such aviation as may be organic therein. The Navy shall be organized, trained, and equipped primarily for prompt and sustained combat incident to operations at sea. It is responsible for the preparation of naval forces necessary for the effective prosecution of war except as otherwise assigned and, in accordance with integrated joint mobilization plans, for the expansion of the peacetime components of the Navy to meet the needs of war.

(b) The naval combat forces of the Navy shall include not less than 11 operational aircraft carriers. For purposes of this subsection, an operational aircraft carrier includes an aircraft carrier that is temporarily unavailable for worldwide deployment due to routine or scheduled maintenance or repair.

(c) All naval aviation shall be integrated with the naval service as part thereof within the Department of the Navy. Naval aviation consists of combat and service and training forces, and includes land-based naval aviation, air transport essential for naval operations, all air weapons and air techniques involved in the operations and activities of the Navy, and the entire remainder of the aeronautical organization of the Navy, together with the personnel necessary therefore.

(d) The Navy shall develop aircraft, weapons, tactics, techniques, organization, and equipment of naval combat and service elements.

Matters of joint concern as to these functions shall be coordinated between the Army, the Air Force, and the Navy.

Composition and Functions of the Marine Corps. As defined in Title 10, USC:

(a) The Marine Corps, within the Department of the Navy, shall be so organized as to include not less than three combat divisions and three air wings and such other land combat, aviation, and other services as may be organic therein. The Marine Corps shall be organized, trained, and equipped to provide fleet marine forces of combined arms, together with supporting air components, for service with the fleet in the seizure or defense of advanced naval bases and for the conduct of such land operations as may be essential to the prosecution of a naval campaign. In addition, the Marine Corps shall provide detachments and organizations for service on armed vessels of the Navy, shall provide security detachments for the protection of naval property at naval stations and bases, and shall perform such other duties as the President may direct. However, these additional duties may not detract from or interfere with the operations for which the Marine Corps is primarily organized.

(b) The Marine Corps shall develop, in coordination with the Army and the Air Force, those phases of amphibious operations that pertain to the tactics, techniques, and equipment used by landing forces.

(c) The Marine Corps is responsible, in accordance with integrated joint mobilization plans, for the expansion of peacetime components of the Marine Corps to meet the needs of war.

History

The government of the United States if founded upon a single document, the Constitution. The Constitution contains provisions for governing the armed forces that have not changed since the document was written.

The Congress, under the powers granted to it by the Constitution, has passed many laws forming and regulating the Navy. In turn, the Secretary of the Navy has approved regulations and orders giving detail to these regulations.

In 1798, *Navy Regulations* provided for the establishment "at the seat of the government an executive known as the Department of the Navy, and a Secretary of the Navy, who shall be the head thereof."

A board of naval commissioners, with three members, was created by an act of 7 February 1815.

On 31 August 1842, the "bureau system" was established by Congress.

The congressional acts of 11 July 1890, 3 March 1891, and 20 June 1940 provided an under secretary and an assistant secretary.

On 3 March 1915, the Office of the Chief of Naval Operations was provided for by an act of Congress.

On 12 July 1921, Congress created the Bureau of Aeronautics, and on 24 June 1926, Congress authorized the Assistant Secretary for Air.

By 1942, *Navy Regulations* read as follows:

The business of the Department of the Navy not specifically assigned by law shall be distributed in such manner as the Secretary of the Navy shall judge to be expedient and proper among the following bureaus:

First, a Bureau of Yards and Docks
Second, a Bureau of Naval Personnel
Third, a Bureau of Ordnance
Fouth, a Bureau of Ships
Fifth, a Bureau of Supplies and Accounts
Sixth, a Bureau of Medicine and Surgery
Seventh, a Bureau of Aeronautics

The National Security Act established the DoD in 1949 as an executive department of the government to include the military departments of the Army, Navy, and Air Force. The Secretary of the Navy was demoted to subcabinet rank. The titles of these positions have changed over the years, and various bureaus have been retitled as commands.

Congress and the Department of the Navy

Of the three branches of government, the legislative branch has the sole power to appropriate funds. From this and from the constitutional responsibility to "raise armies and navies," Congress derives the power to determine the nature of the Navy and Marine Corps and the amount of money used to purchase and operate ships and weapons and to pay personnel. Both the Senate and the House have committees on armed forces. These committees hold annual hearings for the purpose of authorizing ships and weapons. The appropriations committees of both houses then appropriate money for ship and weapon construction and additional funds for supplies, pay, and other support.

The Navy Department has a Chief of Legislative Affairs and an office in the House and the Senate to provide rapid liaison with the committees and members. Members of Congress, by the Department of the Navy or by other offices of DoD, may originate proposals for legislation. Wherever proposals originate, they are referred to appropriation committees of the Congress for hearing and further processing.

Titles 10 and 37 of the USC, which are widely available on the Internet (see appendix E, Sources), contain most of the laws affecting the Navy.

Organization of the Department of the Navy

The Department of the Navy is unique within DoD because it includes two separate services, the Navy and the Marine Corps, each with its own distinct, although interrelated, mission and chain of command (see figure 12-1).

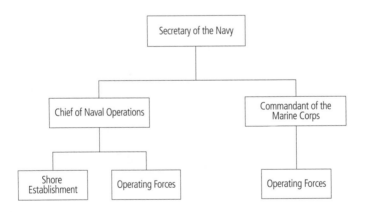

Figure 12-1 Navy Organization

Organization of the Secretariat. The Secretary of the Navy (figure 12-2) is overall in charge of construction, manning, armament, equipment, and maintenance of all vessels and aircraft and performs other duties as assigned by the Secretary of Defense. The Secretary of the Navy has direct cognizance over all officer and enlisted personnel and public and legislative relations and is assisted by the Under Secretary.

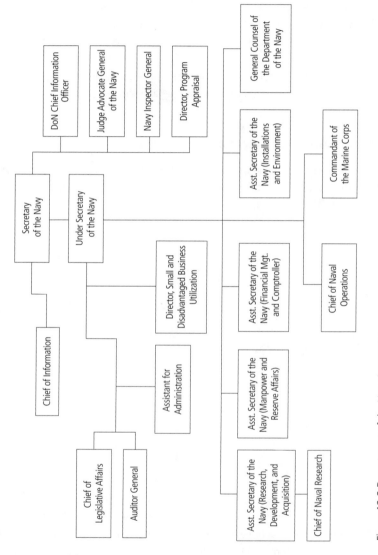

Figure 12-2 Department of the Navy Secretariat

Four assistant secretaries also assist the Secretary of the Navy:

- The Assistant Secretary of the Navy (Research, Development, and Acquisition) manages the department's acquisitions, directs research and development efforts, and oversees procurement and contracting.
- The Assistant Secretary of the Navy (Installations and Environment) determines long-range strategic direction and policy for Navy installations and oversees installations, logistics, environment, and safety programs.
- The Assistant Secretary of the Navy (Financial Management and Comptroller) directs and manages the department's financial activities.
- The Assistant Secretary of the Navy (Manpower and Reserve Affairs) exercises overall supervision of personnel policies for the department.

The Secretary is further assisted by the following individuals:

- The Assistant for Administration manages the various boards, directors, and chiefs reporting to and performing staff functions for the Secretary and his or her civilian executive assistants, which are collectively referred to as the Executive Office of the Secretary.
- The Judge Advocate General (JAG) has cognizance over all major phases of military, administrative, and legislative law pertaining to the operation of the department. The JAG reviews the records of court-martial proceedings and other courts and boards, as well as matters of international law.
- The General Counsel provides legal services and advice throughout the department in the fields of business and commercial law.
- The Chief of Information (CHINFO) handles all aspects of public information and the public affairs program for the department.
- The Chief of Legislative Affairs assists the senior officials of the Navy in their relations with Congress and handles liaison with individual members of Congress and congressional staff members.
- The Director, Office of Program Appraisal, provides appraisals of Navy and defense plans, studies, and proposals.
- The Naval Inspector General inquires and reports on matters affecting military efficiency or discipline; proposes a program of inspections; and makes inspections, investigations, and reports as directed by SECNAV or CNO.
- Department of the Navy Chief Information Officer (CIO) is responsible for the development and use of Information Management (IM)/Information Technology (IT) and for creating a unified IM/IT vision for the department. Additionally, the CIO ensures that the development and acquisition

of IT systems are interoperable and consistent with the department's objectives and vision.

- The Auditor General audits and assesses business risks within the department to provide managers objective feedback on efficiency and effectiveness of DON programs, systems, functions, and funds.
- The Director, Small and Disadvantaged Business Utilization, oversees procurement opportunities for small businesses and minority-serving educational institutions.

The Office of the Chief of Naval Operations

The various offices under the CNO are collectively referred to as the Office of the Chief of Naval Operations, or OPNAV.

The Chief of Naval Operations (OP-00). The CNO is the senior military officer in the Navy and serves as primary naval adviser to the President and Secretary of Defense and as a member of the JCS. The CNO, with the CMC, is responsible for keeping the SECNAV fully informed on matters considered or acted upon by the JCS.

The Vice Chief of Naval Operations (OP-09). The VCNO has authority and duties as delegated by the CNO. Orders issued by the VCNO in performing such duties have the same effect as if issued by the CNO.

The VCNO's principal job is to act as executive for the CNO. In addition, the VCNO coordinates the performance of the various boards, staff assistants, deputy chiefs of staff, and directors of major staff offices.

The following individuals assist the CNO:

- Director, Navy Staff (No9B)
- Deputy CNO, Manpower, Personnel, Education and Training (N1)
- Deputy Chief of Naval Operations for Information Dominance (N2/N6)
- Deputy CNO, Information, Plans and Strategy (N3/N5)
- Director for Material Readiness and Logistics (N4)
- Deputy CNO, Integration of Capabilities and Resources (N8).

OPNAV N-8 (originally, Deputy CNO, Resources, Warfare Requirements and Assessments) was established in 1992. Prior to that time, a different assistant CNO represented each naval warfare area on the OPNAV staff. The reorganization consolidated all of the warfare areas under a single DCNO, N8, to eliminate the barriers between the warfare communities and to ensure that Navy procurement programs were evaluated in terms of their specific contributions to the joint warfighting effort. Currently, the warfare divisions report to N8F, Director, Warfare Integration.

The Shore Establishment

The Navy Personnel Command (NPC), led by the Chief of Naval Personnel, is responsible for the procurement, education, training, discipline, promotion, welfare, morale, and distribution of officers and enlisted personnel. The command also has responsibility for all records of medals and awards and for correctional custody units, and it supervises Navy morale, welfare, and recreation (MWR) activities.

Bureau of Medicine and Surgery (BUMED). BUMED, led by the Navy Surgeon General, provides Navy and Marine Corps members with health care services and quality-of-life services, maintains health records, and conducts research and development of health-related issues.

Naval Sea Systems Command (NAVSEA). NAVSEA develops, acquires, modernizes, and maintains ships, ordnance, and systems for the Navy and Marine Corps. NAVSEA performs acquisition, in-service support, and technical organization functions to meet naval and joint forces warfighting requirements.

Naval Air Systems Command (NAVAIR). NAVAIR provides life-cycle support of naval aviation aircraft, weapons, and systems, which includes research, design, development, and systems engineering; acquisition; test and evaluation; training facilities and equipment; repair and modification; and in-service engineering and logistics support.

Naval Supply Systems Command (NAVSUP). NAVSUP provides supply support to Navy forces worldwide. It supplies parts and equipment to the fleet, performs contracting functions, and operates the Navy Exchange system and other services.

Naval Facilities Engineering Command (NAVFAC). NAVFAC provides facilities life-cycle support, which includes management of installations, environmental programs, base realignment and closure requirements, and engineering planning for contingency operations. NAVFAC also oversees the civil engineer corps, naval construction battalions (SEABEES), Naval Beach Group, and other Naval Special Operating Units.

Space and Naval Warfare Systems Command (SPAWAR). SPAWAR provides the Navy with command, control, communications, computers, intelligence surveillance and reconnaissance (C4ISR), business information technology, and space capabilities.

Strategic Systems Programs (SSP). SSP provides the nation's sea-based deterrent missile system. SSP is the Navy's manager for all aspects of development, manufacture, and support of Trident weapons systems, including development and production of the missiles, guidance, fire control, launcher, and navigation subsystems; the training of weapons systems personnel; logistic support; and equipment maintenance and repair.

Naval Legal Service Command. The Deputy Judge Advocate General of the Navy is assigned additional duty to the CNO as Commander, Naval Legal Service Command, and oversees Navy-wide legal services to ship and shore commands, active-duty military personnel, dependents, and retirees. Legal services include military justice, comprising trial and defense counsel; command support; legal assistance; civil law, including handling personal property, tort, and military claims; administrative law; and environmental law.

Office of Naval Intelligence (ONI). ONI supports the operating forces through the collection of maritime intelligence and moves that intelligence rapidly to key strategic, operational, and tactical decision makers.

Naval Education and Training Command (NETC). NETC conducts education and training of Navy officers and enlisted members. NETC's responsibilities include recruit training, specialized-skills training, and officer precommissioning training.

The United States Naval Academy. USNA educates future officers and prepares them for commissions in the Navy and Marine Corps.

Naval Network Warfare Command (NAVNETWARCOM). NAVNETWARCOM is responsible for delivering integrated cyber mission capabilities in information operations, intelligence, network operations, and space.

Naval Strike and Air Warfare Center (NSAWC). NSAWC, located at Naval Air Station Fallon, Nevada, provides naval aviation training and tactics development. NSAWC supports aircrews, squadrons, and air wings through flight training, academic instructional classes, and direct operational and intelligence support.

The United States Naval Observatory. The observatory determines the positions and motions of celestial bodies, motions of the Earth, and precise time; provides astronomical and timing data required by the Navy, other components of DoD, government agencies, and the general public for navigation, precise positioning, command, control, and communications; and conducts relevant research.

The Naval Safety Center. The center provides safety assistance and advice to the CNO, CMC, and the Deputy Assistant SECNAV for Safety. The Naval Safety Program provides guidance and direction, safety data services, safety program services, and safety marketing information.

Commissioning Programs

The Navy trains future officers through a variety of programs. In addition to the programs described below, programs specifically designed to commission Navy enlisted members are discussed in chapter 7.

Officer Candidate School (OCS). Navy Officer Candidate School, located in Newport, Rhode Island, is an intensive twelve-week course that provides initial training for college graduates to become Navy officers.

The Naval Reserve Officers Training Corps (NROTC) Program. The NROTC program commissions officers into the Navy's unrestricted line and nurse corps as well as the Marine Corps. Two- and four-year NROTC scholarships, offering tuition, fees, a monthly stipend, books, and uniforms, are available at more than 160 colleges and universities. Scholarship midshipmen participate in summer cruises each year. A two- or four-year NROTC nonscholarship college program is also offered; participants in the college program are eligible to compete for scholarships, receive monthly stipends during their junior and senior years, and participate in summer cruises the summer before they are commissioned.

The United States Naval Academy (USNA). The USNA, located in Annapolis, Maryland, is a fully subsidized four-year undergraduate educational program. Naval Academy midshipmen receive active-duty pay while pursuing bachelor's degrees in a wide variety of majors and commissions as Navy or Marine Corps officers. USNA midshipmen also participate in cruises each summer.

Staff Corps Commissioning Programs. Specialized programs exist to commission officers into the civil engineering corps, nurse corps, medical corps, dental corps, JAG corps, and chaplain corps. Some of these programs provide financial benefits while the candidates complete degree requirements. In addition, established specialists in certain professional and scientific fields may qualify for direct commissions.

The U.S. Marine Corps

Origin. On 10 November 1775, a resolution of the Continental Congress established the Continental Marines, which was based on an organization in the British Royal Navy. The Marine Corps was established by an act of Congress on 11 July 1798. Congress intended the Marine Corps to be a strong, versatile, fast-moving, and hard-hitting force that would be prepared to prevent potential conflicts by prompt and vigorous action, be able to hold a full-scale aggressor at bay while the United States mobilized, and be ready when the nation was least ready.

In keeping with this intent, the Marine Corps still provides the nation with an expeditionary military organization capable of responding rapidly to threats to

Marines participate in an amphibious landing exercise with the Royal Brunei Landing Force.

American interests by projecting power through its forward-deployed units and by reacting to crises with combat-ready units tailored to meet any contingency.

Tradition. As they enlist, Marines learn that Marine Corps traditions are as much a part of their equipment as their pack and rifle. These traditions are many: devotion to duty and to discipline, loyalty to the country and the Corps, self-sacrifice, flexibility, and dependability. Marines reinforce this tradition through meticulous maintenance of their distinctive insignia and uniforms and through a continuously fostered readiness to be the first force called upon to respond to a national emergency.

Mission of the Marine Corps. The Marine Corps is the Nation's "force in readiness," prepared for rapid and discriminate employment across the spectrum of conflict on land, sea, and air. This spectrum ranges from general war to mid- or low-intensity conflicts. The Marine Corps provides forces both visible and discreet, on-scene or poised beyond the horizon, forces that possess a conspicuous strike and power projection capability.

Title 10, USC, assigns the Marine Corps several specific roles and functions. In fulfilling these roles, the Marine Corps performs a wide variety of wartime tasks, including seizure and defense of advanced naval bases; crisis response; forward presence; alliance support and special operations, which can include close-quarter battle, reconnaissance and surveillance, seizure and destruction of offshore facilities such as oil or gas platforms, and hostage rescue. Other Marine Corps functions can include various noncombat operations involved with disaster relief, humanitarian assistance, and counternarcotics efforts.

Core Competencies of the Marine Corps. Marine Corps Vision and Strategy 2025 articulated the following core competencies for the Corps:

- The Corps conducts persistent forward naval engagement and is always prepared to respond as the Nation's force in readiness.
- The Corps employs integrated combined arms across the range of military operations and can operate as part of a joint or multinational force.
- The Corps provides forces and specialized detachments for service aboard naval ships, on stations, and for operations ashore.
- The Corps conducts joint forcible entry operations from the sea and develops amphibious landing force capabilities and doctrine.
- The Corps conducts complex expeditionary operations in the urban littorals and other challenging environments.
- The Corps leads joint and multinational operations and enables interagency activities.

The Commandant and Headquarters Staff. The CMC is a member of the JCS and is directly responsible to SECNAV under the administrative chain of command for the procurement, discharge, education, training, discipline, and distribution of Marine Corps officers and enlisted personnel.

The Commandant is assisted by the Assistant Commandant, Sergeant Major of the Marine Corps, and Chief of Staff as well as the following deputies and assistants:

- Deputy Commandant, Plans, Policies, and Operations
- Deputy Commandant, Manpower and Reserve Affairs
- Deputy Commandant, Programs and Resources
- Deputy Commandant, Aviation
- Deputy Commandant, Installations and Logistics
- Deputy Commandant, Combat Development Command
- Director, Intelligence
- Director, Command, Control, Communications, and Computers
- Director, Health Services
- Director, Public Affairs
- Inspector General of the Marine Corps
- Staff Judge Advocate to the Commandant/Director
- Legislative Assistant to the Commandant

Organization of the Marine Corps. Figure 12-3 shows the organization of the Marine Corps.

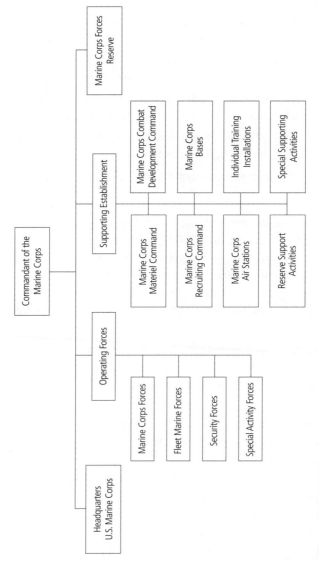

Figure 12-3 USMC Organization

The Marine Corps is organized into two broad categories: operating forces and the supporting establishment. The major elements of the operating forces are the Marine Corps Forces, Fleet Marine Forces (FMF), Security Forces, and Special Activity Forces.

Marine Corps combat, combat support, and combat service support units are part of the assigned Marine Corps Forces. These forces serve under geographic COCOMs to plan and accomplish assigned operational missions. FMF units serve with Navy fleets, to seize or defend advanced naval bases and conduct land operations essential to the prosecution of naval operations. Security Forces deter, detect, and defend against terrorist actions and conduct initial incident response to combat the threat of terrorism worldwide. Special Activity Forces provide security or services or perform duties for agencies other than the Department of the Navy, such as internal security services at Department of State embassies, consulates, and legations.

Organization for Combat. The Marine Corps task-organizes for combat by forming integrated, combined-arms Marine Air Ground Task Forces (MAGTF). These task forces are specifically tailored according to the mission and can be rapidly deployed by air or sea. A task force comprises four elements: command, ground combat, aviation combat, and service support. Combining air and ground combat elements with combat service support under a single commander allows close integration of air and ground units into a single force.

The size of the task force and its elements are mission-dependent. The smallest MAGTF is called a Marine expeditionary unit (MEU). With a strength of about 2,100 personnel, a MEU is embarked aboard a small group of ships configured as an expeditionary strike group (ESG), commanded by an amphibious squadron (PHIBRON) commander. A MEU normally consists of an infantry battalion reinforced with a composite aviation squadron (normally including attack helicopters, transport helicopters, air refuelers/transport aircraft, light attack fixed-wing aircraft, and command and control assets), a MEU service support group, and a command element. The MEU is commanded by a colonel and deploys in austere environments with fifteen days of supplies. Forward-deployed MEUs provide an immediate sea-based response to meet forward-presence and limited power-projection requirements.

Security Cooperation MAGTF (SC MAGTF) A security cooperation MAGTF is similar to a MEU, but task-organized for security cooperation and civil-military operations. Enhanced with additional engineering, medical, dental, and transportation capabilities, the SC MAGTF may also include enhanced civil affairs, operational law, veterinary services, information operations, and interagency liaison capability. Primarily tasked with supporting and developing partner-nation security efforts in a specific regional area, the SC MAGTF is also available to assist in other operations including terrorist interdiction.

Marine Expeditionary Brigade (MEB). A MEB is larger than a MEU and consists of approximately 16,000 Marines commanded by a brigadier general and organized into a command element, an infantry regiment, an aircraft group, and a brigade service support group. MEBs will normally provide the landing force building blocks for larger contingencies and major operations. When combined, two MEB assault echelons constitute the assault echelon of a Marine expeditionary force (MEF).

A MEF is the largest task force. Composed of 50,000 Marines commanded by a lieutenant general, a MEF consists of one or more of the following: an infantry division, comprising three infantry regiments (with a total of nine infantry battalions in the division); an artillery regiment (with four artillery battalions); a tank battalion; a light armored reconnaissance battalion; an amphibious assault battalion; a Marine aircraft wing, which provides both fixed-wing and rotary-wing aircraft; and a force service support group.

Special-Purpose MAGTF. A special-purpose MAGTF (SPMAGTF) is task-organized to accomplish specific missions, including humanitarian assistance, disaster relief, or limited security operations under semipermissive conditions. A SPMAGTF is not organized or equipped for operations in a high or mid-intensity nonpermissive (hostile) environment. The enhanced MAGTF operations (EMO) initiative is refining organization, equipment, and select tactics, techniques, and procedures (TTPs) to provide small units with more agility and robust capabilities against hybrid threats.

Amphibious Warfare. Amphibious warfare integrates all types of ships, aircraft, weapons, and landing forces in an attack against a hostile shore. Initiated in the absence of friendly forces ashore, and exploiting the element of surprise, amphibious warfare requires the rapid landing and buildup of forces and equipment to prosecute further combat operations.

The scale of an amphibious evolution may range from a small incursion to a full-scale assault. When confronting an enemy of significant combat capability, the role of the amphibious force may be to seize initial entry points for introduction of more extensive follow-on forces.

The Marine expeditionary unit is the integral part of an amphibious ready group (ARG), designed to bring the MEU to the theater of operations and to land it on a hostile shore.

Normally, the commander, amphibious task force (CATF) is the Navy officer who commands the ARG. This officer, and the Marine Corps MEU commander known as the commander, landing force (CLF), share equal footing in the planning stage. From there, the CATF is in charge until the Marines have secured a beachhead and control is shifted to the CLF ashore.

The major types of amphibious operations are:

- Amphibious engagement and crisis response, which contributes to conflict prevention or crisis mitigation, may engage in operations such as security cooperation, foreign humanitarian assistance, civil support, noncombatant evacuations, peace operations, recovery operations, or disaster relief.

- Amphibious raid involves a swift incursion into or a temporary occupation of an objective, followed by a planned withdrawal.

- Amphibious assault involves the establishment of a landing force on a hostile or potentially hostile shore.

- Amphibious withdrawal involves the extraction of forces by sea in ships or craft from a hostile or potentially hostile shore.

Commissioning Programs. USMC officers may be commissioned following graduation from the U.S. Naval Academy or an NROTC program, or from Officer Candidate School in Quantico, Virginia.

The U.S. Coast Guard

Under Title 10 and Title 14, USC, the Coast Guard is a military service and a branch of the armed forces; it is also a federal law enforcement agency with broad powers to conduct inspections, searches, seizures, and arrests on the high seas and U.S. waters. The Coast Guard may at any time provide forces and perform military functions in support of naval component commanders or COCOMs; and, upon the declaration of war, or when the President so directs, the Coast Guard operates under the Department of the Navy.

History of the Coast Guard. Created by an act of Congress on 4 August 1790 at the request of the first Secretary of the Treasury, Alexander Hamilton, the Coast Guard has been variously known as the Revenue Marine, the Revenue Service, and the Revenue Cutter Service. As early as 1799, Congress provided for cooperation between the cutters and the Navy whenever the President directed. An act of Congress in 1915 consolidated the Revenue Cutter Service and the Life-Saving Service into the Coast Guard.

In addition to peacetime service to the country, the Coast Guard has given effective service in wartime. It participated with the Navy in the Quasi-War with France in 1798, the War of 1812, the Seminole War, and the Mexican War, and is said to have fired the first maritime shot in the Civil War (the revenue cutter *Harriet Lane* fired across the bow of the steamer *Nashville* while Fort Sumter was being bombarded).

In World War I, the Coast Guard not only hunted submarines but also performed convoy duty, principally between Gibraltar and the British Isles. Peace after World War I brought the Coast Guard its greatest expansion and most difficult duty, the enforcement of Prohibition. With the repeal of Prohibition, the Coast Guard was drastically cut. In 1939 the Lighthouse Service of the Department of Commerce was transferred to the Department of the Treasury and the Coast Guard. In 1940 the Coast Guard established the Atlantic Weather Observation Service, patrolling weather stations for protection of transatlantic air commerce. The Coast Guard Auxiliary (then called the Reserve) was established in 1939 and the Reserve in 1941. By November 1941 the Coast Guard was operating as part of the Navy. In World War II, in addition to guarding the continental coastline, the Coast Guard manned 351 vessels of the Navy. In 2003 the Coast Guard was transferred from the Department of Transportation to the newly created Department of Homeland Security.

The Commandant and Headquarters Staff. The Commandant of the Coast Guard reports to the President, the Secretary of Homeland Security, and, when assigned, the Secretary of Defense. The Commandant is not a member of the Joint Chiefs of Staff. Assistants to the Commandant include:

- Chief of Staff of the Coast Guard
- Vice Commandant of the Coast Guard
- Director of Governmental and Public Affairs
- Judge Advocate General and Chief Counsel
- Assistant Commandant for Human Resources
- Assistant Commandant for Intelligence and Criminal Investigations
- Assistant Commandant for Engineering and Logistics
- Assistant Commandant for Marine Safety, Security, and Stewardship
- Assistant Commandant for Command, Control, Communications, Computers, and Information Technology
- Assistant Commandant for Capability
- Assistant Commandant for Planning, Resources, and Procurement
- Assistant Commandant for Acquisition
- Deputy Commandant for Operations

Organization of the Coast Guard. The operating forces are divided between two area commanders: Commander, Coast Guard Area Atlantic (headquartered in Portsmouth, Virginia) and Commander, Coast Guard Area Pacific (headquartered in Alameda, California). Area commands are further divided into geographic districts, each under a district commander. Figure 12-4 illustrates the organization of the Coast Guard.

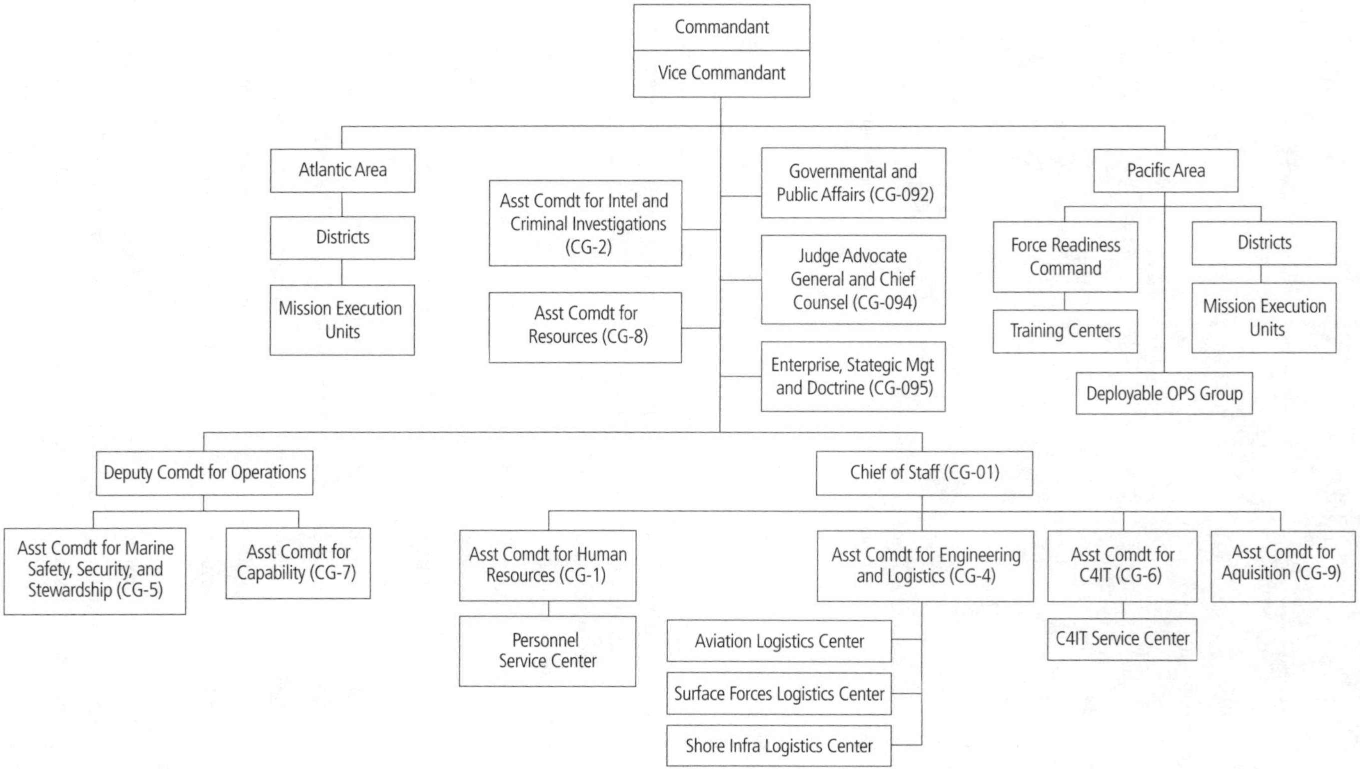

Figure 12-4 USCG Organization

A Coast Guard rescue swimmer deploys during a boating safety event demonstration.

Missions of the Coast Guard. The Coast Guard exercises primary maritime authority within U.S. waters. It is a relatively small, decentralized organization capable of rapid response in a wide variety of situations and of shifts in emphasis on short notice when the need arises. Although operating within the Department of Homeland Security in peacetime, Title 14, USC, specifies that the Coast Guard is "at all times an armed force of the United States."

The Coast Guard's five primary missions are:

- Maritime Safety: Eliminate deaths, injuries, and property damage associated with maritime transportation, fishing, and recreational boating.

- Maritime Security: Protect America's maritime borders from all intrusions by (a) halting the flow of illegal drugs, aliens, and contraband into the United States through maritime routes; (b) preventing illegal fishing; and (c) suppressing violations of federal law in the maritime arena.

- Maritime Mobility: Facilitate maritime commerce and eliminate interruptions and impediments to the efficient and economical movement of goods and people, while maximizing recreational access to and enjoyment of the water.

- National Defense: Defend the nation as one of the five U.S. armed services; enhance regional stability in support of the National Security Strategy, utilizing the Coast Guard's unique and relevant maritime capabilities.

- Protection of Natural Resources: Eliminate environmental damage and the degradation of natural resources associated with maritime transportation, fishing, and recreational boating.

Law Enforcement Operations (LEO). Title 18, USC, sec. 1385, known as the Posse Comitatus Act, proscribes the use of Army and Air Force units for law enforcement except when expressly authorized by the Constitution or Congress. By regulation, this proscription also applies to Navy units. Additional laws specify that DoD activities may provide law enforcement agencies, such as the Coast Guard, with support and technical assistance, such as use of facilities, aircraft, vessels, intelligence, technical expertise, and surveillance.

Posse Comitatus prohibits Navy personnel from directly participating in search, seizure, or arrest of suspected criminals. When engaged in LEO, which are primarily targeted at interdiction of suspected drug smugglers, Navy ships are augmented with Coast Guard law enforcement detachments. Embarked Coast Guard personnel perform the actual boardings of interdicted suspect drug-smuggling vessels and, if needed, place the smugglers under arrest.

Commissioning Programs. Officers receive commissions in the U.S. Coast Guard following graduation from the U.S. Coast Guard Academy in New London, Connecticut, or completion of OCS, also in New London. In addition, direct commissioning programs exist for professionals in specialized fields such as law, aviation, environmental management, and engineering.

CHAPTER THIRTEEN

THE OPERATING FORCES OF THE NAVY

Not only on the deep sea, the broad bay, and the rapid river, but also up the narrow muddy bayou, and wherever the ground was a little damp, they have made their tracks.

—President Abraham Lincoln

It was their task to keep the sea lanes open, to maintain the Navy's traditions of "not giving up the ship," and this they did even though they paid with their lives.

—Navy Department press release, 19 July 1942

The operating forces of the Navy consist of the fleets and their subordinate type commanders, shore-based long-range air forces, strategic submarine forces, the Military Sealift Command (MSC), and shore activities assigned by the President or the Secretary of the Navy.

Operational Control vs. Administrative Control

As discussed in chapter 11, the operating forces have a dual chain of command. They report to the CNO through an administrative chain of command, which is responsible for their training and preparation for employment. This type of command, known as Administrative Control (ADCON) provides seniors with the authority for administration and support, resources and equipment, personnel management, unit logistics, individual and unit training, readiness, mobilization, demobilization, discipline, and other nonoperational matters.

Under the administrative chain of command, ships, aircraft squadrons, and other operating units are assigned to type commanders (TYCOMs). Each TYCOM is further subdivided into groups and squadrons. This organization carries out normal administration, and a ship or squadron is always under the ADCON of its type commander, even when under the operational control (OPCON) of a numbered fleet, task force, or battle group commander.

OPCON provides seniors with the authority to organize commands and forces and to employ those forces to accomplish assigned missions. Tactical control (TACON) is inherent in OPCON and provides the authority for controlling and directing the application of force or tactical use of combat support assets within the assigned mission or task. Navy operating forces report through an operational chain of command to the appropriate combatant commander, as discussed in chapter 11, to fulfill the Navy's warfighting missions. In addition to exercising ADCON over their assigned operating units, TYCOMs exercise OPCON during most phases of training. After the completion of basic and intermediate training, the appropriate numbered fleet commanders assume OPCON of these forces for advanced training and operations. Some elements of these forces are further assigned to task force or expeditionary strike force organizations for specific operations and missions including assignment to combatant commands.

Classifications of Ships and Aircraft

Surface Ships. Commissioned Navy ships with military crews (both surface ships and submarines) are designated by the prefix USS (for United States Ship) preceding the ships' names. In addition to its name, each ship is assigned a hull number, consisting of its designation and sequential number (e.g., CG 73).

The designations of major categories of commissioned surface ships are as follows:

AS	Submarine tender
CVN	Aircraft carrier (nuclear-powered)
CG	Guided-missile cruiser
DDG	Guided-missile destroyer
FFG	Guided-missile frigate
LCC	Command ship
LCS	Littoral combat ship
LHA	Amphibious assault ship (general purpose)
LHD	Amphibious assault ship (multipurpose)
LPD	Amphibious transport dock
LSD	Dock landing ship
MCM	Mine countermeasures ship
PC	Coastal patrol craft

A lieutenant looks over the side of the guided-missile frigate USS *John L. Hall* (FFG 32) as it arrives at Naval Station Rota for a scheduled port visit.

Ships that have the USNS prefix (for United States Naval Ship) before their name are Military Sealift Command ships manned with mostly civilian crews. USNS ships have a *T-* preceding the designation, as follows:

T-AE   Ammunition carrier

T-AFS   Combat stores ship

T-AH   Hospital ship

T-AKE   Dry cargo/ammunition ship

T-AOE   Fast combat-support ship

T-AO   Oiler

T-ARS   Rescue and salvage ship

T-ATF   Fleet ocean tug

Submarines. The U.S. Navy has three categories of nuclear-powered submarines:

SSN   Fast attack submarine

SSGN Guided-missile submarine

SSBN Ballistic-missile submarine

Aircraft Squadrons. There are four basic types of aircraft squadrons: carrier, patrol, composite, and noncombatant. Carrier squadrons include fighter, attack, strike/fighter, antisubmarine, and airborne early warning. Patrol squadrons consist of land-based aircraft with a maritime patrol mission. Composite squadrons perform utility missions including plane guard, search and rescue, replenishment, and personnel transport. Noncombatant squadrons can have development, tactical support (long-range personnel transport and logistics), and training missions.

Aircraft squadron symbols, a group of two or more letters followed by a number, such as HSL-48 or VFA-12, comprise three parts: the squadron prefix, mission, and numerical designation.

The first letter of an aircraft squadron title is called the squadron prefix symbol. An *H* denotes a helicopter squadron; a *V* denotes fixed-wing aircraft. In a Marine Corps squadron, this first letter is followed by an *M*.

The next letter, or letters, in the squadron title is the squadron class symbol, and it indicates the basic mission of the squadron, as follows:

AQ	Electronic warfare
AW	Airborne early warning
C	Combat support or composite
F	Fighter
FA	Strike fighter
FC	Fighter composite (adversary simulation)
M	Mine countermeasures
P	Patrol
Q	Electronic reconnaissance
R, RC	Logistics
S	Antisubmarine warfare
SC	Sea combat (multipurpose)
SL	Antisubmarine warfare (light)
SM	Maritime strike
T	Training
X	Test and evaluation

Administrative Chain of Command

Figure 13-1 illustrates the administrative organization of the Navy's operating forces.

- Commander, U.S. Naval Forces, Europe/U.S. Naval Forces, Africa/U.S. Sixth Fleet provides Navy forces to EUCOM and AFRICOM, as described in chapter 11.

- Commander, Operational Test and Evaluation Force heads the Navy's sole independent agency for operational test and evaluation.
- Commander, Navy Reserve Force oversees the Navy's Reserve units.
- Commander, U.S. Naval Forces, Central Command/U.S. Fifth Fleet provides Navy forces to CENTCOM, as described in chapter 11.
- Commander, U.S. Naval Forces, Southern Command/U.S. Fourth Fleet provides Navy forces to SOUTHCOM, as described in chapter 11.
- Commander, Navy Special Warfare Command provides Navy forces to SOCOM, as described in chapter 11.
- Director, Strategic Systems Programs is the Navy's manager for all aspects of development, manufacture, and support of Trident weapons systems, including missile development and production, guidance, fire control, launcher, and navigation subsystems, training of weapons systems personnel, logistic support, and equipment maintenance and repair.
- Commander, Naval Sea Systems Command is responsible for design, development, and maintenance of ships, submarines, and combat systems.
- Commander, U.S. Fleet Cyber Command/U.S. Tenth Fleet is the Navy component to the U.S. Cyber Command.
- Commander, U.S. Fleet Forces Command (formerly Commander, U.S. Atlantic Fleet) is responsible for total force readiness and exercises ADCON over five warfare enterprises, which serve as the lead for their respective Navy-wide communities:
  — Surface Warfare Enterprise (Commander, Naval Surface Forces, Pacific)
  — Naval Aviation Enterprise (Commander, Naval Air Forces, Pacific)
  — Undersea Warfare Enterprise (Commander, Submarine Forces, Atlantic)
  — Naval NETWAR/FORCEnet Enterprise
  — Navy Expeditionary Combat Enterprise
- In addition, Fleet Forces Command exercises ADCON over:
  — Naval Air Force, Atlantic
  — Naval Surface Force, Atlantic
  — Submarine Force, Atlantic
  — U.S. Second Fleet
  — Navy Expeditionary Combat Command

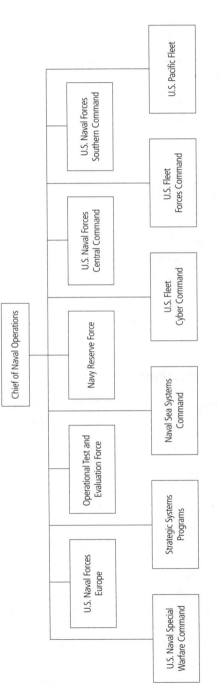

Figure 13-1 Administrative Chain of Command

    — Navy Munitions Command

    — Military Sealift Command

- Commander, U.S. Pacific Fleet exercises ADCON over the following units of the Pacific Fleet:

    — Naval Air Force, Pacific

    — Naval Surface Force, Pacific

    — Submarine Force, Pacific

    — U.S. Third Fleet

    — U.S. Seventh Fleet

    — Naval Forces, Japan

    — Naval Forces, Korea

    — Naval Forces, Marianas

    — Logistic Group, Western Pacific

    — First Naval Construction Division, Pacific

    — Navy Munitions Command, East Asia Division

    — Navy Munitions Command, CONUS West Division

Operational Chain of Command

Operationally, the Navy assigns ships and other units based on geographic location to one of the numbered fleets. The composition of these fleets changes on virtually a daily basis as assets move in and out of their respective areas of responsibility. As units of the Navy enter the area of responsibility for a particular commander, they are operationally assigned ("chop," which means change of operational control) to the appropriate numbered fleet. When a ship home-ported in San Diego transits the Pacific Ocean, its OPCON shifts from Commander, Third Fleet to Commander, Seventh Fleet.

    Second Fleet serves in the Atlantic and reports operationally to Commander, Fleet Forces Command. Similarly, units of the Third and Seventh Fleets report to Commander, U.S. Pacific Fleet; Third Fleet's area of responsibility is the eastern and northern Pacific Ocean, while Seventh Fleet units serve throughout the western Pacific and Indian Ocean region. Fourth Fleet is responsible for ships operating in the Caribbean, and Central and South America, and reports to U.S. Southern Command (SOUTHCOM). Fifth Fleet units serve throughout the Persian Gulf, Red Sea, Arabian Sea, and off the coast of East Africa; Commander, Fifth Fleet is also designated as Commander, U.S. Naval Forces Central Command and reports directly to U.S. Central Command (CENTCOM). Sixth Fleet, serving as U.S. Naval Forces, Europe and U.S. Naval Forces, Africa, reports to both U.S. European Command EUCOM and U.S. Africa Command (AFRICOM). Commander, Tenth Fleet is responsible to U.S. Cyber Command for the operation of Navy networks.

Figure 13-2 shows the Navy's task organization. A task force may consist of a diverse variety of ships, including aircraft carriers, amphibious ships, surface combatants, and submarines brought together to fulfill a particular mission. In order to provide flexibility and ease of communication in meeting the varied military requirements of vast areas, task forces are further divided operationally into task groups (e.g., expeditionary strike group [ESG], carrier strike group [CSG], amphibious ready group [ARG]), which in turn may be subdivided into task units (e.g., air defense ships) and task elements (individual commands). Depending on the type and scope of the operation, the force will be assigned a task force or battle force designation under the operational control of the numbered fleet commander. These subdivisions are designated numerically (e.g., Task Unit 77.3.1 is Task Unit 1 of Task Group 3 of Task Force 7 of the Seventh Fleet).

Deploying Units

On any given day, ships and squadrons from the U.S. Atlantic and Pacific Fleets are on deployment away from home port. Although battle group configurations can vary depending on the mission, deploying forces generally follow a few standard configurations.

Carrier Strike Group (CSG). The CSG is a flexible, heavy strike group that can support initial crisis response missions in nonpermissive environments. CSG are capable against antiship missiles, ballistic missiles, fighter/attack aircraft, electromagnetic jammers, cruise-missile-equipped surface combatants, submarines (nuclear and diesel), and terrorist threats. Typically, a carrier strike group will consist of:

- CSG staff
- Destroyer squadron (DESRON) staff
- One CVN with embarked air wing
- Five surface combatant ships (CG/DDG/FFG/LCS)
- One SSN
- One logistic support ship (T-AOE, T-AKE, or T-AO and T-AE)
- One logistics helicopter detachment

Amphibious Ready Group/Marine Expeditionary Unit (ARG/MEU). The ARG/MEU is the routine rotational amphibious force package, and may deploy with surface combatants and a submarine, depending upon the mission. When led by

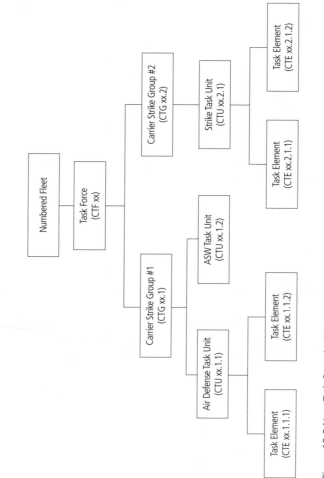

Figure 13-2 Navy Task Organization

a flag or general officer, the group is referred to as an expeditionary strike group (ESG). An ARG/MEU consists of the following:

- One amphibious squadron (PHIBRON) staff
- Three amphibious ships (LHA/LHD, LPD, LSD)
- Naval support elements (NSE), including assault craft, Beachmaster Unit, logistics helicopter detachment, tactical air control squadron, and fleet surgical team
- Marine expeditionary unit (MEU) staff
- Ground combat element (reinforced battalion landing team)
- Air combat element (composite squadron of fixed and rotary wing aircraft)
- Logistics combat element (combat logistics battalion)
- Up to three surface combatant ships (CG/DDG/FFG/LCS), depending on mission, with two SUW/ASW–capable helicopter detachments

Surface Strike Group (SSG). The SSG is a surface group that can operate independently or with other maritime forces to support crisis response or sustained missions. Like CSGs, SSGs can operate in limited nonpermissive environments characterized by multiple threats. SSG capabilities include passive surveillance and tracking, passive defense and early warning, strike operations, and sea control and may include maritime ballistic-missile defense (BMD). A nominal SSG consists of three surface ships, two of which are strike/cruise missile land attack (TLAM)–capable CGs or DDGs, and the third, which may be a surface combatant or amphibious ship.

Fleet Response Plan

The Fleet Response Plan was developed in the early 2000s to better enable the Navy to deploy and sustain naval forces during protracted wars, or to meet other national security requirements. This plan provides the maintenance, training, and operational framework to meet COCOM demand signals for traditional and emerging missions, and it is more capable of surging quickly to deal with unexpected threats, humanitarian disasters, and contingency operations. By enabling ships to surge and reconstitute rapidly, the Fleet Response Plan provides the capability of six CSGs deployed or ready to deploy within thirty days and of two CSGs ready to deploy within ninety days.

The Fleet Response Plan provides flexibility for unscheduled deployments in support of emergent national security operations, but generally limits deployments to six months or fewer out of each twenty-seven-month readiness cycle.

Fleet Response Training Plan

The Fleet Response Training Plan (FRTP) is a twenty-seven-month cycle that aligns with the Fleet Response Plan and replaces the old Interdeployment Training Cycle. The FRTP includes four phases prior to deployment: maintenance, unit-level training, integrated training, and sustainment.

The maintenance phase normally starts the cycle and ranges from nine weeks for a surface combatant to up to ten months for an aircraft carrier. During the maintenance phase, major shipyard- or depot-level repairs, upgrades, and modernization installations are scheduled, and units focus on individual and team training.

The unit-level training phase focuses on completion of TYCOM unit-level training requirements, including team training and unit-level exercises, inspections, assessments, certifications, and qualifications. During this phase the major prerequisites for a surge deployment (manning, maintenance, and basic training) are completed to make a unit available for emergency surge. If necessary the training in this phase may be augmented with additional, tailored training that can be completed rapidly before deployment to support a crisis or contingency operation.

The integrated training phase is intended to coordinate the actions of individual ships into the operations of the group, within a challenging operational environment. This phase provides training that is tailored to individual ship and air-wing strengths and weaknesses. Following completion of this phase, a group is considered surge-ready and able to deploy on short notice if required.

The sustainment phase includes a variety of training evolutions designed to maintain readiness until the group actually deploys.

Battle Effectiveness Award

The Battle Effectiveness Award, or Battle E, replaces the former Battle Efficiency Award. Awarded annually, it recognizes sustained superior performance in an operational environment, and sustained continuous readiness throughout the Fleet Response Training Plan cycle. In order to be eligible for the Battle Effectiveness Award, a ship needs to earn four of the five departmental effectiveness awards.

Crew members of ships awarded the Battle E wear the ribbon, and a painted *E* is displayed on the winning ship.

CHAPTER FOURTEEN

THE INTERAGENCY

*There is perhaps no greater challenge for any government than to
synchronize its component parts so that they function collectively
like a well-oiled machine. No government facing terrorism and other
transnational threats can afford to have anything less.*

—Paul Shemella, Program Manager for Combating Terrorism,
The Center for Civil-Military Relations, Naval Postgraduate School

Military power alone is often insufficient to conduct operations including counterterrorism, counter–drug smuggling, humanitarian assistance, peace operations, counternarcotics, security force assistance,
environmental security, human rights, democratization, and prevention of the
proliferation of weapons of mass destruction. Effective action requires that all of
the elements of U.S. national power be brought to bear: diplomacy, information,
military, economic, financial, intelligence, and law enforcement (DIMEFIL). No
single government agency possesses all of these disparate capabilities; thus, effective coordination across federal agencies is required. The terms "interagency" and
"whole of government" are often used to describe the mechanisms by which this
coordination takes place.

In contrast with the rigid, hierarchical organizational structure that most
Sailors and other DoD personnel are accustomed to, most working-level interagency coordination takes place within an informal network that lacks a clear
chain of command. Although the National Security Council (NSC) is responsible
for interagency coordination at the highest levels of government, at the working
level interagency teams are often assembled in an ad hoc way to address a particular crisis or situation, with only minimal guidance provided to the participants by
their parent organizations.

The ad hoc nature of these organizations demands flexibility on the part of the participants to find common ground, build consensus, and take effective collective action. Such critical and seemingly simple questions as "What is the problem we are trying to solve?" and "How will we know if we are making progress?" may receive surprisingly divergent answers from team members representing different agencies.

A Sailor embarked aboard the Military Sealift Command hospital ship USNS *Comfort* (T-AH 20), carries a patient to be seen by medical professionals as part of Operation Continuing Promise. This humanitarian and civic action mission combines U.S. military and interagency personnel, nongovernmental organizations, civil service mariners, academics, and partner nations to provide medical, dental, veterinary, and engineering services afloat and ashore alongside host-nation personnel.

Civilian Response Corps

Recent conflicts and natural disasters have brought home the need for the United States to be able to rapidly deploy critical members of the civilian workforce in response to a crisis. Established in 2008, the Civilian Response Corps is an inter-agency civilian response capability of the Departments of State, Agriculture, Commerce, Health and Human Services, Homeland Security, Justice, and Treasury, and of the U.S. Agency for International Development (USAID).

The Civilian Response Corps is made up of active, standby, and reserve components. Active members of the Corps are full-time employees who train as first responders, ready to deploy within forty-eight hours of notification. Active members focus on critical needs such as assessment, planning, management, administration, logistics, and resource mobilization. The standby component also consists of full-time employees who are ready to deploy within thirty days of notification, to support reconstruction and stabilization operations. Reserve members possess specialized expertise in areas including policing and rule of law, infrastructure development, economic stabilization, state and local governance, agriculture, and provision of basic services. Reserve members are available to be deployed within forty-five to sixty days after notification and to serve as temporary government employees.

U.S. Government Departments and Agencies

The Department of Agriculture performs public health functions domestically and overseas. The department's programs include the Foreign Agriculture Service, the Rural Development Agency, and the National Water Management Center. In addition to providing support to disaster relief operations, the Department of Agriculture is the lead department for the veterinary response for pandemic and avian influenza.

The Department of Commerce possesses both financial and economic technical expertise, including expertise in international trade databases, economic analysis, business development, and exports and imports. Key offices in the Department of Commerce include the National Institute of Standards and Technology (NIST); the National Oceanic and Atmospheric Administration (NOAA); and the Bureau of Industry and Security (BIS), which includes the Office of Nonproliferation and Treaty Compliance (NPTC).

The Department of Health and Human Services (HHS) provides services in public health. Major Health and Human Services agencies include the Centers for Disease Control and Prevention (CDC), the National Institutes of Health (NIH), the Food and Drug Administration (FDA), the Office of Global Health

Affairs (OGHA), and the U.S. Public Health Service (USPHS). Health and Human Services is the lead department for the medical response for pandemic influenza.

The Environmental Protection Agency (EPA) is an independent agency responsible for the protection of human health and the environment. Key EPA incident-response capabilities include the Environmental Response Team, Regional Response Teams, and the Radiological Emergency Response Teams.

The Department of Homeland Security (DHS) was established by the Homeland Security Act of 2002, which consolidated twenty-two existing agencies focused on securing the U.S. homeland from terrorist attacks and man-made and natural threats. DHS is the lead department for domestic incident management and federal coordination for pandemic influenza. DHS agencies include Customs and Border Protection (CBP), Federal Emergency Management Agency (FEMA), Immigration and Customs Enforcement (ICE), Transportation Security Administration (TSA), U.S. Coast Guard (discussed in more detail in chapter 12), and U.S. Secret Service.

The Intelligence Community (IC) is a federation of executive branch agencies and organizations that engages in intelligence activities for the conduct of foreign relations and the protection of U.S. national security interests. The IC is headed by the Director of National Intelligence (DNI, described in chapter 11), and, with the exception of the office of the Director (ODNI) and the Central Intelligence Agency (CIA), its members are components of other cabinet departments.

Members of the IC include:

- Air Force Intelligence
- Army Intelligence
- Central Intelligence Agency
- Coast Guard Intelligence
- Defense Intelligence Agency
- Department of Energy
- Department of Homeland Security
- Department of State
- Department of the Treasury
- Drug Enforcement Administration
- Federal Bureau of Investigation
- Marine Corps Intelligence
- National Geospatial-Intelligence Agency
- National Reconnaissance Office
- National Security Agency
- Navy Intelligence
- Office of the Director of National Intelligence

The Department of Justice (DOJ) enforces U.S. laws and defends the interests of the United States to provide public safety and federal leadership in preventing and controlling crime. DOJ includes the Bureau of Alcohol, Tobacco, Firearms, and Explosives (ATF), U.S. Drug Enforcement Administration (DEA), and the Federal Bureau of Investigation (FBI).

The Department of Energy (DOE) is responsible for ensuring the integrity and safety of the country's nuclear weapons, promoting international nuclear safety, advancing nuclear nonproliferation, and providing safe, efficient, and effective nuclear power plants. The department includes the National Nuclear Security Administration (NNSA) and the Nuclear Weapons Incident Response program.

The Department of State (DOS) has the mission to "create a more secure, democratic, and prosperous world for the benefit of the American people and the international community." The principal aims of the department are to build and maintain strong bilateral and multilateral relationships; to protect the United States and its allies from common threats including terrorism, international crime, and weapons of mass destruction; and to use diplomacy and aid to foster democracy and prosperity throughout the world.

The State Department plays a key leadership role in coordination overseas. The U.S. has an embassy in the capital of most countries with which diplomatic relations exist. The Ambassador for each country reports to the President through the Secretary of State and serves as the President's representative in his or her assigned country.

The Ambassador leads the Country Team, which coordinates U.S. government activities in that country. Country Teams are configured differently in different countries and may include representatives of many different U.S. departments and agencies. Figure 14-1 shows a notional Country Team organization. Unless directed by the President, other U.S. departments and agencies are required to coordinate their actions through the Ambassador and the Country Team, and the Ambassador has authority over all U.S. executive branch personnel in his or her assigned country, with the exception of those under the command of a U.S. COCOM.

Key State Department offices include:

- Coordinator for Counterterrorism
- Counterterrorism Finance Unit
- Coordinator for Reconstruction and Stabilization
- Coordinator for Diplomatic Security
- International Information Programs
- International Narcotics and Law Enforcement Affairs
- International Security and Nonproliferation
- Political–Military Affairs

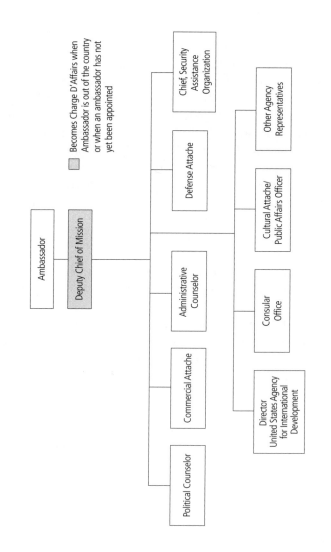

Figure 14-1 Notional Country Team

- Population, Refugees, and Migration
- Trafficking in Persons
- Verification, Compliance, and Implementation

In addition, the department includes the following geographic bureaus:

- African Affairs
- East Asian and Pacific Affairs
- European and Eurasian Affairs
- Near Eastern Affairs
- South and Central Asian Affairs
- Western Hemisphere Affairs

The Department of Transportation (DOT) is responsible for the U.S. transportation system. Transportation agencies include the Federal Aviation Administration (FAA) and the Maritime Administration (MARAD).

The Department of the Treasury is responsible for the sound functioning of the U.S. and international financial systems and for the identifying and targeting of financial support networks established to sustain terrorist and other threats to national security. Key Treasury offices include the Office of Foreign Assets Control (OFAC), Office of Intelligence and Analysis (OIA), Office of International Affairs, and Office of Terrorism and Financial Intelligence (TFI).

U.S. Agency for International Development (USAID), an independent federal government agency under the U.S. Secretary of State, is the principal U.S. agency that provides assistance to countries recovering from disaster, trying to escape poverty, and engaging in democratic reforms. USAID has senior development advisers at each of the DoD geographic COCOMs.

Intergovernmental and Nongovernmental Organizations

Intergovernmental Organizations (IGOs). The interagency team may include members of one or more of these organizations, which have diverse missions and varied membership. Some of the more prominent IGOs include the United Nations, organizations devoted to regional stability and economic interest (e.g., African Union, Association of Southeast Asian Nations, Organization of American States, European Union), law enforcement bodies (e.g., INTERPOL), and economic/financial organizations (e.g., World Bank, International Monetary Fund).

Nongovernmental Organizations (NGOs). No discussion of the interagency coordination process would be complete without considering the vital role played by NGOs. Because NGOs are independent and generally privately funded, they may be reticent to openly cooperate with U.S. government agencies (particularly DoD organizations) under certain circumstances, for fear of losing the goodwill of the people they are supporting. Some of the better-known NGOs include Catholic Relief Services, Médecins Sans Frontières, Oxfam, and Red Cross/Red Crescent.

CHAPTER FIFTEEN

INTERNATIONAL ORGANIZATIONS

We are a strong nation. But we cannot live to ourselves and remain strong.

—General George C. Marshall

The responsibility of the great states is to serve and not to dominate the world.

—President Harry S. Truman

Every Navy officer should have an understanding of the alliances and organizations of which the United States is a member. This chapter includes a discussion of the major alliances.

The United Nations

Origin. The charter of the United Nations developed from proposals made at the Dumbarton Oaks Conference in 1944 by delegates from the United States, Great Britain, the USSR, and China.

In April 1945, fourteen hundred representatives from fifty nations met in San Francisco for a conference on international organization. The Dumbarton Oaks proposals were put before the conference, and the charter was signed after amendments were made. The required number of states ratified the charter on 24 October 1945.

Aims. The United Nations is an association of sovereign nations pledged to maintain international peace and security and to establish the political, economic, and social conditions necessary to that aim. The primary purpose of the United Nations is to keep the peace. The secondary goal is to develop friendly relations among nations based upon respect for the principle of equal rights and self-determination of peoples. The United Nations seeks also to achieve international cooperation in solving economic, cultural, and humanitarian problems. It strives to promote recognition of human rights and of fundamental freedoms for all without distinction as to sex, language, or religion. Finally, the United Nations acts as a center where nations may meet to discuss their problems and try to find peaceful solutions for them.

Organization of the United Nations. The United Nations has six basic divisions called "principal organs," as follows:

- *General Assembly.* The General Assembly includes representatives of all 192 member countries and is the chief deliberative, policymaking, and representative organ of the United Nations. Decisions on ordinary matters require a simple majority; voting on certain important questions is by a two-thirds majority. The assembly holds regular sessions from mid-September through mid-December, and special or emergency sessions when necessary. The General Assembly has the right to discuss and make recommendations on all matters within the scope of the U.N. charter. It has no authority to compel action by any government, although its recommendations carry the weight of world opinion. The General Assembly votes to admit new members and appoints the U.N. Secretary-General.

- *Security Council.* The Security Council is primarily concerned with maintaining international peace and security. There are fifteen members of the Security Council, of which five—France, China, the Russian Federation, the United Kingdom, and the United States—are permanent members. The General Assembly elects the remaining members for two-year terms. Decisions require nine votes, although any permanent member may veto a proposal. Member states are obligated to seek peaceful resolution of disputes, and any member state may bring a dispute before the Security Council. The council seeks to resolve the dispute by peaceful means but may take measures to enforce its decisions. These measures may include imposition of sanctions on countries that threaten the peace, or authorization of military action by coalitions of member states.

- *Economic and Social Council.* This council coordinates the economic and social work of the United Nations and its related agencies to promote economic growth in developing countries and the observance of human rights worldwide. The General Assembly elects eighteen members each year for a three-year term, for a total of fifty-four members. The council normally meets between February and July of each year, adjourning at least six weeks before the General Assembly convenes.

- *Trusteeship Council.* Powers that administer territories that are not ready for self-government place the territories under the international trusteeship system. As of 1994, all trusteeships had attained self-governance or independence; this organ is currently inactive.

- *International Court of Justice.* Also known as the World Court, the International Court of Justice has been located in The Hague since its establishment in 1946. The World Court decides disputes (known as "contentious jurisdiction") between nations that accept its jurisdiction and gives advisory opinions ("advisory jurisdiction") on cases brought before it by U.N. organs and agencies. The World Court has fifteen judges, who are elected by the General Assembly and the Security Council. A judge serves for nine years, and no two judges may be nationals of the same country. Sixty-six nations currently consent to contentious jurisdiction of the World Court; the United States currently does not.

- *Secretariat.* The Secretary-General, who is the chief administrative officer of the United Nations, runs the Secretariat. The General Assembly appoints the Secretary-General on the recommendation of the Security Council. The Secretary-General appoints the staff and carries out the day-to-day work of the United Nations.

U.S. Participation in the United Nations The United States, as the world's leading political, economic, and military power, has a strong interest in U.N. participation. The United States can pursue many of its interests effectively through the United Nations, particularly in circumstances when it would be impracticable or unsafe for the United States to act alone. The United Nations has been instrumental in carrying out many aims of the United States, including containing the spread of weapons of mass destruction, enforcing sanctions on nations hostile to regional peace and cooperation, and combating international terrorism and drug trafficking.

North Atlantic Treaty Organization (NATO)

In the Atlantic and the Mediterranean, U.S. forces operate closely with NATO allies. If you are assigned to this area of the world or visit it on deployment, you should familiarize yourself with the NATO organization. Although it has not been updated since 2003, the *NATO Handbook*, available on the Internet, remains a valuable source of information. Updated information on NATO can be obtained from the NATO issues pages, http://www.nato.int/issues/index.htm.

The Formation of NATO. When World War II came to an end, the Western democracies hoped to enter an era of security and demobilized the majority of their armed forces. The emergence of postwar tensions and threatened expansion by the former Soviet bloc caused the Western nations to unite for a common defense against further Soviet expansionism. In April 1949, in Washington, D.C., the foreign ministers of Belgium, Canada, Denmark, France, Iceland, Italy, Luxembourg, the Netherlands, Norway, Portugal, the United Kingdom, and the United States signed the North Atlantic Treaty to prevent aggression and, if necessary, resist attack against any alliance member. In 1952 Greece and Turkey joined the alliance, followed by the Federal Republic of Germany in 1955 and Spain in 1982. More recent additions to NATO membership include the Czech Republic, Hungary, and Poland (1999); Bulgaria, Estonia, Latvia, Lithuania, Romania, Slovakia, and Slovenia (2004); and Albania and Croatia (2009).

The Treaty. The text of the treaty is short and clear. It conforms to both the letter and the spirit of the U.N. charter. Briefly, it sets forth the following as desirable goals:

- Peaceful settlement of disputes and abstinence from force or threat of force
- Economic collaboration between signatories
- Strengthening the means of resisting aggression by individual effort and mutual assistance
- Consultation in the event that any signatory is threatened

The North Atlantic Council (NAC). The NAC is the principal forum for consultation and cooperation between NATO member governments on all issues affecting their common security. NAC decisions are based on consensus, and all members have an equal right to express their views; each member nation provides an ambassador or permanent representative. The NATO Secretary-General chairs this council as well as other senior committees.

Defense Planning Committee (DPC). The DPC deals with defense planning and other issues related to NATO's integrated military structure. It is composed of representatives of all countries except France (which withdrew from the DPC in 1966). It meets regularly at the ambassadorial level and twice yearly when member countries are represented by their defense ministers.

Commands. The strategic area covered by NATO is divided into two regional commands: Allied Command Europe and Allied Command Atlantic, with a regional planning group for North America. With the exceptions of Iceland (which has no military) and France, all member countries assign forces to the integrated command structure. The NATO defense area covers the territories of member nations in North America, in the Atlantic area north of the Tropic of Cancer, and in Europe, including Turkey. Events occurring outside of this area that affect the preservation of peace and security may also be of concern to NATO.

NATO-Russia Council. The NATO-Russia Founding Act signed in 1997 established a Permanent Joint Council to serve as the principal mode of coordination between NATO and Russia. In 2002 the NRC replaced the Permanent Joint

Council. NATO suspended formal NRC meetings in 2008 following Russia's military action in Georgia, but meetings resumed in 2009.

Shift in Emphasis. Since the close of the Cold War, NATO has revised its strategy in view of the changing global landscape and has accepted many former Soviet bloc nations into its membership. NATO recognizes that the primary threats to NATO's security, such as failed states, proliferation of weapons of mass destruction, and threats of terrorism now require a different approach centered on conflict prevention and crisis management.

Other Organizations and Agreements

Organization for Security and Co-operation in Europe (OSCE). Fifty-six countries in Europe, Central Asia, and North America, including the United States, participate in OSCE, making it the largest regional security organization in the world. OSCE's missions include early warning, conflict prevention, crisis management, and postconflict rehabilitation.

Organization of American States (OAS). OAS, dating back to the First International Conference of American States in 1890, is the world's oldest regional organization. The OAS Charter was signed in 1948 and entered into force in December 1951. There are currently thirty-five member states, including the United States The four pillars of the OAS mission are promoting democracy, defending human rights, coordinating member states' actions to fight threats to security, and fostering development and prosperity in the region. In 2009 the OAS reversed its 1962 decision to exclude Cuba from OAS activities and resolved to enter into dialogue initiated by the Cuban government.

The collective security systems of the 1947 Inter-American Treaty of Reciprocal Assistance—known as the Rio Treaty, which became part of the OAS—represented the American states' general acceptance of the principle underlying the Monroe Doctrine: an attack upon an American state by a non-American state would be an attack upon all.

North American Aerospace Defense Command (NORAD). The North American Aerospace Defense Command is a binational U.S. and Canadian organization charged with the missions of aerospace warning and aerospace control for North America. Aerospace warning includes the monitoring of man-made objects in space and the detection, validation, and warning of attack against North America whether by aircraft, missiles, or space vehicles, utilizing mutual support arrangements with other commands. Aerospace control includes providing surveillance and control of the airspace of Canada and the United States.

The NORAD Commander is appointed by, and responsible to, both the President of the United States and the Prime Minister of Canada. The Commander, headquartered at Peterson Air Force Base, Colorado Springs, Colorado, is also the Commander of U.S. Northern Command (NORTHCOM). The NORAD/NORTHCOM command and control center is located a short distance away from NORAD headquarters, at Cheyenne Mountain Air Station, and is supported by three subordinate region headquarters located at Elmendorf Air Force Base, Alaska; Canadian Forces Base, Winnipeg, Manitoba, Canada; and Tyndall Air Force Base, Florida.

The U.S.–Republic of Korea Mutual Defense Treaty. This treaty, signed in 1953, allows the United States to station troops in South Korea. To coordinate operations between U.S. and Korean armed forces, a Combined Forces Command (CFC) was established in 1978. The head of the CFC also serves as Commander of the United Nations Command (UNC) and U.S. Forces Korea (USFK).

U.S.–Japan Treaty of Mutual Cooperation and Security. This treaty, signed in 1960, provides the basis for the close relationship between the United States and Japan and their defense establishments.

ANZUS Treaty. This treaty, signed in 1951 by Australia, New Zealand, and the United States, provides for cooperation among the armed forces of the three countries. New Zealand's refusal since 1984 to permit visits by U.S. warships unless granted assurances they are not carrying nuclear weapons has caused the United States to suspend its ANZUS security obligations to New Zealand.

Group of Eight (G-8) and Group of Twenty (G-20). The G-8, first established as the G-6 in 1975, is an organization of eight major industrial democracies. The group, whose membership includes the United States, Canada, France, Germany, Italy, Japan, the United Kingdom, and Russia, meets periodically to discuss world economic issues and other mutual concerns. In 1999 the G-20 was established to give emerging market countries representation in global economic decision making. Membership in the G-20 includes Argentina, Australia, Brazil, Canada, China, France, Germany, India, Indonesia, Italy, Japan, Mexico, Russia, Saudi Arabia, South Africa, South Korea, Turkey, the United Kingdom, the United States, and the European Union (EU).

Organization for Economic Cooperation and Development (OECD). This organization, headquartered in Paris, promotes economic and social welfare in the thirty member countries and stimulates growth in developing nations. In addition to the United States, members are Australia, Austria, Belgium, Canada, the Czech Republic, Denmark, Finland, France, Germany, Greece, Hungary, Iceland, Ireland, Italy, Japan, South Korea, Luxembourg, Mexico, the Netherlands, New Zealand, Norway, Poland, Portugal, the Slovak Republic, Spain, Sweden, Switzerland, Turkey, and the United Kingdom.

CHAPTER SIXTEEN

THE NAVY RESERVE

A strong Naval Reserve is essential, because it means a strong Navy. The Naval Reserve is our trained civilian navy, ready, able, and willing to defend our country and suppress her enemies should the need arise again.

—Rear Admiral Felix Johnson, 26 October 1946

We cannot be the Navy we are today without our Reserve component.

—Admiral Gary Roughead, Chief of Naval Operations

Representing 20 percent of the total Navy force, the Navy Reserve plays a larger and more critical role than ever in the Navy's routine operations. Today the Navy Reserve is an important component of the Navy's balanced and affordable force. Every Navy officer should have a basic understanding of the organization and role the Navy Reserve plays in meeting peacetime commitments and wartime requirements.

History of the Navy Reserve

The U.S. Navy Reserve was officially established on 3 March 1915, although historians trace the advent of the Reserve to colonial days and the Revolutionary War. Predecessors of the citizen-sailors of today include the members of naval militias in Massachusetts (1888) and then New York, Pennsylvania, and Rhode Island (1889). In 1891 the Office of Naval Militia was established in the Navy Department. Six years later, sixteen states had naval militia whose personnel served with the Regular Navy during the Spanish-American War.

The Division of Naval Affairs replaced the Office of Naval Militia in the Navy Department by 1914. During World War I, approximately 30,000 reserve officers and 300,000 reserve enlisted members served on active duty at sea and ashore.

In the period between World War I and II, there were no Ready Reserve units as we know them today, and no reserve officers on extended active duty. Reserve officers trained during voluntary two-week active-duty tours on combatant ships or at shore stations. Just prior to World War II, some junior officers went on active duty following their graduation from NROTC, so that in the opening days of the war a few members of the Reserve were serving in fleet units. After Pearl Harbor, larger numbers of reservists helped man and command the Navy's ships, submarines, and aircraft; by the end of the war, four out of five Navy personnel were reservists. Many reservists remained in the Navy after the war, either on extended active duty as reservists or as members of the Regular Navy. Shortly after the end of the war, the Navy set up the framework for the modern-day Navy Reserve by establishing the Naval Air Reserve Training Command and the Naval Surface Reserve Training Command.

During the Korean War, many reservists returned to active duty for the duration of the war. During the conflict in Vietnam, the President decided not to call up the Reserve, except for selected air and Seabee units, but to use the draft to obtain extra manpower. This decision resulted in the widespread perception that the Reserve had become largely irrelevant to the national defense.

In the early 1970s, in response to a Reserve force that had fallen far behind the active forces in its training and equipment readiness, the "Total Force" concept was born. This plan recognized that the Navy Reserve was likely to be an important part of any response to a future national emergency, and that modern equipment and training were essential to ensure the Navy Reserve could rapidly and seamlessly integrate into the fleet.

During the 1980s the Department of Defense introduced a "horizontal integration" strategy, which assigned reservists to train with the active commands they would serve with in time of national emergency. During this period the Navy Reserve increased in size and received the most modern equipment, including F-14 Tomcat and F/A-18 Hornet aircraft, HH-60 Seahawk helicopters, and FFG-7-class–guided missile frigates. Horizontal integration remains a key feature of today's Navy Reserve training and mobilization strategy.

The first major test of the "Total Force" concept came during the Desert Shield/Desert Storm Operations of 1990–91. A large-scale call-up of some 22,000 medical, logistics, Seabee, and other reserve personnel demonstrated that the reserve forces could indeed be rapidly mobilized and deployed in response to a crisis situation.

Following the 11 September 2001 terrorist attacks, more than 20,000 Navy Reservists were mobilized to take part in Operations Noble Eagle (DoD support to homeland security), Enduring Freedom, and Iraqi Freedom. In 2005 Congress officially redesignated the Naval Reserve as the Navy Reserve.

Components of the Reserve

In 2010 the Navy Reserve consisted of approximately 690,000 personnel in three components: the Ready Reserve, which is the primary source of personnel for mobilization, the Standby Reserve, consisting of individuals who have a temporary disability or hardship and those who hold key defense related civilian jobs, and the Retired Reserve. The majority of reservists are in the latter two components, which are at a lower level of readiness, and subject to being called for active duty only in the event of a declared war or other national emergency. Without the concurrence of Congress, the President may order members of the Ready Reserve to active-duty status during war or national emergency.

All individuals obligated to serve in the Navy Reserve are initially assigned to the Ready Reserve, and most remain in the Ready Reserve for the remainder of their service obligation. There are three groups in the Ready Reserve: the Selected Reserve (SELRES), Full Time Support (FTS), and the Individual Ready Reserve (IRR).

SELRES members hold valid mobilization billets and drill for pay. The First Call program provides an expedited mechanism to activate a small number of SELRES members with critical skills, such as crisis action team members, in the early stages of developing crises. SELRES members who elect to fill First Call billets can expect to report to their assigned duty stations within one to seven days of notification and serve on active-duty status in the training and administration of the Navy Reserve Force program.

FTS members serve on active-duty status in the training and administration of the Navy Reserve Force program; the Canvasser Recruiter (CANREC) program includes FTS reservists temporarily recalled to active duty to serve as recruiters.

The IRR includes members of the Voluntary Training Unit (VTU) and Active Status Pool (ASP). VTU members participate in monthly drills for which they receive retirement credit but are not paid. ASP members do not participate in monthly drills but may accrue retirement credits through correspondence courses.

Drilling reservists, the IRR, and some standby reservists are considered to be on "active status." This term, not to be confused with the term "active duty," denotes personnel who are eligible to train (sometimes without pay) as well as to earn points toward retirement, and who may be considered for advancement or promotion. These are also the first reservists called to active duty upon mobilization.

Conversely, reservists who are not on "active status" may not receive drill pay, earn retirement points, or be considered for promotion.

Figure 16-1 illustrates the relationships between the various categories of the Navy Reserve.

Mission and Organization of the Navy Reserve

The mission of the Navy Reserve is to provide strategic depth and deliver the full range of operational capabilities to the Navy and Marine Corps team as well as to Joint forces. The Navy Reserve can provide a broad range of cost-effective, adaptable military capabilities and civilian skills to fulfill mission requirements.

The Navy Reserve is commanded by a vice admiral, with a subordinate rear admiral in charge of Navy Reserve Forces Command. Types of Navy Reserve assignments include aviation, engineering, information warfare, public affairs, intelligence, special operations, surface warfare, and logistics.

Navy Reserve Participation and Administration

Retirement Point Credit. Navy Reserve officers in an active status must maintain minimum participation levels, which are measured in retirement point credits. All officers must earn fifty points per year for that year to count as a qualifying retirement year. All members receive fifteen gratuitous membership points per year; they must earn any additional points. Reservists earn one point for each day of annual training or inactive-duty training period. There are two training periods per day on a typical weekend drill, for a total of four points per drill weekend. Reservists may earn additional points for completion of correspondence courses and other professional training. Members who have completed their minimum service obligations but who are not earning sufficient points to remain in active status are transferred to the inactive component of the Standby Reserve.

Reserve retirement pay, in addition to other retirement benefits discussed in chapter 20, is collected beginning at age sixty by retired members with at least twenty creditable years of combined active duty and reserve service. The amount of retirement pay is calculated based on the member's pay grade and retirement-point total.

Transfer to the Navy Reserve from Active Duty. Many officers who leave active duty elect to retain their commissions in the Navy Reserve. In fact, acceptance of a Reserve Commission is a prerequisite for acceptance of separation pay for officers who are involuntarily discharged prior to reaching retirement eligibility.

Active Status		Inactive Status	Retired Status
READY RESERVE Ready Reserve = SELRES + FTS + IRR			
IRR (Individual Ready Reserve) IRR = VTU + ASP + MMIRRG **45% of Ready Reserve**			
VTU (Volunteer Training Unit) Drill in a non-pay status	**ASP** (Active Status Pool) Non-drilling status	**USNR-S2** (Standby Reserve) <u>Inactive</u> Cannot earn points or promote	Retired Qualified for reserve retirement or FTS retirement
	MMIRRG (Merchant Marine) Non-drilling status		
USNR-S1 (Standby Reserve) <u>Active</u> Key Federal Employees Hardships			
SELRES (Selected Reserve) Hold valid mobilization billets for pay			
FTS (Full Time Support) Reservists on active duty 365 days a year (includes CANREC)			

Figure 16-1 Navy Reserve

CHAPTER SEVENTEEN

CAREER PLANNING

Believe it or not, you are the largest factor in the development of your naval career. If I've learned anything over my own career it's that you must have a plan. . . .

Webster's dictionary defines the word "career" as a course or passage. You wouldn't get underway for sea without a navigational plan or conduct flight operations without a flight plan, so why make a career of the Navy without a plan? Take my advice and set aside some time in your busy schedule to plot a course for success.

—Rear Admiral J. I. Maslowski, USN

You've got to be careful if you don't know where you're going, because you might not get there.

—Yogi Berra

Arguably, the quality of the officer corps in the Navy has never been higher than it is today. Of course, it goes almost without saying that a strong performance record is a prerequisite for success, but in today's competitive environment, being a good performer will not likely be sufficient in itself. To give yourself the best possible chance, you must aggressively manage all aspects of your career.

You should seek out the hard, operational jobs in which your outstanding performance will be noticed. A balanced career of operational, overseas, joint duty, Washington, and staff assignments will demonstrate the diversity of your talents and experiences. In determining your next career move, seek the advice of your detailer, your XO and your CO, and other senior officers whose judgment you trust. You might even want to study the biographies of senior officers in your community to find out more about their assignments and achievements as junior officers.

Accomplishing certain well-defined milestones, although no guarantee of success, will greatly enhance your promotion opportunities. Such milestones include achieving warfare qualification, obtaining a postgraduate degree or attending a War College, and obtaining Joint Qualified Officer (JQO) designation. In addition, you must carefully review and manage your official record to ensure that selection boards have a current and accurate picture of your achievements. It is safe to say that every year great officers fail to select for promotion because they neglect to review their records and correct outdated or incorrect information.

This chapter will give you an overview of the subject of career management and provide you with the tools you need to begin managing your career from the time you begin your first tour.

Detailing

Navy Personnel Command (NPC) executes personnel policies for the Navy. As previously discussed in chapter 3, two groups of officers at NPC, detailers and placement officers, are responsible for assigning officers to appropriate billets. Detailers are responsible for a group of officers in a particular pay grade and designator, and placement officers are responsible for a group of similar ships or commands. Detailers and placement officers have different "customers"; your detailer represents you and is primarily concerned with finding a billet that is a good match for your rank, qualifications, desires, and career needs, while a placement officer represents a command and is primarily concerned with finding the best-qualified officers to fill that command's billets. By working together, they meet the needs of individual Navy officers as well as commands.

When an officer is due for rotation, the placement officer controlling the officer's current billet posts the billet with the appropriate detailer, specifying the requirements of the billet. The detailer takes into account rotation date, personal preferences, and career progression needs of possible candidates for the billet and then confers with placement to write a set of orders for an officer who is a good match.

Three factors, called the detailing triad, come into play as a detailer decides where to send an officer for his or her next tour. The first factor, personal preference, is clearly the most important and visible factor to the officer being detailed. The second factor is based on the best career interests of the officer. Detailers are well aware of the tours that officers require to remain competitive with their peers, and they will not permit officers to stray too far from these requirements, regardless of their personal preferences. The third factor, often called "needs of the Navy," recognizes the sometimes harsh reality that, all other considerations aside, critical billets must be filled with the best possible candidates.

Admiral Nimitz summed it up well while talking with a group of young destroyer captains during World War II. Being asked for advice on career planning, he said,

> First, determine what career you want to follow, and plan it all the way to the top. Then ask for the best and toughest job available that suits your career path. If you present your case well to your detailer, you should get your requested job, then just continue on up the ladder as far as you can. If you don't get it, plead your case firmly and honestly. If you are turned down a second time, keep quiet, go to your assigned duty, and carry it out better than it was ever done before. If you do so, the chances are that your detailer will ask you what job you want the next time around. After all, he has to fill difficult and prestigious jobs with good men. If you have proved that you are a good man, he will need you. Remember, you are always allowed one objection. If you don't succeed, never say another word about it.

Duty-Preference Information. Not too long after you arrive at a new duty station, you should start working with your detailer on your next set of orders. If you are coming up for a new set of orders and your detailer has no preferences on file for you, he or she may assume that you don't care where you go and detail you accordingly.

To avoid this situation, there are several methods you can use to advise your detailer of your desires for your next assignment. The first is the "dream sheet," Officer Duty-Preference and Personal Information Card, NAVPERS 1301/1. In it, you will fill out your top three choices for type of command, type of billet and geographic location, and then you will rank those three factors from most to least important. There is also space on the card for free-form text to describe any special circumstances or desires. The same information may be submitted electronically using BUPERS Online, described later in this chapter. As another alternative, although it is generally preferable to put your desires in writing, you may also telephone your detailer. Detailers are difficult to get on the telephone directly, but you may leave a voice mail message or request that he or she call back so you can speak in person at a later time.

Communication with NPC

BUPERS Online. First established as a direct dial-in computer bulletin board in 1991, this site has steadily evolved and is now a secure web portal known as BUPERS Online (https://www.bol.navy.mil). BUPERS Online provides the fleet with easy access to detailers, up-to-date policies, news and information, personal information on promotion boards or advancement results, orders status, status of various packages submitted for approval, and more. This technology allows members to communicate with NPC from virtually anywhere. To maintain the security and integrity of personnel files, a common access card (CAC) is required to access the site.

BUPERS Online provides access to your Official Military Personnel File (OMPF) as well as medical and dental records. Other services available on BUPERS Online include communication with detailers or other NPC departments, retention, career information and Navy policy bulletins, NAVADMIN and NAVOP messages, advancement exam and board results, orders-status information, and duty-preference submissions.

Email. One of the easiest and most direct methods of communicating with your detailer is email. Use of email instead of the telephone prevents those lengthy "on-hold" sessions waiting for your detailer to have a free minute and allows him or her to research the answers to your questions before responding.

Selection Boards

Precedence. Many selection boards consider officers within certain eligibility criteria, including designator and precedence number. Following one year of service, ensigns are assigned six-digit precedence numbers, which represent their relative seniority on the Navy active-duty list, based on their year of commissioning (Year Group) and lineal standing within that Year Group. All May and June graduates of the Naval Academy and Naval ROTC are normally assigned the same date of rank, with their relative precedence determined by their final class standing, which is based on a weighted average of academic average, Naval Science course average, and Naval Aptitude grade. The *Register of Commissioned and Warrant Officers of the United States Navy and Marine Corps and Reserve Officers of Active Duty* (NAVPERS 15.018 series)—a.k.a., "The Blue Book," provides the official precedence list.

Statutory Boards. Statutory boards are those governed by law, primarily Title 10, USC. These boards affect promotion, selective early retirement (SERB), and continuation of officers who have reached the maximum years of service for their rank and would otherwise be subject to statutory retirement. Statutory boards are convened by the Secretary of the Navy, and results are approved by the President and Secretary of Defense or Secretary of the Navy. Membership on statutory boards is set by statute and SECNAVINST 1401.3 (which is very specific as to designator mix and pay grade of board members).

Administrative Boards. All other boards are administrative and governed by instruction or policy rather than law. Administrative boards are convened to decide such matters as selection for department head, XO, and CO and selection for postgraduate education or War College attendance, and also to consider requests for redesignation to another officer community. Administrative boards are convened and approved by either the Chief of Naval Personnel (CNP) or the Deputy CNP. The board sponsor determines membership requirements for administrative boards.

Administrative boards can be every bit as critical to an officer's career as statutory boards, because virtually all officers have career milestones, determined through administrative board action, that they must meet to maintain upward mobility. An officer's failure to select for his or her next career milestone determined by an administrative board often foreshadows failure to select for promotion during a future statutory board.

Preparation. Order and review your record on CD for accuracy at least six months in advance of the board, as discussed in chapter 3. You may do this in person at NPC, or you may request a copy on CD to be sent to you. You may submit correspondence to the board offering evidence of corrections to augment your record. However, because at adjournment each board will destroy all submitted correspondence, it is important that you ensure that permanent corrections to your record are also made. This is your record, and ultimately you are responsible for its accuracy. Some professional military associations will review your record for a nominal fee to help you identify any errors that may need to be corrected. When reviewing your record, check the following:

- Ensure a current officer photograph is included.
- Verify awards are correct.
- Check all special qualifications and education sections.
- Make sure all fitness reports are present and there are no gaps over thirty days.
- Submit missing information to Navy Personnel Command (PERS-312) via the NPC Web site (http://www.npc.navy.mil/Channels). Drill down as follows: Boards > Active Duty officer > Letter to the Board FAQ's (located in lower right, under "board preparation").

In addition to your preparations, the fitness report master file is queried six weeks prior to the board convening for fitness report continuity. If a fitness report is missing, your command will be sent a message.

If time is short before the board convening date, and you believe important documentation is missing from your file, you should contact your detailer for assistance and advice and send a copy of any missing documentation directly to the president of the board in accordance with guidance in the MILPERSMAN. A command endorsement of your letter to the president of the board is not necessary.

Only those officers who are eligible before a selection board may correspond with the president. The board will return without action any endorsement or letter written on your behalf that is not sent via you, as well as any correspondence received after the convening date of the board.

Take special care to ensure that your official full-length photograph, as discussed in chapter 3, is current and in the appropriate uniform and format. Before mailing your photograph, show it to your department head, XO, CO, or other officers you trust. Ask them for their opinion of the photograph. Is your posture poor or do you appear overweight? Does your uniform or personal grooming look sloppy? Don't send in a photograph that puts you in a less than favorable light; correct any discrepancy and have a new photograph taken.

The Precept. A precept is a document, signed by the convening authority and directed to the president of the board, giving general and specific guidance to the board regarding the criteria upon which their selections should be based. The precept is the only guidance for selection provided to a board.

The mission of any selection board is to select those "best qualified." The precept provides detailed guidance on how the board should assess the relative qualifications of the individuals under consideration, and it may provide specific instruction to ensure equal consideration for minority and women officers as well as officers with nontraditional career paths. A precept may direct the board to emphasize certain particularly relevant aspects of the officers' records, such as performance of duty in a joint billet or in other positions relating to the selection.

Precepts for administrative boards may also contain additional specific guidance, including quotas or numbers of primary selectees and alternates, additional program eligibility criteria, and other information the board sponsor deems necessary.

Information Considered by the Board. Statutory boards are only allowed to consider an officer's official service record and any correspondence the officer submits to the board about his or her record. The board will not consider information submitted from any other source. Administrative boards follow a similar procedure, except for those boards that require application packages (i.e., Federal Executive Fellowship (FEF), test pilot, lateral transfer/redesignation, etc.). In such cases, the boards also review the application packages.

Board Procedures. Board membership is kept secret until the board convenes. To ensure a level playing field, officers under consideration by a board may not visit their detailers prior to or during board deliberations. When the board convenes, the precept is discussed and the board gets to work.

As an initial step, two board members review each individual record. One of these members annotates a copy of his or her assigned officers' PSRs and is responsible for briefing the officers' careers to the rest of the board. After this records review phase, the board moves into a room called the "tank" (a private, theater-like room) for the selection phase. The annotated PSRs are projected onto large screens in the tank and the appropriate board members brief each officer's record.

After each record is presented, the board members, using the precept as guidance, use handsets to vote a confidence level for the selection of the candidate. Each member may vote either 100 percent (if 100 percent sure the candidate should be selected), 75 percent, 50 percent, 25 percent, or 0 percent (if certain that the candidate should *not* be selected). After all the votes are cast, a computer in the tank combines them into an overall confidence rating, which is then displayed as a percentage on a monitor for all the board members to see.

The confidence rating of each candidate is recorded and then ranked after all the records have been reviewed. At this point, the board normally votes to consider some number of top scorers to be "tentatively selected" as well as some number of the bottom-scoring candidates to be "dropped from further contention." All the candidates between the "selected" and "dropped" scores are then re-reviewed. Several tank sessions are usually required before the board comes up with the number of candidates they feel are best qualified.

Releasing the Results. After the board completes its deliberations and votes to confirm the tentative selections, a "select" list is provided by the Chief of Naval Personnel to the Secretary of the Navy via the VCNO/CNO and Navy JAG. Board results for promotions to the rank of lieutenant commander and above are subject to additional levels of review; from SECNAV, reports go to Chairman, Joint Chiefs of Staff, for review of board selection statistics related to joint duty. The board report is then forwarded to SECDEF, who approves the list of selectees and forwards it to the White House. The White House forwards the nomination to the Senate Armed Services Committee (SASC), which reviews the list and may then raise questions about individual names. Following this review, the SASC delivers the list to the full Senate and recommends confirmation. The entire process normally takes four months from SECNAV board callout to Senate confirmation. SECNAV's goal is to have the selection message released within one hundred days. Generally, only promotion lists are published in an ALNAV Navy message; individual notification is the rule for SERBs, continuations, and administrative board results.

Special Board Procedures. Failure of selection (FOS) for promotion is not in itself grounds for requesting a special board. The only time a special board is granted is when the Secretary of the Navy (or other designated authority) determines that an eligible officer was not considered by a regularly scheduled promotion selection board because the action of the board was contrary to law or involved material error of fact or material administrative error, or that the board did not have certain material information before it for consideration. Special board procedures apply to active-duty officers only.

Education Programs and Subspecialties

A postgraduate education is becoming an absolute necessity in today's ever more competitive Navy. A master's degree demonstrates your initiative and provides you with necessary skills that allow you to develop an area of expertise in addition to your primary warfare specialty.

There are many windows in your career to pursue a master's degree and a number of ways to do it. Many postgraduate programs require some type of obligated service. Close consultation with your detailer is essential to determine which program and what time to attend are best for you.

In almost every competitive category and grade, officers who have attended or are attending postgraduate school fare better than the fleet average in selection for promotion. The following is an excerpt from a recent promotion board precept: "The board

The School of Business and Public Policy, one of four schools at the Naval Postgraduate School, delivers solid business school lessons for officers in the U.S. military.

shall give favorable consideration to those officers with relevant graduate education, experience in specialized areas, and Professional Military Education (PME). Best-qualified officers seek opportunities to broaden their cultural awareness through experiences and education and to enable better communication in a global operating environment."

Naval Postgraduate School (NPS). The Navy's graduate institution, NPS, located in Monterey, California, offers master's and doctoral degree programs in fifty-five technical and managerial curricula that are relevant to a Navy officer's career. Of the approximately two thousand students enrolled in degree programs, almost half are Navy and Marine Corps officers, and the remainder are officers and civilians from other U.S. services and federal agencies, and military officers from sixty other nations. Attending NPS is contingent upon a strong professional record and past academic performance.

Academic performance is determined by use of the academic profile code (APC), which is computed by the NPS admissions office, based on previous academic transcripts. All applicants to NPS must submit an online application and transcripts for all undergraduate and graduate academic work. Enclosure (3) to OPNAVNOTE 1520 provides an explanation of the APC.

Civilian Universities. Many specialized curricula that are not taught at NPS are instead offered at civilian universities, with tuition funded by NPS. OPNAVNOTE 1520 provides a list of these curricula and schools.

Tuition Assistance (TA). This popular financial benefit pays off-duty college tuition, up to a maximum fiscal year credit limit of sixteen semester hours, or twenty-four quarter hours. Payment for tuition and fees will not exceed $250.00 per semester hour or $166.67 per quarter hour. You may be eligible to receive tuition assistance toward the completion of a master's degree earned during off-duty hours. To receive funds you must agree to remain on active duty for at least two years after the completion of the last course for which you used TA benefits.

Navy College Program. The Navy College Center (NCC) offers a call center that is open seven days a week to provide educational counseling, testing, and referrals about off-duty voluntary education programs and services. Each major shore installation has a Navy College Office (NCO) staffed by professionals who advise Navy members on academic programs and administer on-base education programs. Before you enroll in any college course funded by TA, you must file an individual education plan with the NCO.

Sailor/Marine American Council on Education Registry Transcript (SMART). SMART provides an academically accepted record of college credit for military training and occupational experience.

Servicemembers Opportunity Colleges, Navy (SOCNAV). SOCNAV is a consortium of over 1,800 colleges and universities that permit Navy members to easily transfer credits between member institutions to complete degree requirements.

VA Educational Programs. You may be eligible to participate in one or more programs administered by the Department of Veterans Affairs, including the Montgomery GI Bill (MGIB), the Post-9/11 GI Bill, and the Reserve Educational Assistance Program (REAP).

Olmsted Scholarships. A small number of junior officers with between three and eleven years of service are selected for this program each year. Nominations are solicited annually by NAVADMIN in the June/July time frame. The Olmsted Scholarship program offers Navy officers with exceptional foreign language aptitude the opportunity to pursue two years of graduate study at a foreign university.

Subspecialty Codes (SSCs). SSCs apply to billets that require special qualifications beyond those of a particular designator or group of designators. SSCs define the field of application and additional education, experience, or training that are required to satisfy those requirements and that are applicable to unrestricted line, restricted line, and staff corps officers. The subspecialty system is also the basis for generating the Navy's advanced education and training program requirements. An officer may be designated as a proven subspecialist following successful completion of a qualifying billet assignment.

Your eligibility for subspecialty coding is based on your education and experience. You may receive a subspecialty code by completing a graduate education program. You may also earn a subspecialty code by serving in certain types of billets. Make sure that your fitness reports accurately document your subspecialty experience and that your transcripts are included in your record.

The following is a list of subspecialty code areas for unrestricted line (URL), restricted line (RL), and staff corps officers:

2XXX	National security studies
3XXX	Resource management and analysis
4XXX	Applied disciplines
5XXX	Engineering and technology
6XXX	Operations
11XX	Civil Engineering corps subspecialties
12XX	Judge Advocate General (JAG) corps subspecialties
13XX	Supply corps subspecialties
14XX	Chaplain corps subspecialties
15XX and 16XX	Medical corps subspecialties
17XX	Dental corps subspecialties
18XX	Medical Service corps subspecialties
19XX	Nurse corps subspecialties

Suffixes given to personnel and billets to indicate the level of experience that an individual has, or that the billet requires, are as follows:

A Associates level of education (personnel only)

B Validated requirement for master's or higher level of education (billets only)

C PhD level of education—proven subspecialist

D PhD level of education—non-proven

E Baccalaureate level of education (personnel only)

F Master's degree not fully meeting Navy criteria in a degree program—proven subspecialist

G Master's degree not fully meeting Navy criteria in a degree program—non-proven

I Master's degree completed by immediate graduate education program not fully meeting Navy criteria in a degree program (personnel only)

J Fully trained (Medical corps only)

K Board certified/Board equivalency certified (Medical corps only)

L Post-bachelor's certificate level of education (personnel only)

M Post-master's graduate degree or certificate level of education (e.g., engineer's degree or certificate)—proven subspecialist

N Post-master's graduate degree or certificate level of education—non-proven

P Master's level of education—non-proven

Q Master's level of education—proven subspecialist

R Significant experience—proven subspecialist

S Significant experience—non-proven

T In training for a subspecialty code (personnel only)

V Formal preparation beyond basic professional education in a program approved by Bureau of Medicine and Surgery (Medical corps only)

Specialty Career Paths (SCPs). Through this option, officers in the surface, aviation, and submarine communities can develop skills in one of a number of mission areas. Providing an alternative to the traditional command at sea career path, SCPs provide the Navy with midgrade and senior officer expertise in the following critical skills:

- Operations analysis
- Financial management
- Naval operational planner
- Antiterrorism/Force protection
- Shore installation management
- Antisubmarine warfare
- Mine warefare
- Missile defense
- Strategic sealife
- Education and training management

Officers selected for this program are eligible for postgraduate education, training, and experience in their specialty area and for competition for CO/XO or equivalent assignments.

Fellowship Programs

White House Fellowship. The White House Fellows program was established in 1964 to provide a few motivated young Americans with the experience of direct and personal involvement in the process of governing the nation. Fellows are assigned to the White House staff, the Vice President, members of the Cabinet, and to other top-level executives. In addition to their duties as special assistants, White House fellows participate in an educational program revolving around the government's processes, personalities, and problems.

Federal Executive Fellowship (FEF) and Cyber FEF (CFEF). The Navy's Federal Executive Fellowship program helps fill the Navy's requirements for senior-level officers knowledgeable in the formulation and conduct of foreign policy and in the intricacies of the decision-making process at the highest levels of government. To be eligible you must be an unrestricted or restricted line officer in the permanent pay grade of lieutenant commander or above. Graduate-level education or a subspecialty in political-military affairs or national security affairs is desired but not required. CFEF places officers with the 1600 designator in select nonprofit research organizations to increase their understanding of information technology and cyberspace policy.

Secretary of Defense Corporate Fellowship Program (SDCFP). The SDCFP was established in 1995 to foster innovation by providing officers with firsthand experience in the strategic management practices of U.S. corporations. Officers participating in this program can expect to utilize their experiences to improve innovation in the Navy in a subsequent shore tour.

Legislative Fellows Program (LEGIS). The LEGIS provides an annual opportunity for Navy officers to broaden their experience and knowledge in operations and organization of Congress while enhancing the Navy's ability to fulfill its role in the national policy development process.

Professional Military Education: U.S. Service Colleges

In order to attend a Service College (also called a War College) you must have completed your bachelor's degree and been screened through a selection board. Most War College curricula are ten to twelve months in length and require an active service obligation of two years following graduation. Some War Colleges award a master's degree upon successful completion; the Navy awards subspecialty codes to the graduates of many War Colleges. Additional information is available in MILPERSMAN 1520-010.

Senior War Colleges. Senior war colleges (open to officers in pay grades O-5 and senior) are in the following locations: Air War College, Maxwell Air Force Base, Alabama; Army War College, Carlisle Barracks, Pennsylvania; Industrial College of the Armed Forces (ICAF) Fort McNair, Washington, D.C.; USMC "Top Level" Quantico, Virginia; National War College, Fort McNair, Washington, D.C.; and Naval War College, Newport, Rhode Island.

Intermediate War Colleges. These war colleges, which are open to officers in pay grade O-4 (select) and senior, are located at Air Command and Staff, Maxwell Air Force Base, Alabama; Army Command/General Staff, Fort Leavenworth, Kansas; USMC Command and Staff, Quantico, Virginia; and Naval Command and Staff, Newport, Rhode Island.

In addition to the resident programs listed above, the following war colleges offer nonresident programs that may be offered by correspondence courses or evening classes in certain areas: Naval Command and Staff, Air Command and Staff, and Army Command and Staff. Some distance learning programs are self-paced, while others conform to a specific schedule; some require a selection board for acceptance, but others offer open enrollment. There are also some opportunities to attend certain foreign war colleges.

Joint Qualifications System

Title 10, USC, sec. 619a, commonly referred to as the Goldwater-Nichols Act, requires that any officer appointed to flag rank must have completed a tour of duty in a joint duty assignment. Although the wording of the law is clear, until recently the definition of the term "joint duty assignment" was subject to some interpretation.

Effective as of 2008, active-component officers must be designated as a joint qualified officer (JQO) prior to appointment to flag rank. JQS allows officers to earn joint qualification through a combination of joint education, experience, training, and other military education.

Officer Communities

Navy officers can be broadly grouped into three categories: URL, RL, and staff corps. Within each broad grouping are more specific categories, called designators.

Designators. Each officer in the Navy is assigned a designator, which consists of a four-digit number. The first three numbers correspond to the community in which the officer serves; the fourth number indicates whether the officer's status is in the regular Navy or some component of the Navy Reserve. A "0" as the final number indicates the officer is in the Regular Navy (USN), a "5" indicates the officer is in the active component of the Navy Reserve, and a "7" indicates the officer is assigned to the Full Time Support (FTS) component of the Navy Reserve. The designator for each of the officer communities described below is in parentheses following the noun name of the community. Where two designators are listed, the first is for officers in training and the second is for fully qualified officers.

Unrestricted Line. The distinguishing feature of an unrestricted line (URL) officer is that he or she is eligible for command at sea, meaning command of a warfighting unit. (Officers in the restricted line and staff corps are also eligible for command, but only ashore, and only within their respective specialties.) The designators of URL officers are:

- Surface warfare (116X /111X). An officer entering this field is initially assigned designator 116X until achieving surface warfare qualification, at which time his or her designator is changed to 111X. A subcategory of surface warfare is nuclear surface warfare (116XN /111XN).
- Aviation warfare (pilots: 139X/131X; naval flight officers [NFOs]: 137X/132X). All pilots and NFOs receive initial training at Naval Flight School in Pensacola, Florida, and then continue with training in specific aircraft types in fleet-readiness squadrons.
- Submarine warfare (117X/112X). Submarine warfare officers attend Nuclear Power School in Orlando, Florida, followed by prototype training before receiving their assignments to their first submarines.
- Special warfare (118X/113X). These officers serve in the areas of unconventional warfare, counterinsurgency, coastal and riverine interdictions, and tactical intelligence collection. Officers are initially assigned to Basic Underwater Demolition/SEALs (BUDS) training in Coronado, California.
- Explosive ordnance disposal (119X/114X). These officers perform explosive ordnance disposal (EOD) duties, operational diving, and expendable ordnance management (EOM). EOD officers receive their initial training at the Navy Diving and Salvage Training Center in Panama City, Florida, and the Naval School Explosive Ordnance Disposal at Eglin Air Force Base in Eglin, Florida.

Restricted Line. These are line officers who are restricted in the performance of their duties to certain specialized fields. RL designators include:

- Human resources (120X). Human resources officers plan, program, and execute manpower life cycle management.
- Engineering duty (EDO; 146X/144X). EDOs specialize in ship engineering, including research, design, acquisition, construction, maintenance, and modernization of weapons and combat systems.
- Aerospace engineering duty (AEDO; 151X). AED officers are specialists in aerospace engineering, including design, development, procurement, production, and support of air weapons systems and aircraft.

- Aerospace maintenance duty (AMDO; 152X). AMD officers are specialists in aviation maintenance management and related logistics support.
- Information professional (160X). Information professionals provide planning, acquisition, operation, maintenance, and security expertise in information, command and control, and space systems.
- Information warfare (161X). Information warfare officers are specialists in tactical cryptology, command and control, computer network operations, and space systems.
- Intelligence (163X). Intelligence officers are specialists in counterintelligence and investigations and information collection, analysis, and dissemination.
- Public affairs (PAO; 165X). PAOs are specialists in public and internal information and community relations.
- Foreign area officer (FAO; 171X). FAOs advise and assist in planning and implementing policy with respect to political–military aspects of international affairs; provide background information on international development, interpret and evaluate the political–military significance; advise, assist, and support the development of plans and policies; and maintain liaison with government agencies concerned with international affairs.
- Meteorology and oceanography (METOC; 180X). METOC officers are specialists in meteorologic and oceanographic mapping, charting, and geodesy.

Staff Corps. Staff corps officers are qualified professionals who are limited to service in their own fields of expertise. Staff corps designators are as follows:

- Medical corps (210X). Medical corps officers are licensed practicing physicians and osteopaths, or officers attending accredited schools of medicine or osteopathy. These officers may be general practitioners or specialists in a particular field of medicine. Medical corps officers serve aboard larger ships as well as in clinics and naval hospitals ashore.
- Dental corps (220X). Dental corps officers are licensed practicing dentists. These officers serve in hospitals and dental clinics, although some large ships with dental treatment facilities have dental officers assigned.
- Medical service corps (MSC; 230X). MSC officers are health care professionals other than physicians and nurses. This designator encompasses a wide variety of specialties, including pharmacy, hospital administration, occupational safety and health, physical therapy, and other health care fields.
- Judge advocate general (JAG) corps (250X). JAG officers are practicing attorneys who are responsible for administering the Navy's justice system as well as matters related to contract and business law.

- Nurse corps (290X). Nurse corps officers are graduates of accredited nursing schools. These officers generally rotate between shore and overseas commands; those who are specialists in particular fields may have different career paths.

- Supply corps (310X). Supply corps officers are specialists in business and logistics management including financial acquisition and contracts, system inventory, transportation and physical distribution, automated data processing, integrated logistics support, petroleum management, merchandising, and food service.

- Chaplain corps (410X). Members of the chaplain corps are ordained in their particular denominations and serve afloat and ashore. The chaplain corps is responsible for implementation of religious ministries throughout the naval service.

- Civil engineering corps (CEC; 510X). Civil engineering corps officers are engineers and architects specializing in facilities management, operations, maintenance, and planning, construction and contracting, petroleum engineering, or ocean and environmental engineering.

Warrant Officers and Limited Duty Officers. Officers commissioned through these programs have risen through the enlisted ranks and are assigned designators and follow career paths that make use of their specific areas of expertise. Chapter 7 provides additional information on these commissioning programs. Depending on their designator, warrant officers and LDOs may be either unrestricted line or staff corps.

CHAPTER EIGHTEEN

SUCCESSFUL LEADERSHIP

You don't manage people; you manage things. You lead people.

—Rear Admiral Grace Hopper

If you want an army to fight and risk death, you've got to get up there and lead it. An army is like spaghetti. You can't push a piece of spaghetti, you've got to pull it!

—General George S. Patton Jr.

In the program that prepared you for your commission, the instructors probably spent time discussing the traits of superior leaders. You may have read essays written by flag officers and been tasked with memorizing a list of leadership traits. Perhaps you wondered how such activities would ever make you into a good leader.

The answer is, they won't—at least not by themselves. Classroom study plants the seeds of knowledge so that, with practice and maturity, you will be able to train yourself to become the sort of leader you admire. No training program, however well designed, can make you into a leader. This is a voyage you must undertake of your own will and sustain under your own power.

A great leader won't necessarily have all of the traits that will be discussed in this chapter, but he or she will have put considerable effort into developing as many of them as possible.

Leadership Qualities

Knowledge. Your first requirement as a naval leader is to have a knowledge of yourself, your profession, and your ship or unit. Do you know your own strengths and weaknesses? Are you prepared to play to your strengths and compensate for or correct your weaknesses? Even John Paul Jones had his faults, but he led in such a way that his strengths overcame his weaknesses.

Do you know your profession? You can't maintain the respect of your people if you don't know your business. Your immediate goal should be to achieve journeyman-level proficiency in your chosen specialty, but beyond that, you must also develop your knowledge of the broader aspects of naval warfare.

Finally, do you know your ship or unit? Knowledge of your own command, and your responsibilities in it, are prerequisites to success in any position. Once you have such a knowledge base, you will be better able to assess any new situation that arises, make a decision, and come up with a plan of action to deal with it.

Throughout your career, never be satisfied with your current level of training or qualification or knowledge. Strive for continuous self-improvement.

Watchstanders on the bridge of littoral combat ship USS *Independence* (LCS 2).

Integrity. One of the Navy's core values discussed in chapter 2, integrity is the cornerstone of what Navy officers do. More than simply standing up for your beliefs, the development of integrity is an active process that begins when you identify what you believe in and determine what you are willing to sacrifice for your beliefs. If you don't know what your beliefs are, decide what you want them to be, and adopt them. If you wait until you are under duress before doing this kind of introspection, you may ultimately regret the choices you make. Set aside some

time early in your career to give some thought to your values, because the decisions you make will lie at the heart of your performance as a leader.

Loyalty. Many different kinds of loyalty will be demanded of you. Your para-
mount loyalty, of course, lies with the oath you have taken to defend the United
States and the Constitution, but you also will, and should, feel loyalty to the U.S.
Navy, to your ship or unit, to your superiors in command, to your subordinates, to
your shipmates, and, of course, to your family and friends.

Seniors in the Navy rightfully demand a high degree of personal loyalty from
their subordinates. The so-called acid test of loyalty is the ability to pass on the
order of a superior, perhaps an unpopular order with which you don't agree, and
make it appear to your subordinates as if the order originated with you.

Equally important as loyalty up the chain of command to your superiors is loyalty down the chain of command to your subordinates. Look after your people,
their interests, their welfare, and their careers. Such loyalty will help your subordinates build their own loyalty to you.

There will be occasions when your different loyalties will pull you in opposing
directions, when you find that you cannot be loyal to a shipmate, a superior, or a
friend without sacrificing your loyalty to the United States. If that is the case, your
choice is clear.

Maturity. More than simply the state of being fully grown, maturity entails a
sense of responsibility, of willingness to take "ownership" of a problem and see the
solution through to its completion. The absence of this quality is demonstrated
by someone who believes that a problem, whatever it is, will always be taken care
of by someone else. This kind of attitude can be absolute poison in an organization in which individuals must rely on each other to take care of problems without being told.

Displays of temper and incidents of ridicule and verbal abuse of subordinates
are signs of immaturity. This type of behavior, although it has never been condoned
in the Navy, has been drawing increased scrutiny in recent years. COs have been
relieved of their commands for such conduct, and junior officers have cut short
otherwise promising careers.

Will. In war, it is insufficient to simply "try" to win; the only alternative to winning a battle is losing it. To have will means to not give up in the face of over-
whelming obstacles, to find a way around them, over them, or through them to
achieve your goal. Will means not undertaking a mission with the thought that
you will do your best—it means never allowing yourself any thought but that you
will succeed.

Followership. You cannot successfully lead without in turn being a successful
follower of your own leaders. Your ability to do this will reinforce the followership
skills of your own subordinates.

Self-Discipline. Learn to set realistic goals and hold yourself to them. From your boss's perspective, discipline is probably the most highly prized quality that you can have. You cannot impose discipline on your subordinates without first imposing it on yourself.

Confidence. In an emergency situation, your subordinates will be looking to you to be cool and confident. If you seem frightened or indecisive, or if you lack self-confidence or appear not to trust your own judgment, you will put yourself and your people at unnecessary risk. Mental rehearsals will help you learn to maintain your composure in stressful situations, as will repetition and drill.

You can't expect to have confidence in your ability to perform as a Navy officer right away—true confidence comes at least in part from knowledge and experience. Hone and practice your skills, and learn from your own mistakes as well as the mistakes of others until you are comfortable with your expertise and have learned to rely on your own judgment.

Flexibility. The need for flexibility is often mistakenly used as an excuse not to make plans, but this is the wrong approach. In order to be flexible you must not only make plans, but also backup plans, and backup plans for your backup plans. Don't become too accustomed to the status quo, and be ready to adapt without complaint when the situation changes without notice.

Endurance. Serving in the Navy can be hard work and is often both physically and mentally stressful. The sometimes extreme demands of this profession are one reason the Navy places so much emphasis on the requirement to maintain yourself in good physical condition. You can't effectively lead your people if you are exhausted and stressed out.

Decisiveness. There is a feeling among some officers that decisiveness means voicing an instant and unchanging opinion on every subject. A better name for this is stupidity.

Decisiveness means the ability to commit yourself, and your subordinates, to a course of action. Once you have announced a decision and set a plan in motion, you risk sabotaging your success every time you have to change your plans. Although you should not hesitate to reverse your decision when necessary, you should bear in mind the costs of this change and only make that change with good reason.

In peacetime you may have the luxury of taking some time to make up your mind on a possible course of action. If the matter is not urgent, and if the situation is sufficiently complex to warrant it, spend time gathering information and consulting with others before you make your final decision. Don't announce your decision until it is necessary for you to do so; this permits you to keep evaluating new information with an open mind.

Initiative. Initiative has several allied qualities: imagination, aggressiveness, and the ability to look and think ahead. Don't wait for your superiors to tell you what needs to be done. A wise old seaman once said, "Initiative is the ability to do the right thing without being told."

Justice. Endeavor to treat your subordinates with absolute fairness. Personal prejudice—against race, gender, ethnic origin, personal appearance, or other similarly irrelevant factors—has no legitimate place in a leader's decision making.

Compassion. While you must insist on loyalty, discipline, performance, and dedication, you must remember that the men and women who work for you are not always motivated by the same things that you are. Make an effort to find out what motivates your subordinates, and keep it in mind in your dealings with them.

Be considerate of your subordinates' feelings. Remember the adage "Praise in public, criticize in private." It is equally important to be considerate of the feelings of your superiors and peers.

Forcefulness. The meek may someday inherit the earth, but in the interim they are unlikely to succeed as Navy officers. You will have to learn to stand up to your peers, recalcitrant subordinates, and occasionally with your superiors to do your job effectively.

Positive Attitude. Your attitude is incredibly contagious. If you radiate negativity, everyone who works for you will radiate negativity as well, and they won't perform at their best. Be enthusiastic, and demonstrate your enthusiasm to your people at every opportunity.

Communications Skills. It is not critical for you as a junior officer to be known as a great speaker or writer. However, you must be reasonably competent in both written and oral communications, or your lack of skill will adversely affect your performance and the performance of your people. Chapter 8 discusses oral and written communications in detail.

Personal Behavior. It is not enough to behave ethically and morally; as a leader and a role model you must also be perceived as ethical and moral. Strive to set an example for your subordinates. Set the highest standard you possibly can; the standard to which you hold yourself will determine the standard you can set for your subordinates.

Courage. Courage comes in two forms, physical and moral. Physical courage is overcoming your fears to carry out your duties in a dangerous situation. Moral courage can be even more difficult; it means having the courage of your convictions, "calling them like you see them," admitting your own mistakes, and speaking up when you feel a senior is about to make an error. Moral courage includes the ability to honestly counsel subordinates on their weaknesses, one of the hardest and most painful tasks of any leader.

Leadership Continuum Training

Although there is no substitute for leadership learned through on-the-job training (OJT), the Navy recognizes that these lessons should be augmented by formal classroom leadership training.

The Navy's Leadership Development Continuum provides progressive leadership development programs (LDP), addressing the requirements of sequential levels of leadership from initial entry through retirement. Each LDP is tailored to the needs of specific leadership positions, from leading petty officer (LPO) to commanding officer. LDPs include classroom training, e-learning, OJT, and other training events.

Officer Leadership Development courses include Division Officer Leadership, Department Head Leadership, Advanced Officer Leadership, Executive Officer Leadership, Command Leadership, and Major Command Leadership.

CHAPTER NINETEEN

COMMAND

You should enter the Navy for one purpose, to command ships, submarines and aircraft. Once you get such a command enjoy every minute of it.

—Fleet Admiral Chester Nimitz

The Captain of a ship, like the captain of a state, is given honor and privileges and trust beyond other men. But let him set the wrong course, let him touch ground, let him bring disaster to his ship or to his men, and he must answer for what he has done. No matter what, he cannot escape.

—*Wall Street Journal,* 14 May 1952

N*avy Regulations* art. 0801 states, "The responsibility of the commanding officer for his or her command is absolute. . . . The authority of the commanding officer is commensurate with his or her responsibility."

Preparation for Command

You will often hear that command is, as it should be, the aspiration of every Navy officer. Up to the point when you assume your first command, you will spend your entire career preparing for it. It isn't too early to start your preparations now. The book *Command at Sea* contains more detailed information on preparations for, and responsibilities of, command.

General Preparation. As you progress in your career, you should make an effort to learn all you can about the different aspects of your ships or units. You should pursue your professional education with a vigor, through reading, seminars, and classes, and by asking questions of your seniors and engaging your peers in discussion.

Observe your seniors and how they do their jobs. Study the careers of officers you admire and who have held the kinds of positions you aspire to hold. Find out all you can about what made these officers successful, base your own goals on their achievements, and emulate their personal qualities as much as possible. Maintain a familiarity with the notional career path for your designator, as discussed in chapter 17, as well as any new opportunities announced in message traffic and the NPC publication, *Perspective.*

Shiphandling. Every ship CO, regardless of his or her background, must be an outstanding shiphandler. The CO must be able to train the ship's junior officers in all aspects of shiphandling, and must, when necessary in an emergency, be prepared to make rapid decisions or even relieve the conning officer.

Like any other skill, shiphandling is an art that must be practiced. As a junior officer, take every possible opportunity to rehearse making approaches on other ships for underway replenishment, coming into an anchorage, conducting shipboard recovery during man-overboard drills, and other similar shiphandling evolutions. Many junior officers shy away from these opportunities because they are afraid of being embarrassed by their lack of skill. All novice shiphandlers make mistakes, but if you allow yourself to be discouraged by such fears, your skills will never improve. It is far better to perform poorly in a man-overboard drill, or in many man-overboard drills, than to perform poorly when a real sailor is lost over the side. If you are always the first junior officer on the bridge when you hear a

USS *Bunker Hill* (CG 52) makes an approach on the *Nimitz*-class aircraft carrier USS *Carl Vinson* (CVN 70) during a replenishment at sea.

training opportunity announced, you will make a favorable impression on your CO and your skills will develop rapidly.

If your duties permit, when you aren't actively engaged in conning the ship you should study the actions of the officer who is. Continually ask yourself what orders you would be giving to the helm and lee helm in the same situation, and attempt to project, based on the conning officer's orders, how the ship will respond. You can learn nearly as much by observing the actions of a skilled boat coxswain as you can from observing a skilled OOD. Because different classes of ships can handle quite differently, you should also ask your chain of command to allow you to spend time under way on other types of ships to broaden your experience.

Watchstanding. It is natural to look on your watchstanding requirements as a chore to be gotten through, but your watches are also your most valuable opportunities for learning your profession. When you become qualified as OOD underway, it means that your CO has the confidence in your judgment to allow you to make decisions in his or her absence. This is not only an enormous responsibility, but also an opportunity to practice, to some small degree, the experience of command. Similarly, when you become qualified to stand CDO in port, you will be completely responsible for the ship in your CO's absence. Treat these watches as rehearsals for your future command.

Training and Qualification for Command. As you progress through the ranks, selection boards will periodically review your record to determine your fitness for the next career milestone: department head, XO, and CO. Start early to find out what it takes to ensure that your record will compare favorably with those of your peers. Always ask your detailer to give you the most challenging assignments possible—provided you perform well, these are the jobs that will make you stand out in your peer group. Prior to the time you will be considered for command, make sure you have completed whatever your designator requires for command qualification. This process is at least partially intended to separate those who are committed to their desire to command from those who are not.

It is critically important that COs possess comprehensive knowledge of all aspects of their commands. If you are a surface warfare officer, it is well worth your while, regardless of your billet, to spend sufficient time standing watches in engineering as a junior officer to complete your EOOW qualification, and similarly to complete your tactical action officer (TAO) qualification at the earliest opportunity. Regardless of your community, you should seek out opportunities to add to your qualifications and to continue to hone the qualifications you already have.

Mental Preparation. In addition to the qualities of successful leaders discussed in the previous chapter, successful commanding officers share certain values that have been ingrained in the Navy's culture for hundreds of years. If you hope to follow in their footsteps, you should work to develop these values in yourself.

A CO's reputation is based in large part on the appearance and military smartness of the crew and ship because the CO's own example is what sets the standards for his or her subordinates. You should become familiar with the rules of military etiquette and practice them diligently. In addition, make sure that your appearance, grooming, and personal conduct are always above reproach, and demand no less from your subordinates.

Not solely a health and safety issue, cleanliness is as much a part of the Navy's culture as nearly any other visible quality. Cleanliness in work spaces, living spaces, and the exterior of the ship or unit represents visible evidence of a crew that takes pride in its command. Begin early to cultivate this habit in yourself, both by demanding the highest standards in your own spaces and by enforcing these standards throughout the command when you are standing watch as CDO.

Although commanding officers are not averse to risk, nor could they be, they are willing to work hard and ensure the same of their subordinates in order to minimize *unnecessary* risk. Examples of this are repetitive drills and exercises to keep a crew's readiness at its peak, and making extensive preparations for heavy weather whenever the possibility of a storm exists. It is far better to take precautions that later turn out to have been unnecessary than to find out too late that you should have made more extensive preparations.

You probably were exposed to the importance of "attention to detail" during your preparation for commissioning. Attention to detail means never leaving anything to chance or assuming that someone else will take care of it. An officer who exhibits this characteristic will ensure his organization works through an entire inspection checklist before the inspection team ever steps aboard, to preclude the possibility of unpleasant surprises.

Under the concept of "command by negation," a senior empowers a junior to make decisions, with the understanding that it is the junior's responsibility to keep the senior apprised of key aspects of the situation and his or her decisions; the senior will provide guidance or other direction only when required. This practice relieves seniors of some of the burdens of routine decision making, yet allows them to step in when they disagree with the proposed action. As a corollary to this concept, you may notice that your COs use "UNODIR" (unless otherwise directed) whenever possible in their communications with superiors.

Similarly, a good CO will help subordinates develop good judgment by telling them *what* to do without telling them *how* to do it. In the short run, this makes the CO's job harder, as there is a good chance inexperienced subordinates will make mistakes that could have been avoided had the CO offered additional "rudder orders." In the long run, however, the subordinates will learn more, develop more initiative and confidence in their own judgment, and be better prepared to respond in an emergency.

Assumption of Command

Relieving Command. Prior to reporting aboard, you will attend any necessary pipeline schools designated in your orders. Once reporting aboard, turnover can take as little as a few days or as long as a month. One to two weeks is normal. You will have to be flexible in arranging your turnover schedule, because the schedule of the ship or other deployable unit will likely be relatively fixed, and you owe the officer you will be relieving the courtesy of accommodating his or her scheduling needs.

Navy Regulations art. 08070 provides guidance on turnover procedures, and your type commander will likely have a separate, more detailed list of procedures. *Navy Regulations* require, at a minimum, the following of the offgoing commanding officer:

- Inspect the command in company with the relieving officer.
- In the case of a ship or other operational command, exercise the crew at general quarters and general drills, unless impracticable.
- Advise the relieving officer of any known defects or peculiarities in the command, particularly safety, operational readiness, training, habitability, or material conditions.
- Deliver to the relieving officer all unexecuted orders, all regulations and orders in force, and all official correspondence and information concerning the command and its personnel.
- Deliver to the relieving officer all documents required to be held by the CO and inventory the postal account (if the command has a post office).
- Deliver to the relieving officer all magazine keys and other keys in his or her possession.
- Inventory all communications security material.
- Submit fitness reports on all assigned officers and sign all logs, records, and other documents prior to the date of relief.
- Call the crew to muster for the change-of-command ceremony. Shore commands may modify this procedure.

In addition to these required turnover items, if time permits you should review the ship's bills, conduct a supply inventory and review the results of recent inspections and subsequent corrective actions on any discrepancies, the status of any equipment that is reported as out of commission, and other similar matters. It is customary for the offgoing CO to refrain from offering personal opinions of the members of the wardroom, so that the relieving CO has an open mind on the matter.

The offgoing CO prepares a letter listing any unsatisfactory conditions in the command at the time of turnover—particularly those dealing with safety, inoperative machinery or armament, significant lack of spare parts, ordnance or supplies, notable personnel deficiencies or training shortfalls, fiscal integrity or command performance—and proposing a plan of corrective actions. The relieving officer endorses this letter, noting any areas of disagreement and allowing the offgoing CO the opportunity to respond.

The offgoing CO has the primary responsibility for making arrangements for the change-of-command ceremony, although the relieving CO will be asked to provide a list of his or her personal guests. If a reception is held following the ceremony, the new and old COs share the expenses.

Organization and Administration

The *Standard Organization and Regulations Manual (SORM)* describes the basic principles of ship organization as well as the duties of officers and enlisted personnel. Your type commander and immediate superior in command (ISIC) may provide additional guidance. You or your XO will need to stay in frequent contact with your officer and enlisted placement officers to anticipate arrivals and detachments and to deal with other detailing contingencies that may arise.

Command Excellence

In a 1985 study, *Command Excellence* interviewed hundreds of officers and enlisted members at twenty-one commands in order to identify those qualities that distinguish the outstanding CO from the merely average CO. The study identified the following twelve characteristics of an outstanding CO:

- Targets key issues. Outstanding COs recognize that no commander, and no crew, can do everything that someone else wants done. Instead, these COs learned to set priorities to accomplish their most important tasks first.

- Gets crew support for command philosophy. Whether transcribed into a formal document or not, the successful CO has a command philosophy, and he or she communicates this philosophy to the wardrooms and crews both formally and through personal example.

- Develops the XO. The successful CO recognizes his or her responsibility to prepare the XO for command.

- Staffs to optimize performance. Although few commanders have the luxury of being able to choose their own crews, the CO who is most successful make an effort to put the best person in each position to take advantage of his or her talents.

- Gets out and about. The successful CO doesn't hide in his or her stateroom but practices what some have called MBWA ("management by walking around.") This keeps the CO in touch with the individual members of the command on a daily basis.

- Builds esprit de corps. The morale, pride, and teamwork of a command are the intangibles that make the difference between an outstanding command and an ordinary one. The best CO projects a "can-do" positive attitude, works to overcome conflicts among the crew, and praises and rewards good performance.

- Keeps his or her cool. An outstanding CO is not a "screamer," and doesn't react emotionally or impulsively.

- Develops a strong wardroom. The best wardrooms are cohesive, cooperative, and supportive of each other. A CO can do much to foster this environment by encouraging teamwork among members of the wardroom and taking a personal interest in the career development of each individual officer.

- Values the chiefs' quarters. The outstanding CO recognizes that the range of expertise and experience in the chiefs' mess is one of a command's most valuable assets, and the CO treats the chiefs accordingly.

- Ensures training is effective. The best CO believes the old Chinese proverb "The more you sweat in peace, the less you bleed in war." Such COs stress frequent, realistic, and thorough training.

- Builds positive external relationships. The outstanding CO understands the importance of establishing and maintaining strong relationships with external organizations such as the staff, shipyards and contractors, placement officers, base commanders, and others. Strong ties help the command to better accomplish its mission

- Influences successfully. An outstanding CO is able to persuade the crew to do an unpleasant job enthusiastically rather than grudgingly.

Setting Command Vision and Philosophy

By the time you achieve your first command, you will have had ample opportunity to formulate your own command vision—how you picture your unit will operate—through the study of leadership and daily observations of your seniors' practices. Before you arrive at your new command, you should plan to spend time formalizing this vision into a command philosophy statement that describes how you intend to achieve this vision, a statement that you can share with your new wardroom and crew. They will be eager to find out what you expect of them, and their learning curve will be considerably steeper if you provide them with written guidance than if they have to figure out what you expect based solely on trial and error. Once you have determined your command philosophy, you should consider holding an all-officers meeting and a series of "captain's calls" to personally put the word out to your wardroom and crew. Periodically you should review your decisions and actions to ensure that they are consistent with your command vision and philosophy.

The following are some considerations you may want to include in your command philosophy.

Safety. There is no higher priority in peacetime operations than the safety and well-being of the ship and crew. Make clear to the crew that this is your highest priority and that you expect it to be theirs as well.

Standards. What are your standards for excellence? However self-evident you may feel your standards are, it is still a good idea to put them in writing.

Priorities and Goals. Make sure every member of your crew is aware of what your top priorities are and what goals you have set for them.

Command Policies. Different COs have different philosophies about such mundane but important matters as leave and liberty, discipline, habitability, appropriate civilian attire, watchstanding, and qualifications. Particularly if your policies differ from those of your predecessor, make them known.

Support for Navy Policies. Your crew will be looking to you to endorse the Navy's policies on such issues as diversity, equal opportunity, drug- and alcohol-abuse prevention, sexual-harassment prevention, smoking cessation, and mental health and physical readiness. If you fail such endorsements, they may conclude that these issues are not important to you.

CHAPTER TWENTY

Separation and Retirement

*My sword I give him that shall succeed me in my pilgrimage, and my
courage and skill to him that can get it. My marks and scars I carry
with me, to be a witness for me, that I have fought his battles who will
now be my rewarder.*

—John Bunyan

*So safe on shore the pensioned sailor lies,
and all the malice of the storm defies . . .*

—William Somerville

Sooner or later, whether you decide to separate at the end of your initial obligated service or reluctantly retire after a thirty-year distinguished career, you will face the prospect of leaving the Navy. It is never too early to start planning for this eventuality, and this chapter is intended to help you in this effort.

Preseparation Plan

Like any complex undertaking, your successful transition to civilian life requires a plan. The following suggestions for developing a transition plan are drawn from the *Department of Defense Preseparation Guide*. This publication includes many more suggestions for retirees, as well as a comprehensive list of other preseparation resources.

One Year Prior to Separation. Schedule your Preseparation Counseling appointment. Review "Preseparation Counseling Checklist" (DD Form 2648) and develop your individual transition plan. Attend a Transition Assistance Program workshop. Begin working on your resume and researching the job market in your career field.

180 Days Prior to Separation. Begin actively networking with friends and colleagues and attending job fairs. Review and copy your medical and dental records. Request your DD Form 2586, "Verification of Military Experience and Training."

150 Days Prior to Separation. Begin building your career wardrobe and start actively applying for jobs and posting resumes to career Web sites. Schedule your separation physical examination.

120 Days Prior to Separation. If you have an interest in pursuing federal employment, begin investigating special federal programs and hiring opportunities for veterans and reviewing jobs and applying on the USAJOBS Web site (http://www .usajobs.opm.gov/). Begin arrangements to vacate government housing. Investigate options for transitional health care, if required. Explore the option of joining the Reserve or National Guard. Visit the area to which you plan to move and schedule job interviews there.

90 Days Prior to Separation. Investigate housing options in the area you plan to locate to and begin arrangements for shipment and storage of your household goods.

30 Days Prior to Separation. Make final decisions on your need for interim health care and life insurance. Review your DD Form 214, "Certificate of Release or Discharge from Active Duty" worksheet.

Separation

Officers who are not eligible for retirement may separate from the Navy. Such separation may be voluntary or involuntary.

Voluntary Separation. Officers who have fulfilled their initial active obligated service may submit a resignation from active duty. Such a resignation is termed "unqualified" for officers eligible for an honorable discharge upon separation. Officers may also request early separation in special circumstances including hardship. Subject to the needs of the Navy, separations are normally approved when the officer has completed minimum time on station for the particular type of assignment and has fulfilled any other active-service obligations due to receipt of educational benefits or special pay or due to other circumstances. When requesting separation, submit your letter of unqualified resignation nine to twelve months in advance of the date you desire to separate. Regular officers who have not yet completed their minimum service obligation will be automatically considered for appointment in the Navy Reserve, and approval of such a resignation request will generally be contingent on acceptance of a reserve appointment, if offered.

A "qualified" resignation may be submitted in response to administrative separation proceedings, in which case the officer may be granted an honorable or general discharge, or an other than honorable discharge in lieu of a board of inquiry.

Involuntary Separation. Officers in the Navy Reserve may be involuntarily separated after twice failing to select for promotion, or after being involuntarily released from active duty due to demobilization or drawdown. Officers in the Regular Navy may generally be involuntarily separated only for twice failing to select for promotion. In addition, administrative separations "in the best interest of the service" may be awarded to officers under certain circumstances, and courts-martial may award punitive dismissals for violations of the Uniform Code of Military Justice.

Separation Pay. Officers who are involuntarily separated from the Navy may be entitled to separation pay if they meet the following criteria:

- Officers must be retention-eligible and not separated due to substandard performance or dereliction of duty. Officers who are separated due to failure to select for promotion, as well as reserve officers involuntarily released from active duty, meet this requirement.

- The separation must be truly involuntary and not initiated by the officer or caused by the officer's own conduct.

- Officers must have served at least six, but less than twenty, years of active duty. Reserve officers not on the active-duty list must have served at least six years of continuous active duty immediately before separation.

- Officers must agree to serve in the Ready Reserve for a minimum of three years in addition to any existing obligation. (This agreement does not obligate the Reserve to accept the officer for service.)

The amount of separation-pay entitlement is equal to 10 percent of the product of the officer's years of service (each full month of service is counted as one-twelfth of one year), times twelve, times the amount of the officer's monthly basic pay at the time of separation.

Officers separated under certain adverse circumstances are entitled to one-half of the normal amount of separation pay.

Navy Reserve Affiliation. Officers who separate from the Navy prior to completing eight years of active service, and officers who receive separation pay, are required to affiliate with the Navy Reserve upon separation. Such officers may voluntarily affiliate with the Selected Reserve or be involuntarily assigned to the Individual Ready Reserve (IRR). Other separating officers may also request to affiliate with the Selected Reserve. Chapter 16 provides descriptions of these reserve categories.

Retirement

Eligibility. Active-duty officers are eligible to retire upon completion of twenty years of active service. You should plan to submit your request for retirement six to nine months prior to your desired retirement date if it coincides with the PRD of your tour, and nine to twelve months in advance if your desired retirement date is prior to your PRD. A retirement request will not normally be approved from an officer who is within six months of his or her PRD, if that officer has been notified of impending change of station orders.

Retirement Pay. There are three formulas for computing nondisability retirement pay:

1. The "final basic pay" plan applies to members who first entered military service prior to 8 September 1980. Multiply your basic monthly pay at the time of retirement by 2.5 percent for each whole year of service (each whole additional month counts as one-twelfth of one year).

2. The "high 3" plan applies to members who first entered military service between 8 September 1980 and 31 July 1986. Compute pay using the same formula as paragraph 1, except use the average basic pay for your three highest-earning years rather than your final basic pay.

3. Members who first entered military service on or after 1 August 1986 may choose either the "high 3" plan described above or the "Redux" option. Under the latter plan, the member receives a $30,000 career status bonus (CSB) at fifteen years of service in exchange for agreeing to serve to at least twenty years of service and then retire under the less-generous Redux plan. Retired pay under Redux consists of 2.5 percent times the years of service, minus one percentage point from the product for each year less than thirty years, times the average of the highest thirty-six months of basic pay. At age 62, retired pay is recalculated without deducting the one percentage point for each year less than thirty years, which allows retired pay to catch up to what it would have been without the Redux penalty.

Military retired pay is usually cost-of-living-adjusted annually based on the change in the consumer price index (CPI). Redux retirement pay is adjusted based on the change in CPI, minus 1 percent.

Loss of Citizenship. Loss of U.S. citizenship generally results in the loss of retired pay. Because payment of retired pay is contingent on a member maintaining his or her military status, the Comptroller General has held that loss of citizenship is "inconsistent" with a continuation of that status.

Veterans' Benefits

Eligibility for most Department of Veterans Affairs (VA) benefits is based upon the type of discharge from active service. Honorable and general discharges qualify a veteran for most VA benefits, and punitive discharges issued by courts-martial bar most VA benefits. Certain types of benefits and medical care require wartime service. Your service discharge form (DD 214), which documents your service dates and type of discharge, will be an important document when seeking any type of VA benefit.

Educational Benefits. The VA administers education benefits discussed in chapter 17. In addition, the VA administers the Vocational Rehabilitation and Employment (VR&E) program for veterans with service-connected disabilities, and the Dependents' Educational Assistance, which provides education and training opportunities to eligible dependents of certain veterans.

Home Loan Guaranties. The VA guarantees loans made to servicemembers and veterans for purchasing or refinancing homes. The VA guarantees part of the total loan, which permits the purchaser to obtain a mortgage with a competitive interest rate, in some circumstances with no down payment. Applicants must have a good credit rating, have an income sufficient to support mortgage payments, and agree to live in the property.

Life Insurance. The VA oversees Servicemembers' Group Life Insurance (SGLI), discussed in chapter 3. Within 120 days of separation or retirement, you may convert SGLI to Veterans' Group Life Insurance (VGLI), which is renewable five-year term coverage. VGLI coverage is issued in multiples of $10,000 up to a maximum of $400,000, but coverage cannot exceed the amount of SGLI you had at the time of separation. In addition to VGLI, the VA offers Service Disabled Insurance to veterans with service-connected disabilities and Veterans' Mortgage Life Insurance to veterans granted specially adapted housing grants.

VetSuccess. The VA administers a comprehensive employment Web site at http://www.vetsuccess.gov.

Disability Compensation. The VA pays monetary benefits to veterans who are disabled by injury or disease that was incurred or aggravated during active military service. Benefits, based on the level of disability and the number of dependents, are set by Congress and are not subject to federal or state income tax. Disability compensation is also affected by eligibility for military retirement pay, receipt of disability severance pay, and separation incentive payments. Veterans whose service-connected disabilities are rated at 30 percent or more are entitled to additional allowances for dependents, based on the number of dependents and the degree of disability.

Hospital and Outpatient Care. There are eight different priority groups of eligibility for VA hospital and outpatient care, based on severity of disability and means-testing criteria. Group 1, with the highest priority, includes veterans with service-connected disabilities rated 50 percent or more, and veterans determined by VA to be unemployable due to service-connected conditions.

VA medical benefits are separate and distinct from TRICARE medical benefits. Retirees and their dependents are eligible to participate in these programs, which are discussed in chapter 3. Transitional medical coverage programs for separatees are described later in this chapter.

Other Benefits

Permissive Temporary Duty. Retirees and members who are being involuntarily separated are eligible for permissive temporary duty for job hunting and house hunting activities, subject to the needs of their commands. Retirees are eligible for up to twenty days; involuntary separatees are eligible for up to ten days. Members of either group who are stationed outside the continental United States may be authorized an additional ten days.

Terminal Leave. Subject to the approval of their commands, all separatees and retirees may detach from their commands in sufficient time to use the remainder of their accrued leave prior to separation from active duty. In the case of separating officers, if early detachment is not authorized, they may sell back up to sixty days of accrued leave.

Storage and Relocation of Household Goods. All separatees are entitled to store household goods for up to six months following separation, and to move their possessions to their homes of record or other locations a shorter distance away. Retirees and involuntary separatees are entitled to store household goods for up to one year, and to move their possessions to any location in the United States or to an overseas home of record. Retirees may request extensions beyond the one-year limit for medical, training, educational, or other deserving reasons.

Government Housing Extensions. Under certain circumstances, separatees may request to remain in their government quarters for a brief period following separation. When granted such an extension, the former member is charged rent equal to the appropriate amount of local basic allowance for housing (BAH).

Transitional Health Care for Separatees. The Transitional Assistance Management Program (TAMP) provides 180 days of transitional health care benefits to those servicemembers, and their families, who are being involuntarily separated from active duty under honorable conditions. The Continued Health Care Benefit Program (CHCBP), which can provide temporary transitional health coverage for eighteen to thirty-six months after TRICARE or TAMP eligibility ends, must be purchased within sixty days of loss of eligibility for either program. Although you must pay the premium yourself, CHCBP benefits are comparable to TRICARE Standard with the same benefits, providers, and program rules.

Survivor Benefit Plan (SBP). Under SBP, a retiree contributes 6.5 percent of retired pay each month to provide his or her surviving spouse or children an annuity equal to 55 percent of retired pay. Enrollment in SBP is automatic, unless the retiree and the spouse elect in writing not to participate, or to participate to a lesser extent. An election into the plan is irrevocable except by death or divorce. A retiree who had no eligible spouse when first eligible to enroll in SBP, or who subsequently divorced and married a different spouse, may elect during the first year of marriage to cover the new spouse.

Postservice Employment Regulations

Seeking Postservice Employment. Various laws restrict the employment activities of former military members. There are additional restrictions on regular retired officers and on officers who retired above certain pay grades or who were involved in procurement activities. These restrictions are based upon the need to prevent activity that conflicts with the interests of the United States and to preserve the public's confidence in government integrity.

Before beginning negotiations with a prospective employer, you should consult with a Navy ethics counselor (a designated JAG corps officer) to assist you in determining the restrictions that apply to your situation. If a potential violation exists, you should disqualify yourself from taking any action on behalf of the government that could affect your prospective employer. The standards of conduct not only prohibit actual violations of the rules, but also any act that could create the appearance of using public office for private gain or for giving preferential treatment, or that could result in conflict of interest or loss of impartiality.

The Procurement Integrity Act imposes additional restrictions on federal employees who are involved in procurement. This act bars employees who were involved in large procurements from employment with the private employers concerned for a period of one year.

Working during Terminal Leave. With several exceptions, if there is no bar to your employment with a specific employer, you may begin working for that employer while on terminal leave. Surprisingly, if you take a federal civil service job, you may legally receive both military and civil service compensation at the same time. Retired military members may not be appointed to a civil service position in DoD within 180 days of retirement without obtaining a waiver.

Employment with Foreign Governments and Foreign Principals. Retired military members may not accept employment from any foreign government, including corporations owned or controlled by foreign governments, without consent of the Service Secretary and the Secretary of State. Before accepting an offer of foreign employment, submit a written request for approval to the Bureau of Naval Personnel, Office of Legal Counsel (Pers-06), Washington, D.C. 20370-5006.

Navy Professional Reading List

Books in the Navy Professional Reading Program (http://www.navyreading.navy
.mil/) are selected by the Navy Professional Reading Program Advisory Group at
the Naval War College. Separate lists have been developed for each of the following groups:

- junior enlisted
- leading petty officer
- division leader
- department/command leader
- senior leaders

The following is the 2010 Division Leader list, intended for junior officers and
senior enlisted members:

Boot, Max. *The Savage Wars of Peace: Small Wars and the Rise of American Power.* New
York: Basic, 2003.

Christensen, Clayton M. *The Innovator's Dilemma: The Revolutionary Book That Will
Change the Way You Do Business.* New York: HarperCollins, 2003.

Forester, C. S. *The Good Shepherd.* Annapolis, Md.: Naval Institute Press, 1955.

Friedman, Thomas L. *The World Is Flat: A Brief History of the Twenty-First Century.*
New York: Farrar, Straus and Giroux, 2005.

Hirsch, James S. *Two Souls Indivisible: The Friendship That Saved Two POWs in
Vietnam.* Boston: Mariner, 2005.

Kagan, Donald. *On the Origins of War and the Preservation of Peace.* New York: Anchor,
1996.

Levitt, Steven D., and Stephen J. Dubner. *Freakonomics: A Rogue Economist Explores
the Hidden Side of Everything.* New York: William Morrow, 2005.

Marolda, Edward J., and Robert John Schneller. *Shield and Sword: The United States
Navy and the Persian Gulf War.* Annapolis, Md.: Naval Institute Press, 2001.

Reid, Michael. *Forgotten Continent: The Battle for Latin America's Soul.* New Haven,
Conn.: Yale University Press, 2007.

Sobel, Dava. *Longitude: The True Story of a Lone Genius Who Solved the Greatest Scientific Problem of His Time.* New York: Penguin, 1996.

Stillwell, Paul. *The Golden Thirteen: Recollections of the First Black Naval Officers.* Annapolis, Md.: Naval Institute Press, 1993.

Toll, Ian W. *Six Frigates: The Epic History of the Founding of the U.S. Navy.* New York: W. W. Norton, 2008.

MILITARY JUSTICE

Justice and power must be brought together, so whatever is just may be powerful, and whatever is powerful may be just.

—Blaise Pascal

Justice is the first virtue of those who command, and stops the complaints of those who obey.

—Denis Diderot

You should be familiar with the fundamentals of military law and naval discipline. As a junior officer, you are likely to be called to serve as the investigating officer for a crime, mishap, or complaint; to serve as a witness at a court-martial or nonjudicial punishment hearing; to conduct a summary court-martial or serve as a member of a special or general court-martial; or to serve as a member of an administrative discharge board. Each of these duties carries with it the responsibility to act honorably and fairly, to carefully consider the particulars of the case as well as the applicable military law, and to act in accordance with the rights of individual members as well as the good of the Naval Service.

Sources of Military Law

Until relatively recent times, the administration of justice in the Navy was largely the sole prerogative of the CO, according to the law and customs of the sea. The sea is a cruel place, and ship's captains have traditionally had the power of life or death over the members of their crew. More recently, this power has been somewhat tempered by the standardization of laws and regulations designed to prevent the mistreatment and arbitrary punishment of military personnel.

Constitution. Article 1, section 8 of the Constitution states "Congress shall have the power . . . to make rules for the government and regulation of the land and naval forces." The Constitution is printed in its entirety in appendix 1 to the *Manual for Courts-Martial (MCM)*, described below.

Uniform Code of Military Justice (UCMJ). The UCMJ is the fundamental military law that applies to all members in every branch of the armed services. This publication is printed in its entirety in appendix 2 to the *MCM*.

Manual for Courts-Martial (MCM). This publication explains the UCMJ and prescribes regulations that carry out the basic rules of the UCMJ for all branches of the service.

Manual of the Judge Advocate General (JAG Manual, or JAGMAN). The *JAG Manual* applies only to the Navy and Marine Corps. It implements the UCMJ and *MCM* within the Department of the Navy and contains regulations pertaining to administrative law.

Criminal Justice

Punitive Articles and Specifications. A crime is a violation of the penal law. Arts. 78–134 of the UCMJ define military crimes. Each crime is defined in terms of a group of facts or elements, each of which must exist for the crime to have taken place.

Part IV of the *MCM* describes the elements of each article of the UCMJ. Each section provides the text of a UCMJ article, the elements of that crime, and a short explanation of the elements. In addition, each section identifies the permissible maximum punishment for the crime and contains a sample showing the language that should be used to charge a servicemember with the crime.

Alternatives of the Commander. When faced with a crew member who has apparently committed a crime, the CO may take no action, or he or she may take any of the following actions:

- Administrative actions
- Nonjudicial punishment
- Court-martial

Administrative actions

Administrative actions include use of the Navy's informal resolution system for minor misconduct, oral performance counseling, written counseling in the form of a nonpunitive letter of caution or letter of instruction, extra military instruction (EMI, discussed in chapter 6), denial of privileges, appropriate comments or downgraded marks in fitness reports or evaluations, adjustment or withdrawal of security clearances (in cases where a servicemember's conduct brings into question his or her trustworthiness), withholding or withdrawal of advancement or promotion recommendations, reassignment or delay of reassignment, detachment for cause, or administrative separation from the Navy.

In the case of withholding of privileges, an individual with the power to grant a privilege (such as special liberty, the wearing of civilian clothing, and on-base driving) also has the power to revoke that privilege. Although privileges may be withheld, rights such as compensation, medical care, quarters, food, and normal liberty may not be administratively withheld.

Normal liberty may be withheld administratively only by the use of EMI, the extension of working hours as necessary to accomplish mission requirements, limited authorized health and safety reasons (i.e., drunk watch, immunization, and family advocacy 72-hour cooling-off period), and the overseas liberty risk program. The once-common use of so-called voluntary restraint ("hack") is not authorized.

Administrative actions are not legally considered punishment and are not intended to serve in lieu of punishment; punishment may only be awarded at NJP or by a court-martial. Administrative actions may be taken in addition to or instead of disciplinary action as circumstances warrant. Such action does not preclude further disciplinary action, and in many cases, both disciplinary action and appropriate administrative actions are taken.

Jurisdiction

In order for an offense to be disposed of under the military justice system, both the accused and the crime must be under military jurisdiction. In addition, certain other procedural requirements must be met.

Jurisdiction over the Accused. The accused is subject to military jurisdiction if he or she is an active-duty servicemember or a cadet, midshipman, or Reserve member performing active duty. Reservists who have been released from a period of active duty in which an offense was committed may be subsequently recalled for disciplinary proceedings.

Jurisdiction over the Offense. An offense is subject to military jurisdiction if it is related in some way to the servicemember's military service. An offense occurring onboard a naval vessel or shore installation would always be considered service connected, although an offense that takes place off base may not be, depending on the circumstances. As described later in this appendix, certain types of offenses must always be investigated by Naval Criminal Investigative Service (NCIS), regardless of where they occur.

Statute of Limitations. The statute of limitations contained in art. 43, UCMJ, requires the trial of most types of offenses to begin within five years. Exceptions to this rule are unauthorized absence or missing a movement of a ship in wartime, murder, rape, or the rape of a child, or any other offense punishable by death, which can be tried at any time, or child abuse, which may be tried during the life of the child or within five years after the date on which the offense was committed, whichever is longer. For periods of unauthorized absence, the statute of limitations clock begins to run when the period of absence ends.

Former Jeopardy. This concept, often referred to in crime novels as "double jeopardy," means that an accused cannot be tried twice for the same offense. A previous trial that did not result in an acquittal is not considered a "complete" trial for purposes of former jeopardy, and that trial is not a bar to a second trial. A trial by a state or foreign country, whatever the outcome, is also not a bar to a trial by court-martial, which is conducted under federal law.

Former Punishment. A servicemember who has received nonjudicial punishment for a particular minor offense may not then be tried at court-martial for the same offense. The word "minor" is key; if the offense is not minor, or if it turns out to be more serious than it appeared at the time NJP was held, punishment at NJP will not serve as a bar to trial by court-martial.

Procedural Rules

Apprehension. Apprehension is the act of taking a person into custody. Officers, noncommissioned officers, petty officers, masters-at-arms, military police, and NCIS agents or agents of other DoD criminal investigative agencies have the authority to apprehend any individual who is subject to the UCMJ. However, enlisted personnel may apprehend commissioned officers only when actually performing law enforcement duties or when so directed by a commissioned officer.

Apprehension may consist of voluntary submission by the person apprehended, or it may consist of physical force. The individual performing the apprehension is required to make the situation clear by stating, "I am placing you in custody" or similar words, followed by identifying himself or herself to the person being apprehended and stating a reason for the apprehension. There are limitations on the authority to apprehend servicemembers off base or in private dwellings.

All apprehensions must be based on probable cause; that is, facts and circumstances must exist that would lead a reasonable person to conclude that an offense has or is being committed, and that the person to be apprehended committed or is in the process of committing the offense.

Restraint. Once a suspect is apprehended, the appropriate authority may impose restraint. Restraint may be moral rather than physical, as when a suspect is ordered to remain within the limits of a particular command. Restraint may also, of course, be physical. A servicemember may be placed in restraint pending disciplinary action if the appropriate authority, acting in a neutral and detached manner, has a reasonable belief that an offense has been committed, that the person to be restrained committed it, and that restraint is warranted under the circumstances. Restraint is considered to be warranted when the servicemember is a flight risk or when there is reasonable grounds to believe the member will engage in serious future acts of misconduct if not restrained.

Searches and Seizures. The Fourth Amendment to the Bill of Rights, which protects the people against unreasonable searches and seizures, also applies to military personnel. Evidence obtained by an unlawful search may not be admissible in a court-martial proceeding. Inspections whose primary purpose is not to seek evidence of a crime (e.g., a health and welfare inspection of a berthing area or an inventory of a supply storeroom) are not considered searches, and evidence that turns up during such inspections is always admissible in a trial by court-martial. The products of searches that are conducted specifically to seek evidence of crimes are also admissible, provided the searches are legally conducted.

Legal searches may be divided into two categories: those that require probable cause and those that do not. Probable cause is not required for border searches, searches of persons and vehicles entering or leaving naval installations or ships, searches of government property, or searches for which the cognizant individual gives consent. In addition, a frisk for weapons incident to a lawful stop by a law enforcement official, a search incident to an apprehension by such an official, searches of confinement facilities, or searches under emergency situations do not require a finding of probable cause. All other kinds of searches are subject to the requirement for probable cause—that is, the CO with jurisdiction over the person or place to be searched must determine that a reasonable person would conclude that a crime was committed, and that the search would be likely to produce evidence of this crime. A CO may *not* delegate this authority.

Investigations

Initiation of Charges. Any civilian or servicemember may initiate charges against another servicemember, either orally or in writing. Once charges have been initiated, and the CO or designated command representative determines that the situation warrants further investigation, the command initiates an investigation.

Investigation by NCIS. Certain types of incidents and suspected offenses must always be referred to NCIS for investigation, regardless of where they occurred and whether or not civilian authorities are conducting an investigation. Such offenses include espionage, terrorism, sabotage, assassinations, attempted defection, non-combat deaths not medically attributable to disease or natural causes, fires or explosions of unknown origin affecting military property, theft or loss of ordnance, narcotics, dangerous drugs or controlled substances, disappearance of a military member when foul play cannot be excluded, suspected fraud against the government within the Navy or Marine Corps, certain security incidents, national security cases, and sexual assaults.

Informal Investigations. For most minor offenses, a preliminary inquiry officer (PIO), appointed by the CO conducts the investigation. This officer interviews witnesses, examines any physical or documentary evidence, and advises the accused of his or her rights before taking an oral or written statement. After concluding the investigation, the PIO forwards up the chain of command a report that includes a brief summary of the evidence, comments on the performance and prior disciplinary record of the accused, and a recommendation for the disposition of the offense.

For more serious offenses that are subject to referral to court-martial, a so-called article 32 investigation (set forth in art. 32 of the UCMJ) is initiated. A pretrial investigating officer in pay grade O-4 or above, or a JAG officer, is appointed to investigate the charges. The investigating officer's function is similar to that of the PIO as described above, except that the procedures for conducting the investigation are considerably more formal. After concluding the investigation, the investigating officer forwards a written report to the court-martial convening authority to take action as appropriate.

Nonjudicial Punishment (NJP)

Authority to Impose NJP. This authority rests with the commander, CO, or officer in charge (OIC) of a unit, and it may normally be delegated only in the case of a flag officer to a principal assistant who acts as NJP authority for the unit. For the purposes of this appendix, the person with the authority to administer NJP at a unit is called the CO.

The CO has NJP authority over all military personnel who are members of the command at the time the punishment is imposed, regardless of whether such authority existed at the time the crime occurred. This authority extends to all personnel temporarily assigned to the command and members of embarked staffs and units.

Types of Offenses. The CO has broad discretion to decide whether to handle an offense administratively, to pursue NJP, or to refer it to a court-martial. In general,

NJP is used for minor offenses that could not result in a dishonorable discharge or in confinement of more one year if tried at a court-martial.

Executive Officer's Inquiry (XOI). Most commands precede NJP with an informal hearing called the executive officer's inquiry (XOI). The XO reviews the report of the PIO and may personally examine the evidence and interview witnesses, the chain of command, and the accused before making a determination whether to forward the case to the CO for NJP. Some commands utilize a disciplinary review board (DRB) consisting of the command master chief and other senior enlisted members who review the evidence and make recommendations for disposition of the case prior to, or instead of, XOI. The DRB or XO may not impose punishment, but he or she may take administrative measures.

Refusal of NJP. Enlisted personnel who are not attached to or embarked in a vessel may refuse NJP and request court-martial, as may all officers. The right to refuse NJP expires when punishment is imposed. A member has the right to be present at NJP. Although a member may request to waive the right to a personal appearance, the CO may require appearance. NJP may not be held on a member who is an unauthorized absentee or is otherwise in absentia.

Rights at NJP. A member has the right to remain silent, to have a personal representative (not necessarily an attorney), to examine the evidence against him or her, to present matters in defense or in mitigation and extenuation, and to call any reasonably available witnesses (although civilian witnesses may not be subpoenaed to appear at an NJP hearing). A member does not have the right to consult with an attorney, and military attorneys are not appointed to represent members at NJP, although members who have the right to refuse NJP must be afforded the opportunity to consult with an attorney specifically about that right. A member may hire a civilian lawyer at his or her own expense, but this lawyer enjoys no special status at NJP beyond that of any other personal representative. A member has the right to a public hearing or may request a "closed mast." If the CO grants the request for a closed mast, at least one other witness, such as the command master chief, generally remains present.

As the name indicates, NJP is not a judicial proceeding, and imposition of punishment is not considered a finding of guilt or a conviction. Military rules of evidence do not apply at NJP; the CO's standard in order to impose punishment is a preponderance of the evidence rather than proof beyond a reasonable doubt. However, COs generally do not pursue NJP in cases in which the evidence would not be sufficient for a court-martial conviction.

At NJP, the CO may take the following actions:

- Dismiss the charges, with or without warning and/or imposition of administrative measures

- Impose authorized punishment
- Refer the charges to a court-martial
- Postpone the proceedings, such as when waiting for additional evidence to become available

For a CO in the pay grade of O-4 or above, authorized punishments for enlisted personnel at NJP include:

- Punitive reprimand or admonition
- Restriction to the limits of the ship (or, for a shore command, to prescribed limits of the command) for up to sixty days; or correctional custody for up to thirty days; or, if attached to or embarked in a vessel, confinement on bread and water for up to three days
- Extra duties of no more than two hours per day for up to forty-five days
- Reduction in rate one pay grade
- Forfeiture of up to one-half of one month's pay for up to two months

Commanding officers below the pay grade O-4 and OICs of all ranks have lesser maximum punishment limits, and there are different limits for imposition of punishment on officers, depending on the pay grade of the CO imposing punishment.

The authority to set aside the entire punishment or to remit the unexecuted portion of the punishment rests with the officer imposing NJP, his or her successor in command, the servicemember's next CO (if the member is transferred), or a higher appellate authority. Such actions must normally be taken within four months of the date of the imposition of punishment, and they are undertaken only to correct a clear injustice. In addition, these same authorities may mitigate the punishment, by reducing it in quantity or severity, or suspend the punishment for up to six months. Suspension is normally contingent on another action being performed by the member, such as completion of a rehabilitation course or restitution to a victim of theft or vandalism. Someone who violates the terms of suspension or UCMJ may have his or her initial sentence vacated by any authority competent to impose punishment.

A servicemember may appeal any punishment awarded at NJP to the area coordinator or flag officer with general court-martial authority. There are only two grounds for appeals: that the punishment was unjust (the evidence did not indicate that the member committed the offense), or that the punishment was disproportionate (excessively harsh or unfair) in relation to the offense. Appeals must be filed in writing via the officer imposing the punishment within five calendar days, although extensions for good cause may be requested and granted. A member appealing NJP may request a stay of any restriction, extra duty, or confinement on bread and water pending the outcome of the appeal.

Courts-Martial

Courts-martial are used to try more serious offenses than those normally disposed of at nonjudicial punishment, although less serious offenses may also be referred to court-martial when a servicemember refuses NJP. The standard of proof for conviction at a court-martial is "beyond a reasonable doubt."

Summary Court-Martial (SCM). The function of a summary court-martial is to exercise justice promptly for relatively minor offenses. Any CO may convene an SCM. Any person subject to UCMJ, except officers, cadets, and midshipmen, may be tried by SCM. A summary court-marital is composed of one commissioned officer in pay grade O-3 or above in the same armed force as the accused. All personnel have the right to consult with counsel prior to the court-martial, but not to be represented by counsel. Members may refuse trial by SCM, in which case the offense will likely be referred to a higher court-martial.

The maximum punishment awarded at an SCM is

- Reprimand
- Confinement at hard labor for thirty days (for members in pay grade E-4 and below)
- Restriction for sixty days
- Hard labor without confinement for forty-five days (for members in pay grade E-4 and below)
- Reduction in rate to pay grade E-1 (for members in pay grade E-4 and below) or reduction in rate one pay grade.
- Fine or forfeiture of two-thirds pay for one month.

Special Court-Martial (SPCM). A special court-martial is convened for non-capital or capital crimes for which the mandatory sentence for the crime does not exceed the maximum punishment that such a court may impose. A CO or anyone senior to the CO in the chain of command may convene an SPCM. The court consists of at least three members; any commissioned or warrant officers are eligible to serve on a court martial. If the accused so requests, enlisted members may serve on the court-martial. A two-thirds majority is required to convict. The accused may also request a trial by military judge alone.

A servicemember appearing before a SPCM has the right to be represented by counsel, which may be either a military lawyer or a civilian lawyer retained at the accused's own expense. A trial counsel represents the government.

The maximum punishment that an SPCM may impose on an enlisted member is the lesser of the maximum punishment for the particular offense, or

- Reprimand
- Bad conduct discharge
- Confinement at hard labor for one year
- Restriction for sixty days
- Hard labor without confinement for ninety days
- Fine or forfeiture of two-thirds pay per month for one year
- Reduction in rate to pay grade E-1
- Officers are subject to lesser punishments

General Court-Martial (GCM). The convening authority for a general court-martial is generally a flag officer or other senior officer serving as an area coordinator. A general court-martial is convened for serious noncapital crimes and capital crimes. The court consists of at least five servicemembers; as in the special court-martial, the court may include any commissioned or warrant officers or, if the accused so requests, enlisted members. In most circumstances, a two-thirds majority is required to convict; imposition of more than ten years at hard labor requires a three-fourths majority, and imposition of the death penalty must be unanimous. In noncapital cases, an accused may request a trial by military judge alone.

A member appearing before a GCM has the right to be represented by counsel, either a military lawyer or a civilian lawyer retained at his or her own expense. A trial counsel represents the government.

The maximum punishment that may be imposed on an officer or enlisted member by a GCM is the maximum punishment for the particular offense. This may include the following:

- Reprimand
- Death
- Dishonorable discharge (enlisted members) or dismissal (officers)
- Confinement at hard labor for life; confinement for life, without eligibility for parole, may generally be awarded in cases where the death penalty is authorized
- Restriction for sixty days
- Total forfeiture of pay
- Reduction in rate to pay grade E-1

Administrative Law

Administrative Fact-Finding Body. An administrative fact-finding body, which may be as small as one individual, is constituted under the *Manual of the Judge Advocate*

General to collect and record information on a particular incident. Such investigations are commonly referred to as *JAG Manual* investigations. Common situations in which such an investigation is initiated are accidents resulting in serious injury, death, or significant damage or loss to government property. An administrative fact-finding body is not judicial; its findings and opinions do not represent legal judgments. The findings may, however, be used as the basis for a convening authority's decision to pursue a trial by court-martial. *JAG Manual* investigations may be informal fact-finding bodies, formal fact-finding bodies, or courts of inquiry, depending on the seriousness of the incidents under investigation.

Line of Duty/Misconduct Investigations. Whenever a servicemember is seriously injured or contracts a serious disease, a specific type of *JAG Manual* investigation, called a line of duty/misconduct investigation, must be conducted. This investigation reviews the circumstances of the injury or illness, and makes specific recommendations on whether the injury/illness occurred in the line of duty and whether it was due to the member's own misconduct.

Line of duty is not synonymous with "on duty" or "while performing official duties," but rather indicates the member's good standing at the time of the incident. Injuries and illnesses that occur while the member is not an unauthorized absentee, or as a result of the member's own misconduct, are presumed to have occurred in the line of duty.

"Misconduct" is wrongful conduct. An illness or injury is considered to be due to the member's own misconduct when it results from gross negligence, reckless disregard of the consequences, or the commission of a crime. A finding of misconduct always results in a finding of "not in the line of duty."

Although a similar investigation is done when a member's injury or illness results in death, opinions as to line of duty and misconduct are not expressed in the investigation report. In such cases, the Department of Veterans Affairs makes this determination.

Administrative Discharges. There are four types of administrative discharges that may be awarded to enlisted personnel:

1. Honorable. This discharge is awarded when the servicemember has performed honorable and proper military service.

2. General under honorable conditions. This discharge is awarded to those members whose military records are satisfactory, but less than that required for an honorable discharge.

3. Other-than-honorable (OTH). This is the most negative administrative discharge and is awarded to members whose performance in the military has not been satisfactory. The long-term effects of an OTH discharge on an

individual's VA benefits and future employability in the civilian sector are nearly as severe as the effects of a punitive discharge.

4. Entry-level separation. This discharge is awarded to members within the first 180 days of service. This type of separation is neutral in nature and is intended as a means to separate individuals who are truly not suited for the service.

Bad-conduct discharges and dishonorable discharges are not administrative and may be awarded only as the result of a trial by court-martial.

Enlisted members may be involuntarily separated from the Navy for a variety of reasons that include (but are not limited to) misconduct, unsatisfactory performance, and drug abuse. When the reason for the separation could result in an other-than-honorable discharge, or when the individual has six or more years of military service, or separation processing is mandatory, he or she is permitted the opportunity to appear before an administrative discharge board. This board, consisting of three or more commissioned officers, warrant officers, or senior enlisted members in pay grade E-7 and senior, evaluates the circumstances and makes a determination on whether the misconduct (or other reason for discharge) occurred, and whether to retain or discharge that individual. If the board determines that the servicemember should be discharged, it also recommends the characterization of discharge.

The findings of the board are forwarded through the chain of command to the Chief of Naval Personnel for final disposition. In circumstances where the board recommends separation, the Chief of Naval Personnel may retain the member or separate him or her with a more favorable type of discharge. If the board recommends retention, the Chief of Naval Personnel may only overrule the retention recommendation with the approval of the Secretary of the Navy. In such cases, servicemembers may not receive OTH discharges.

Appendix C

NAVY TERMINOLOGY

above zone. An officer being considered by a selection board who is more senior (i.e., previously passed over) than the officers who are **in zone**.

ADCON. Administrative Control. Direction or exercise of authority over subordinate or other organizations with respect to administration and support, including organization of Service forces, control of resources and equipment, personnel management, unit logistics, individual and unit training, readiness, mobilization, demobilization, discipline, and other matters not included in the operational missions of the subordinate or other organizations.

A-gang. Auxiliaries division of the engineering department.

Airedale. Slang term for a member of the aviation community.

allotment. A selected amount of a member's take-home pay that is designated to be automatically withheld for a certain purpose. Allotments may be designated to be sent to certain charitable organizations or bank accounts or toward loan repayments.

allowance. A component of military compensation that is not taxable (e.g., BAH, BAS).

Attention on deck. A response given by a junior when a senior officer enters the room.

augmentation. The process by which active-duty Navy Reserve officers become officers in the Regular Navy, which generally requires attainment of the appropriate warfare qualification, submission of an augmentation request letter, and selection by a transfer/redesignation board.

Aye, aye. A response to an order signifying that the order is heard, is understood, and will be carried out.

BAH. Basic allowance for housing. A component of compensation to help offset the cost of off-base housing; varies by pay grade and location.

BAS. Basic allowance for subsistence. A component of compensation to help defray food costs for servicemembers who are not required to take their meals "in kind."

base pay. The primary component of military compensation. Base pay increases with pay grade (rank) and length of service. *See also* **fogey.**

below zone. An officer being considered by a selection board who is junior to the officers in zone. If selected, this officer would be an early selectee.

bilge. The rounded interior of the hull. When used as a verb, a slang term to indicate utter failure.

binnacle list. Sick list.

black shoe (or shoe). Slang term for a member of the surface or submarine community. Refers to the black shoes traditionally worn by nonaviators.

blue water. Literally, "deep water," but more traditionally, "away from land."

BLUF. Abbreviation of "bottom line up front," the practice of providing a summary of important points at the beginning of a lengthier report.

boat. A small vessel that may be hoisted aboard a ship. Also used to refer to a submarine.

boomer. Slang term for a ballistic-missile submarine.

boondoggle. Slang term for a temporary assignment viewed as largely recreational in nature.

Bravo Zulu. Phonetic pronunciation of BZ, from the NATO signal codes, signifying "Well done."

bridge. The location on board ship from which the conning officer gives orders to the helm.

brown shoe. Slang term for a member of the aviation community. Refers to the brown shoes traditionally worn by aviators.

brown water. Shallow, inland water.

bubblehead. Slang term for submariner.

bull ensign. Senior ensign in a command, who traditionally wears oversized ensign insignia.

bullnose. A chock placed right over the stem of the ship.

Captain's Mast. Nonjudicial disciplinary procedure.

Carry on. An order to resume or continue previous activity, given by a senior after juniors have come to attention.

Cheng. Chief engineer.

chit. A form used to request leave, liberty, or other special requests.

CMAA. Chief master-at-arms. The enlisted member serving as the head of a command's law enforcement organization.

CM/C. Command master chief. Senior enlisted person in the command. See COB for submarines.

CO. Commanding officer. The captain or skipper of a vessel.

COB. Chief of the boat. Senior enlisted person on board a submarine.

CONUS. Continental United States.

crow. Slang term for the rate insignia of a petty officer (E-4 and above), so called because of the eagle surmounting the rate chevrons.

cumshaw. Unauthorized, unofficial procurement of needed material outside the supply system, usually involving barter.

DC. Damage control.

DCA. Damage control assistant. This officer is responsible, under the chief engineer, for damage control and stability of a ship.

DDS. Direct deposit system. A mandatory process of directly depositing a servicemember's paycheck to his or her bank account.

dead horse. A pay advance (usually one to three months' base pay) taken in conjunction with a PCS move, generally paid back over the following twenty-four months. The equivalent of an interest-free loan.

designated striker. A sailor in pay grades E-1 through E-3 who has a rating.

designator. The four-digit code (e.g., 1165, 1700) assigned to an officer to designate his or her community/warfare specialty.

DFAS. Defense Finance and Accounting Service. Managers of the military pay system.

dink. Slang term for delinquent watch qualifications.

DITY. Do it yourself. Refers to a type of PCS move in which the servicemember moves some or all of his or her own household goods and is reimbursed by the government some percentage of what a commercial mover would have charged.

dog watch. A shortened watch period. Generally, breaking up the four-hour 1600–2000 watch into two two-hour watches, 1600–1800 and 1800–2000, so that personnel on watch can eat the evening meal. This practice also provides an odd number of watches to rotate sections through the daily watches.

dolphins. Slang term for the warfare insignia of submariners.

due course. A "due course" officer is one who has been promoted in zone (as opposed to above zone or below zone).

duty-preference card. A.k.a. "dream sheet." Form used to advise detailers of service-members' duty-assignment preferences.

EAOS. End of active obligated service. The end of an enlistment or extension to an enlistment. Term is only applicable to enlisted members; all officers have "indefinite" EAOSs, even if they are obligated for a certain amount of continued service.

8 o'clock reports. Equipment status reports made by all department heads to the XO, usually at 2130, who then takes them to the CO.

EMI. Extra military instruction. Additional duties assigned to improve a Sailor's performance of duties or military knowledge. Not legally considered a form of punishment.

ensign. The national colors, or the most junior commissioned officer rank.

EOOW. Engineering officer of the watch.

field day. To thoroughly clean a ship's spaces.

first lieutenant. Deck division officer or department head aboard a surface ship.

FITREP. Fitness report. Performance assessment issued to officers and senior enlisted members. (Similar form for junior enlisted members is called an enlisted evaluation.)

flag officer. Admiral (pay grade O-7 and senior).

fogey. Slang term for an increase in base pay as a result of longevity (time in service).

FOS. Failure of selection (for promotion).

gedunk. Slang term for junk food or candy, or a place to buy it.

george. Slang term for the junior ensign in a command.

goat locker. Slang term for chiefs' mess.

gouge. Slang term for valuable information; the naval equivalent of "scoop."

green water. The littoral, or coastal, areas. Intermediate between open ocean (blue water) and inland (brown water).

GQ. General Quarters. The call for all hands to man battle stations.

gundecking. Intentional falsification, generally in reference to maintenance or training records.

hack. Informal (and not legally sanctioned) confinement to quarters or to the ship.

head. Naval term for bathroom.

Hollywood shower. An excessively long shower that wastes water.

interagency. U.S. government agencies and departments, including the Department of Defense.

in zone. That group of officers, delineated by date of rank, who are to be considered by a promotion selection board. Most officers selected are those who are "in zone."

ISIC. Immediate superior in command. The officer who is next senior in the chain of command to a unit's CO.

jack. A triangular replica of the blue star-studded field of the national ensign. It is flown at the bow by ships at anchor or moored to a pier from 0800 to sunset.

Jacob's ladder. A portable ladder used to board a ship.

joint duty. Specifically designated duty with a "joint" (i.e., multiservice) command, staff, or mission. Joint duty credit is generally required for selection to flag rank.

leave. All servicemembers earn thirty days of paid leave each year (two and a half days per month) and (under most circumstances) may carry up to sixty days of leave on the books.

LES. Leave and earnings statement. Monthly statement of a servicemember's pay and allowance entitlements, taxes withheld, and leave balance.

liberty. Authorized absence from an enlisted member's duty station. The correct equivalent term for officers is "shore leave."

line. The naval term for rope.

lose the bubble. Originally, to assume such an extreme up- or down-angle in a submarine that the bubble of the inclinometer is no longer visible. In common slang usage, to lose situational awareness or to panic.

lucky bag. Lost and found administered by the chief master at arms.

main control. The engineering space from which the EOOW controls operations of the engineering plant.

main space. The engine room.

manning the rails. The practice of stationing sailors along the rails of a ship when rendering honors or entering port, or upon returning to home port at the end of a deployment.

mess. A space where meals are served (e.g., the chiefs' mess).

midwatch. A watch stood from midnight until 0400.

MPA. Main propulsion assistant. This officer is responsible, under the chief engineer, for the maintenance and operation of the ship's main propulsion equipment.

mustang. An officer who started out as an enlisted member and rose through the ranks.

MWR. Morale, welfare, and recreation.

Navy shower. A shower that utilizes appropriate water conservation measures. The procedure is to turn on the water to get wet, turn it off while soaping up, then turn it on to rinse.

NEC codes. Navy enlisted classification codes. Numerical codes used to designate special skills and qualifications of enlisted personnel.

NFO. Naval flight officer.

NJP. Nonjudicial punishment, a.k.a. Captain's Mast.

nuc or nuke. Slang term for nuclear-trained officer or enlisted member.

OBE. Overcome by events. A previous concern or question is no longer applicable because of changed circumstances.

ODC. Officer data card. A summary sheet containing information on an officer's training, qualifications, billets held, designator and promotion history, and other key information.

oh dark thirty. Slang term meaning "the middle of the night."

OPCON. Operational control. The authority to perform those functions of command over subordinate forces involving organizing and employing commands and forces, assigning tasks, designating objectives, and giving authoritative direction necessary to accomplish the mission.

Oscar. The dummy used for man-overboard drills, so named for the international signal flag hoisted for "man overboard."

OUTUS. Outside the continental United States (includes Alaska and Hawaii).

padeye. A recessed tie-down point or anchor point on a bulkhead or deck.

pay. A component of military compensation that is taxable (e.g., base pay, sea pay, special duty assignment pay).

pay grade. Alphanumeric designation corresponding to relative seniority of a member of the service. O designates an officer, W a warrant officer, and E an enlisted member. For example, O-1 is an ensign, W-2 a CWO2, and E-1 a recruit.

PCS. Permanent change of station. Used in reference to orders that permanently move a member from one duty station to another.

PEBD. Pay entry base date. The date (usually the day a member begins active duty service) from which all fogeys are calculated.

per diem. Daily allowance to cover cost of meals, lodging, and certain other authorized expenses incurred while in a TAD or travel status.

pilothouse. The location on board ship in which the helmsman stands watch.

police. To inspect and clean up.

POV. Privately owned vehicle.

PQS. Personnel Qualification System. A method of formalizing and tracking the qualification process of personnel toward watch-station certification.

PRD. Projected rotation date. The date (generally month and year) a servicemember's tour at a given duty station is anticipated to end.

proceed time. Additional time, not charged as leave, allowed for PCS transfers to or from certain types of duty.

PSD. Personnel support detachment. A shore-based organization that handles service records and pay for a group of commands in the geographic area.

quarterdeck. The ceremonial area of a ship where the OOD stands watch in port.

rack. Slang term for bunk.

rate. Combination of enlisted rating and pay grade. For example, a servicemember in the YN rating with a pay grade of E-5 has the rate YN2.

rating. Enlisted occupational specialty—for example, YN (yeoman), MM (machinist's mate), and so forth.

ring knocker. Slang term for a graduate of the U.S. Naval Academy,

scuttle. A watertight opening set in a hatch or bulkhead, or the act of intentionally sinking a ship to prevent its capture.

scuttlebutt. A drinking fountain, or a rumor.

sea daddy. Slang term for a mentor who takes a less-experienced crew member under his or her wing.

sea lawyer. Slang term for a sailor who has or professes to have significant knowledge of military laws and regulations and attempts to use this knowledge for personal benefit.

SGLI. Servicemembers' Group Life Insurance. A type of term life insurance available to military members, which is charged at a flat rate of $.065/mo. per $1,000 coverage, to a maximum of $400,000 coverage.

shift colors. When a ship moors or anchors, the ensign is broken on the stern and the jack is broken on the bow; simultaneously the ensign is being hauled down from the main mast. "Shift colors" occurs when the first line is made fast to the pier or the anchor touches the bottom. When a ship gets under way, the process is reversed as soon as the last line is let go from the pier or the anchor breaks free of the bottom.

shore leave. The correct term for the officer equivalent of liberty.

small boy. Slang term for a small combatant, such as a littoral combat ship or destroyer.

smoking lamp. From the days of sail, a lamp from which personnel could light their pipes or cigars. In contemporary usage, the phrase "The smoking lamp is lighted," (never "lit"), signifies that smoking is permitted.

snipe. Slang term for an engineer.

soft power. A term originated by Harvard professor Joseph Nye. Encompasses aspects of a nation's culture, political values, and foreign policy that can attract a population from competing ideologies and complement "hard power" of military force.

subspecialty code. A code assigned to an officer to document specific advanced education or significant experience in a particular, recognized area.

TACON. Tactical control. Command authority over assigned or attached forces or commands, or military capability or forces made available for tasking. Limited to the detailed direction and control of movements or maneuvers within the operational area necessary to accomplish missions or tasks assigned. Tactical control is inherent in operational control.

TAD. Temporary additional duty. Describes duty under orders issued by a permanent duty station for a relatively brief assignment in another location.

TEMDUINS. Temporary duty under instruction. Assignment to a training facility while en route to a permanent duty station.

turn to. Commence work.

12 o'clock reports. Reports on various administrative matters, including fuel and water, magazine temperature, and position, and other reports provided to the OOD by the appropriate officers for delivery to the CO just prior to 1200.

two-blocked. To have reached the maximum limit of something. The term originated from the use of block and tackle for hoisting. When the two blocks touch, lifting can proceed no further.

UA. Unauthorized absence. The naval equivalent of the Army's AWOL (absent without leave).

UIC. Unit identification code. A five-digit numerical code used to identify a particular command or an individual component of a large command.

UNREP. Underway replenishment. The transfer of supplies, fuel, munitions, and personnel from one ship to another while at sea.

VERTREP. Vertical replenishment. The transfer of supplies, munitions, or personnel via helicopter.

Very well. A response given by a senior to a junior who has made a report. Never said by a junior to a senior.

wardroom. The space aboard ship where officers take their meals, relax, and socialize. Also used as a collective term for a command's officers.

XO. Executive officer. Second in command.

Zulu time. Coordinated Universal Time (UTC), formerly known as Greenwich Mean Time (GMT).

ACRONYMS AND ABBREVIATIONS

1MC	general announcing system
3M	maintenance, material, and management
ADCON	Administrative Control
ADP	automated data processing
AEDO	aerospace engineering duty officer
AFRICOM	U.S. Africa Command
AMDO	aerospace maintenance duty officer
ANZUS	Australia, New Zealand, United States (treaty)
APC	academic profile code
ARG	amphibious ready group
ASP	Active Status Pool
ASVAB	Armed Services Vocational Aptitude Battery (test)
ASW	anti-submarine warfare
ATF	Bureau of Alcohol, Tobacco, Firearms, and Explosives (DOJ)
BAH	basic allowance for housing
BAS	basic allowance for subsistence
Battle E	Battle Effectiveness Award
BLUF	bottom line up front
BMD	ballistic missile defense
BUMED	Bureau of Medicine and Surgery
BUPERS	Bureau of Naval Personnel
C	Confidential
C4ISR	command, control, communications, computers, intelligence, surveillance and reconnaissance
CAC	common access card
CACO	casualty assistance calls officer
CAG	Carrier Air Group
CAP	Command Advancement Program
CATF	commander, amphibious task force

CBP	Customs and Border Protection (DHS)
CCC	command career counselor
CDC	combat direction center
CDC	Centers for Disease Control and Prevention (HHS)
CDO	command duty officer
CEC	civil engineering corps
CENTCOM	U.S. Central Command
CFC	Combined Federal Campaign
CFC	Combined Forces Command
CFEF	Cyber Federal Executive Fellowship
CFO	chief financial officer
CHCBP	Continued Health Care Benefit Program
Cheng	chief engineer
CHINFO	chief of information
CHOP	Change of Operational Control
CIA	Central Intelligence Agency
CIC	combat information center
CIO	chief information officer
CMAA	chief master-at-arms
CMC	Commandant of the Marine Corps
CM/C	command master chief
CMS	communications security material
CNO	Chief of Naval Operations
CO	commanding officer
COB	chief of the boat
COCOM	combatant commander
COLA	cost-of-living allowance
CONUS	continental United States
COOL	credentialing opportunities online
COS	chief of staff
CPI	consumer price index
CSB	career status bonus
CSG	carrier strike group
CSO	chief staff officer
CTE	Commander Task Element
CTF	Commander, Task Force
CTG	Commander, Task Group
CTU	Commander, Task Unit
CWO	chief warrant officer
DAPA	drug/alcohol program advisor

DARPA	Defense Advanced Research Projects Agency
DC	damage control
DCA	damage control assistant
DCAA	Defense Contract Audit Agency
DCMA	Defense Contract Management Agency
DDS	direct deposit system
DEA	Drug Enforcement Administration (DOJ)
DeCA	Defense Commissary Agency
DEERS	Defense Enrollment Eligibility Reporting System
DESRON	destroyer squadron
DFAS	Defense Finance and Accounting Service
DHS	Department of Homeland Security
DIA	Defense Intelligence Agency
DIC	Dependency and Indemnity Compensation
DIEMS	day initially entered military service
DISA	Defense Information Systems Agency
DITY	do it yourself
DLA	Defense Logistics Agency
DLSA	Defense Legal Services Agency
DNI	Director of National Intelligence
DoD	Department of Defense
DOE	Department of Energy
DOJ	Department of Justice
DON	Department of the Navy
DOS	Department of State
DOT	Department of Transportation
DPC	Defense Planning Committee (NATO)
DSCA	Defense Security Cooperation Agency
DSS	Defense Security Service
DTRA	Defense Threat Reduction Agency
EAOS	end of active obligated service
EDO	engineering duty officer
EMI	extra military instruction
EMO	electronics material officer
EMPRS	Electronic Military Personnel Records System
EOOW	engineering officer of the watch
EPA	U.S. Environmental Protection Agency
ESG	expeditionary strike group
ESO	educational services officer
ESR	electronic service record

EU	European Union
EUCOM	U.S. European Command
EW	electronics warfare
FAA	Federal Aviation Administration (DOT)
FAO	foreign area officer
FAR	Federal Acquisition Regulations
FBI	Federal Bureau of Investigation
FCB	Functional Capability Board
FDA	Food and Drug Administration (HHS)
FEF	Federal Executive Fellowship
FEMA	Federal Emergency Management Agency (DHS)
FICA	Federal Insurance Contributions Act
FITREP	fitness report
FITW	federal income tax withholding
FMF	Fleet Marine Forces
FMFIA	Federal Managers Financial Integrity Act
FOS	failure of selection
FRTP	Fleet Response Training Plan
FSA	family separation allowance
FSGLI	Family Servicemembers' Group Life Insurance
FTS	Full-Time Support
GMT	General Military Training
GQ	General Quarters
HA/DR	humanitarian assistance and disaster response
HBA	health benefits advisor
HHS	U.S. Department of Health and Human Services
HYT	high-year tenure
IC	intelligence community
ICE	Immigration and Customs Enforcement (DHS)
IGO	intergovernmental organization
IM/IT	Information Management/Information Technology
IRA	individual retirement account
IRR	Individual Ready Reserve
ISIC	immediate superior in command
JAG	Judge Advocate General
JCB	Joint Capability Board
JCS	Joint Chiefs of Staff
JFCOM	U.S. Joint Forces Command
JOOD	junior officer of the deck
JQO	joint qualified officer

JQR	job qualification requirement
JQS	Joint Qualifications System
JROC	Joint Requirements Oversight Council
JS	Joint Staff
JSPS	Joint Strategic Planning System
LaDR	Learning and Development Roadmap
LDO	limited duty officer
LDP	leadership development program
LEGIS	Legislative Fellows program
LEO	law enforcement operations
LES	leave and earnings statement
MAGTF	Marine Air Ground Task Force
MARAD	U.S. Maritime Administration (DOT)
MC	intercommunications voice system
MCM	*Manual for Courts-Martial*
MCPC	Management Control Program coordinator
MCPON	Master Chief Petty Officer of the Navy
MDA	Missile Defense Agency
MEB	Marine expeditionary brigade
MEPS	military entrance processing station
METOC	meteorology and oceanography officer
MEU	Marine expeditionary unit
MGIB	Montgomery GI Bill
MPA	main propulsion assistant
MSC	Military Sealift Command
MTF	military treatment facility
MWR	morale, welfare, and recreation
NAC	North Atlantic Council (NATO)
NATO	North Atlantic Treaty Organization
NAVAIR	Naval Air Systems Command
NAVFAC	Naval Facilities Engineering Command
NAVNETWARCOM	Naval Network Warfare Command
NAVSEA	Naval Sea Systems Command
NAVSUP	Naval Supply Systems Command
NCA	National Command Authorities
NCC	Navy College Center
NCO	Navy College Office
NCPACE	Navy College Program for Advanced College Education
NEAS	Navy Enlisted Advancement System
NEC	Navy enlisted classification

NETC	Navy Education and Training Command
NFO	naval flight officer
NGA	National Geospatial-Intelligence Agency
NGO	nongovernmental organization
NIH	National Institutes of Health (HHS)
NIMA	National Imagery and Mapping Agency
NJP	non-judicial punishment
NMCRS	Navy Marine Corps Relief Society
NNSA	National Nuclear Security Administration (DOE)
NOAA	National Oceanic and Atmospheric Administration
NOFORN	Not Releasable to Foreign Nationals
NORAD	North American Aerospace Defense Command
NORTHCOM	U.S. Northern Command
NPC	Navy Personnel Command
NPS	Naval Postgraduate School
NPTC	Office of Nonproliferation and Treaty Compliance (Commerce)
NRO	National Reconnaissance Office
NROTC	Naval Reserve Officer Training Corps
NSA	National Security Agency
NSAWC	Naval Strike and Air Warfare Center
NSC	National Security Council
NTCSS	Navy Tactical Command Support System
OAS	Organization of American States
OBE	overcome by events
OCS	Officer Candidate School
ODC	officer data card
ODNI	Office of the Director of National Intelligence
OECD	Organization for Economic Cooperation and Development
OFAC	Office of Foreign Assets Control (Treasury)
OGHA	Office of Global Health Affairs (HHS)
OIA	Office of Intelligence Analysis (Treasury)
OMPF	Official Military Personnel File
ONI	Office of Naval Intelligence
OOD	officer of the deck
OPCON	operational control
OPNAV	Office of the Chief of Naval Operations
OSCE	Organization for Security and Cooperation in Europe
OSD	Office of the Secretary of Defense

OTC	officer in tactical command
OTS	Officer Training School (Air Force)
OUTUS	outside United States
PACOM	U.S. Pacific Command
PAO	public affairs office/public affairs officer
PBFT	planning board for training
PCM	primary care manager
PCS	permanent change of station
PDB	Professional Development Board
PEBD	pay entry base date
PHIBRON	amphibious squadron
PHS	Public Health Service
PME	professional military education
PNA	passed, not advanced
POD	plan of the day
POV	privately owned vehicle
PQS	Personnel Qualification System
PRD	projected rotation date
PSD	personnel support detachment
PSR	performance summary record
PTS	perform to serve
REAP	Reserve Educational Assistance Program
REGA	rating entry for general apprentices
RL	restricted line
ROMO	range of military operations
RSO	recreational services officer
RTC	Recruit Training Command
S	Secret
SASC	Senate Armed Services Committee
SBP	Survivor Benefit Plan
SBU	Sensitive but Unclassified
SC MAGTF	Security Cooperation Marine Air Ground Task Force
SCORE	Selective Conversion and Reenlistment
SCP	specialty career path
SDCFP	Secretary of Defense Corporate Fellowship program
SECDEF	Secretary of Defense
SECNAV	Secretary of the Navy
SELRES	Selected Reserve
SERB	Selective Early Retirement Board
SGLI	Servicemembers' Group Life Insurance

SMART	Sailor/Marine American Council on Education Registry Transcript
SOCNAV	Servicemembers Opportunity Colleges
SOCOM	U.S. Special Operations Command
SOPA	senior officer present afloat/ashore
SORM	*Standard Organization and Regulations Manual*
SOUTHCOM	U.S. Southern Command
SPAWAR	Space and Naval Warfare Systems Center
SP MAGTF	Special-Purpose Marine Air Ground Task Force
SRB	selective reenlistment bonus
SSC	subspecialty code
SSG	surface strike group
SSIC	standard subject identification code
SSN	social security number
SSP	Strategic Systems Programs
STA-21	Seaman to Admiral-21
STAR	Selective Training and Reenlistment (program)
STRATCOM	U.S. Strategic Command
SWO	surface warfare officer
TA	tuition assistance
TACON	tactical control
TAD	temporary additional duty
TAMP	Transitional Assistance Management Program
TAO	tactical action officer
TEMDUINS	temporary duty under instruction
TFI	Office of Terrorism and Financial Intelligence (Treasury)
TFL	TRICARE for Life
TRANSCOM	U.S. Transportation Command
TS	Top Secret
TSA	Transportation Security Administration (DHS)
TSP	Thrift Savings Plan
TTP	tactics, techniques, and procedures
TYCOM	type commander
U	Unclassified
UA	unauthorized absence
UCMJ	Uniform Code of Military Justice
UIC	unit identification code
U.N.	United Nations
UNC	United Nations Command
UNODIR	unless otherwise directed

UNREP	underway replenishment
URL	unrestricted line
USAID	U.S. Agency for International Development
USC	U.S. Code
USFK	U.S. Forces, Korea
USMAP	United Services Military Apprenticeship Program
USNA	U.S. Naval Academy
USPHS	U.S. Public Health Service
VA	Department of Veterans Affairs
VERTREP	vertical replenishment
VOLED	off-duty voluntary education
VR&E	Vocational Rehabilitation and Employment (VA)
VTU	Voluntary Training Unit
WHMO	White House Military Office
WQSB	watch, quarter, and station bill
XO	executive officer

SOURCES

In preparing this book the author consulted various instructions, directives, and general messages published by the Department of Defense, the Department of the Navy, OPNAV, NPC, and other DoD and Navy commands. The following specific sources, organized by category, were particularly useful.

AIR FORCE

Air Force: http://www.af.mil/

Air Force Basic Doctrine, Air Force Doctrine Document 1, Headquarters, U.S. Air Force, Washington, D.C., 17 November 2003 (http://www.dtic.mil/doctrine/jel/service_pubs/afdd1.pdf).

Operations and Organization, Air Force Doctrine Document 2, Headquarters, U.S. Air Force, Washington, D.C., 3 April 2007 (http://www.dtic.mil/doctrine/jel/service_pubs/afdd2.pdf).

ARMY

Army: http://www.army.mil

The Soldier's Guide, FM 7-21.13, Headquarters, Department of the Army, Washington, D.C., October 2003 (http://www.hqusareur.army.mil/NCOoutlook/Documents/FM%207-21.13.pdf).

Staff Organization and Operations, FM 101-5, Headquarters, Department of the Army, Washington, D.C., 31 May 1997 (http://www.dtic.mil/doctrine/jel/service_pubs/101_5.pdf).

A Statement on the Posture of the United States Army 2010 submitted by the Honorable John M. Mchugh and General George W. Casey, Jr. to the Committees and Subcommittees of the United States Senate and the House of Representatives 2nd Session, 111th Congress February 2010 (https://secureweb2.hqda.pentagon.mil/VDAS_ArmyPostureStatement/2010/2010_army_posture_statement.pdf).

COAST GUARD

Coast Guard: http://www.uscg.mil

U.S. *Coast Guard: America's Maritime Guardian,* Coast Guard Publication 1, Commandant, U.S. Coast Guard, Washington, D.C., May 2009 (http://www.uscg.mil/top/about/pub1.asp).

COMBATANT COMMANDS

AFRICOM: http://www.africom.mil

CENTCOM: http://www.centcom.mil

EUCOM: http://www.eucom.mil

JFCOM: http://www.jfcom.mil

NORTHCOM: http://www.northcom.mil

PACOM: http://www.pacom.mil

SOCOM: http://www.socom.mil

STRATCOM: http://www.stratcom.mil

TRANSCOM: http://www.transcom.mil

DEPARTMENT OF DEFENSE ORGANIZATION AND FUNCTIONS

Department of Defense Directive 5100.1, Functions of the Department of Defense and Its Major Components (http://odam.defense.gov/omp/pubs/GuideBook/Pdf/510001.pdf).

The United States Naval War College Joint Military Operations Reference Guide, "Forces/Capabilities Handbook," NWC 3153K, July 2009.

INTERAGENCY

Department of Homeland Security: http://www.dhs.gov

Department of State: http://www.state.gov

Diplomacy: The U.S. Department of State at Work. Department of State, June 2008 (http://www.state.gov/documents/organization/46839.pdf).

Introduction to the Civilian Response Corps (http://www.crs.state.gov/index.cfm?fuseaction=public.display&shortcut=4QRB).

One Team, One Mission, Securing Our Homeland: U.S. Department of Homeland Security Strategic Plan Fiscal Years 2008–2013, Department of Homeland Security, Washington, D.C. (http: www.dhs.gov/xlibrary/assets/DHS_StratPlan_FINAL_spread.pdf).

Strategic Plan Fiscal Years 2007–2012. U.S. Department of Justice (http://www.justice.gov/jmd/mps/strategic2007-2012/index.html).

Strategic Plan Fiscal Years 2007–2012. U.S. Department of State, U.S. Agency for International Development, May 2007 (http://www.state.gov/documents/organization/86291.pdf).

Strategic Plan Fiscal Years 2007–2012. U.S. Department of the Treasury (http://www
.ustreas.gov/offices/management/budget/strategic-plan/2007-2012/home.html).

INTERNATIONAL ORGANIZATIONS

NATO: http://www.nato.int

NATO Handbook 2001 (http://www.nato.int/docu/handbook/2001/pdf/handbook
.pdf).

NORAD: http://www.norad.mil

OAS: http://www.oas.org

Organization for Security and Co-operation in Europe: http://www.osce.org/

United Nations: http://www.un.org

LEGAL

Manual for Courts-Martial (MCM) 2008 (http://www.jag.navy.mil/documents/
mcm2008.pdf).

Manual of the Judge Advocate General (JAGMAN) 2007 (http://www.jag.navy.mil/
library/instructions/JAGMAN2007.pdf).

USN/USMC Commander's Quick Reference Handbook for Legal Issues 2007 (http://www
.i-mef.usmc.mil/div/hqbn/hq/_downloads/sja/CMDRS%20Handbook.pdf).

MARITIME STRATEGY

CNO Guidance for 2010, Executing the Maritime Strategy, September 2009 (http://
www.navy.mil/features/CNOG%20201.pdf).

A Cooperative Strategy for 21st Century Seapower, October 2007 (http://www.navy
.mil/maritime/Maritimestrategy.pdf).

Marine Corps Vision and Strategy 2025 (http://www.marines.mil/news/publications/
Documents/Vision%20Strat%20lo%20res.pdf).

Naval Operations Concept 2010; Implementing the Maritime Strategy (http://www
.navy.mil/maritime/noc/NOC2010.pdf).

MARINE CORPS

Amphibious Operations in the 21st Century, U.S. Marine Corps, Marine Corps Combat
Development Command, Quantico VA, 18 March 2009 (http://www.quantico
.usmc.mil/seabasing/resources/Articles/amphib%20Ops%20in%20the%20
21st%20Century.pdf).

Headquarters Marine Corps (HQMC) Organization and Organization Codes, Marine
Corps Order 5216.9U, Headquarters, United States Marine Corps, 2 Navy Annex,
Washington, D.C., 28 January 2005 (http://www.usmc.mil/news/publications/
Documents/MCO%205216.9U.pdf).

The Long War; Send in the Marines: A Marine Corps Operational Employment Concept to Meet an Uncertain Security Environment, Commandant of the Marine Corps, Washington, D.C., January 2008 (http://smallwarsjournal.com/documents/thelongwarsendinthemarines.pdf).

Marine Corps Operations, MCDP 1-0, U.S. Marine Corps, Washington, D.C., 27 September 2001 (http://www.dtic.mil/doctrine/jel/service_pubs/mcdp10.pdf).

Organization of Marine Corps Forces, MCRP 5-12D, U.S. Marine Corps, Washington, D.C., 13 October 1998 (http://www.usmc.mil/news/publications/Documents/MCRP%205-12D%20Organization%20of%20Marine%20Corps%20Forces.pdf).

Policy for the Organization of Fleet Marine Forces for Combat, Marine Corps Order 3120.8A, 26 June 1992 (http://www.usmc.mil/news/publications/Documents/MCO%203120.8A.pdf).

Seabasing for the Range of Military Operations, U.S. Marine Corps, Marine Corps Combat Development Command, Quantico, VA, 26 March 2009.

U.S. Marine Corps: http://www.usmc.mil

USMC Concepts and Programs 2010 (http://www.usmc.mil/unit/pandr/Documents/Concepts/2010/CP2010Index.html).

USMC Vision and Strategy 2025, Commandant of the Marine Corps (http://www.quantico.usmc.mil/download.aspx?Path=./Uploads/Files/SVG_MCVS%2015%20Aug.pdf).

NATIONAL SECURITY

2010 Quadrennial Defense Review (QDR), February 2010 (http://defense.gov/QDR/).

Capstone Concept for Joint Operations (CCJO), Version 3.0, Chairman, JCS, Secretary of Defense, Washington, D.C., 15 January 2009 (http://www.jfcom.mil/newslink/storyarchive/2009/CCJO_2009.pdf).

Joint Operating Environment (JOE) 2010, Commander, Joint Forces Command (http://www.ifcom.mil/newslink/storyarchive/2010/JOE_2010_0.pdf).

National Defense Strategy, Joint Forces Command, Norfolk, VA, June 2008 (http://www.jfcom.mil/newslink/storyarchive/2010/JOE_2010_0.pdf).

National Security Strategy, May 2010, The White House (http://www.jfcom.mil/newslink/storyarchive/2010/JOE_2010_0.pdf).

The National Strategy for Maritime Security, NSPD-41/HSPD-13, September 2005 (http://www.dhs.gov/xlibrary/assets/HSPD13_MaritimeSecurityStrategy.pdf).

NAVY

Career Handbook 2009, Supplement to All Hands Magazine, Navy Personnel Command, Millington, TN, 2009 (http://www.npc.navy.mil/ReferenceLibrary/Publications/NPCCareerHandbook/default.htm).

Manual of Navy Officer Manpower and Personnel Classifications (Vol. I and II), Navy Personnel Command, Millington, TN, October 2009.

Naval Historical Center Dining In/Dining Out: A Navy Tradition (http://www.navy .mil/navco/pages/ssp/reference/dining-in_out.pdf).

Naval Historical Center, Mess Night Manual (http://www.history.navy.mil/Library/special/mess_night.htm).

Naval Military Personnel Manual (MILPERSMAN), NAVPERS 15560D, 22 August 2002 (http://www.npc.navy.mil/ReferenceLibrary/Publications/NPCCareerHandbook/default.htm).

Naval Orientation, Naval Education and Training Command, NAVEDTRA 12966, July 1991.

NAVEDTRA 12018 Basic Military Requirements (BMR).

Navy: http://www.navy.mil

Navy Program Guide 2010, Chief of Naval Operations, Department of the Navy, Washington, D.C. (http:/www.navy.mil/navydata/policy/seapower/sne10/sne10 -all.pdf).

Navy Reserve: http://www.navyreserve.com

Standard Organization and Regulations of the U.S. Navy (SORM), OPNAVINST 3120.32C CH-6, Office of the Chief of Naval Operations, Washington, D.C., 26 May 2005 (http://doni.daps.dla.mil/Directives/03000%20Naval%20Operations%20and%20Readiness/03-100%20Naval%20Operations%20Support/3120.32c.pdf).

Useful Information for Newly Commissioned Officers, NAVEDTRA 12967, Naval Education and Training Professional Development and Technology Center, November 1992 (http://doni.daps.dla.mil/Directives/03000%20Naval%20Operations%20and%20Readiness/03-100%20Naval%20Operations%20Support/3120.32c.pdf).

Separation and Retirement

Department of Defense Preseparation Guide, Active Duty, February 2007 (http://www.turbotap.org/portal/transition/resources/Active_Duty_Presep_Guide).

Preseparation Counseling Checklist for Active Component Service Members, DD FORM 2648, June 2005 (http://www.dtic.mil/whs/directives/infomgt/forms/eforms/dd2648.pdf).

U.S. Department of Veterans Affairs

GI Bill: http://www.gibill.va.gov/

U.S. Department of Veterans Affairs: http://www.va.gov

Vet Success portal: http://www.vetsuccess.gov

OTHER GOVERNMENTAL AND DEFENSE DEPARTMENT ONLINE RESOURCES, NAVAL PUBLICATIONS, AND DIRECTIVES

Air Force Air University (http://www.au.af.mil/au/awc/awcgate/awcgate.htm) maintains an extensive library of military publications, as well as references and links to other online resources.

BUPERS Online (https://www.bol.navy.mil/) provides a secure means for Navy members to review their records and conduct business with NPC.

BUPERS Reference Library (http://www.npc.navy.mil/ReferenceLibrary/) contains BUPERS Directives, Instructions and Notices; Navy Medicine Directives; DoD Directives/Instructions/ Publications and Regulations; and OPNAV/SECNAV Instructions.

Defense Finance and Accounting Service (http://www.dfas.mil) contains information on pay and allowances as well as links to related resources.

Defense Technical Information Center (DTIC) provides a central resource for DoD and government-funded scientific-, technical-, engineering-, and business-related information. DTIC contains links to many databases, including

CJCS Directive Electronic Library (http://www.dtic.mil/cjcs_directives/) contains unclassified CJCS Instructions, Manuals, Notices, Guides, and other policy and procedures.

Joint Electronic Library (http://www.dtic.mil/doctrine/) contains joint publications and doctrine, training information, Universal Joint Task List (UJTL), lessons learned, and other information.

The Federation of American Scientists (FAS) maintains an online library of Presidential Directives and Executive Orders (http://www.fas.org/irp/offdocs/direct.htm).

The Library of Congress maintains a Web site (http://www.thomas.gov) that includes bills and resolutions, and other congressional activity.

Navy Professional Reading Program (http://www.navyreading.navy.mil/) contains the Navy's recommended reading list.

Thrift Savings Plan (http://www.tsp.gov/) provides calculators, forms, and information about TSP.

TRICARE (http://www.tricare.mil) contains TRICARE plan details and eligibility information.

The United States Code (USC) can be accessed on sites maintained by the Cornell University Law School Legal Information Institute (http://www.law.cornell.edu/uscode/), the Government Printing Office (http://www.gpoaccess.gov/uscode/), or the U.S. House of Representatives (http://uscode.house.gov/).

ADDITIONAL PUBLICATIONS

Connell, Royal, and William P. Mack. *Naval Ceremonies, Customs, and Traditions.* 6th edition. Annapolis: Naval Institute Press, 2004.

Department of the Navy (DON) Information Security Program Instruction, SECNAV INSTRUCTION 5510.36A (http://www.ncis.navy.mil/securitypolicy/Information/SECNAVINST/SECNAVINST%205510.36A.pdf).

Naval Military Personnel Command, Leadership and Command Effectiveness Division. *Command Excellence: What It takes to Be the Best!* December 1985.

Navy Regulations, 1990 (http://doni.daps.dla.mil/navyregs.aspx).

The Register of Commissioned and Warrant Officers of the United States Navy and Marine Corps and Reserve Officers of Active Duty (https://navalregister.bol.navy.mil/).

Shenk, Robert. *The Naval Institute Guide to Naval Writing.* 3rd edition. Annapolis: Naval Institute Press, 2008.

Stavridis, James, and Robert Girrier. *Command at Sea.* 6th edition. Annapolis: Naval Institute Press, 2010.

Stavridis, James, and Robert Girrier. *Division Officer's Guide.* 11th edition. Annapolis: Naval Institute Press, 2004.

Stavridis, James, and Robert Girrier. *Watch Officer's Guide.* 15th edition. Annapolis: Naval Institute Press, 2007.

Index

ABOUT THE AUTHOR

Lesa McComas is a former Navy surface warfare officer and the coauthor of the 11th edition of *Naval Officer's Guide*. She is currently an operations analyst at the Johns Hopkins University Applied Physics Laboratory supporting a variety of sponsors in qualitative and quantitative analytic efforts associated with irregular warfare.